The Rise of the Mormons

The *Mormons* Series

The Rise of the Mormons:
Latter-day Saint Growth in the 21st Century

What Mormons Believe:
*Latter-day Saint Beliefs about Christ,
Eternity—and Becoming Like God*
(forthcoming)

Mormon Controversies:
Money, Sex, Death, and the Latter-day Saints
(forthcoming)

Other Books by the Author

Freemasonry: An Introduction
(Tarcher/Penguin, 2011)

The Rise of the Mormons

Latter-day Saint Growth in the 21st Century

Mark Koltko-Rivera

7th Street Books
an imprint of
LVX Publications
New York City
2012

Copyright © 2012 Mark Koltko-Rivera. All rights reserved.

Except as permitted under the United States Copyright Act of 1976, no part of this publication may be reproduced or transmitted in any form or by any means, or stored in a database or retrieval system, without the prior written permission of the copyright holder.

The Rise of the Mormons: Latter-day Saint Growth in the 21St Century by Mark Koltko-Rivera.
Corrected edition, published October 2012 by 7th Street Books, an imprint of LVX Publications, New York City.

7th Street Books, PO Box 20223, New York, NY 10023

ISBN-13: 978-0-6157-1031-0   ISBN-10: 0-6157-1031-X
U.S. editions printed in the United States of America.

Booksellers: This book is likely available through your distributor.

The contents of this book do not necessarily represent the policies or views of either the publisher or The Church of Jesus Christ of Latter-day Saints. This book is not sponsored, sanctioned, or approved by The Church of Jesus Christ of Latter-day Saints.

Front cover: Digitally altered image of a night launch of the NASA Space Shuttle, widely available on the Internet—but without attribution. The author requests the original photographer to come forward for credit.
Back cover author photo by Katherine Finkelstein: katherinefinkelstein.com

Dedicated to

Glen Steenblik and Scott Smith
two 'returned missionaries'
who first taught me the Gospel
as preached by the Latter-day Saints

and to my son
Elder Viktor Edward Koltko
who, at this writing, has just returned from
completing an honorable term of service as a
Latvian-speaking missionary
in the
LDS Baltic States Mission.

Well done, son.
Welcome home.

Table of Contents

List of Illustrations	ix
List of Figures	xi
List of Tables	xv
Important! How to Read This Book	xvii
Preface	xix
Acknowledgements	xxiv
Introduction	1
1 Mormon Growth and Why It Happened, 1830-2011	15
2 The Matrix of Future Mormon Growth: The Mormon World in 2012	53
3 Future Mormon Growth Worldwide through 2120	63
4 Future Mormon Growth in the U.S. through 2120	85
5 Objections and Responses	97
6 Why Religions Grow: A Model	135
7 Exterior Forces "Pulling" for Mormon Growth	139
8 Interior Forces "Pushing" for Mormon Growth	177

(continued)

9 Knowledge Forces and Mormon Growth	223
10 The Potential Impact of High Mormon Growth: A 'More Mormon' World	237
Afterword: The Meaning of Mormon Growth	281
Appendix A: Sources of Statistical Data and Methods of Projections	291
Appendix B: The Slowing of Mormon Growth Post-1990: A Statistical Analysis	297
Appendix C: Why Do People Convert to Mormonism?	311
Appendix D: Tracking Charts: Projected vs. Actual Mormon Growth, 2011-2040	317
References	323
Index	369
About the Author	385

List of Illustrations

The Church website, "lds.org"	226
The Church website, "mormon.org"	229
The author's "I'm a Mormon" web page on www.mormon.org	229
The author's blog, "The Manhattan Mormon™"	230
The author's blog, "LDS 101™"	231

List of Figures

1-1	Global LDS membership, 1830-2010	24
1-2	LDS growth, 1830-2010, on a logarithmic scale	24
1-3	Annual LDS convert baptisms worldwide, 1970-2011	28
3-1	LDS global presence and growth rate, 2011	66-67
3-2	**Projected global LDS membership, 2010-2120, according to the Koltko-Rivera global models**	**71**
3-3	LDS low-growth projection and other global Christian groups, 2020-2120	75
3-4	LDS moderate-growth projection and other global Christian groups, 2020-2120	75
3-5	LDS high-growth projection and other global Christian groups, 2020-2120	76
3-6	LDS low-growth projection and global non-Christian groups, 2020-2120	79
3-7	LDS moderate-growth projection and global non-Christian groups, 2020-2120	79
3-8	LDS high-growth projection and global non-Christian groups, 2020-2120	80
3-9	Comparison: Projections of global Mormon membership, 2020-2120	83

(continued)

4-1	2010 membership distribution across major American churches	87
4-2	Median annual change rates, 1991-2010, major American churches	87
4-3	**Projected LDS membership in U.S.A., 2020-2120, according to the Koltko-Rivera American models**	**92**
4-4	LDS low-growth projection and other American Christian groups, 2020-2120	94
4-5	LDS moderate-growth projection and other American Christian groups, 2020-2120	94
4-6	LDS high-growth projection and other American Christian groups, 2020-2120	95
5-1	Global LDS membership, actual vs. "projected" from the vantage point of 1912	101
7-1	Religious origins of American Latter-day Saints (2007)	143
7-2	Religious origins of American LDS converts (2007)	144
7-3	American population by faith group (2007)	144
7-4	Degree to which faiths are over- and under-represented among those Americans currently LDS who are converts from other religions (2007)	146
7-5	Subgroups of religiously "Unaffiliated" Americans (2007)	149

(continued)

7-6	Proportion of each American age cohort that is Unaffiliated (2007)	151
B-1	Convert baptisms and missionaries serving, 1977-1990	303
B-2	Convert baptisms and countries with LDS congregations, 1977-1990	304
B-3	Convert baptisms and missionaries serving, 1991-2012	308
B-4	Convert baptisms and countries with LDS congregations, 1991-2012	309

List of Tables

1-1	Global LDS membership and growth rate by decade, 1830-2010	23
3-1	Major religious groups worldwide, 2011	64
3-2	**Three models of projected LDS growth worldwide, 2020-2120 ("the Koltko-Rivera global models")**	**70**
3-3	Projections for the global Christian religious scene, 2020-2120 (membership in millions)	74
3-4	Projections for the global non-Christian and LDS religious scene, 2020-2120	78
3-5	Comparison of projections for LDS world membership, 2020-2120	82
4-1	Membership and change rates in major American Christian churches (2010)	86
4-2	**Three models of projected LDS growth in the U.S.A., 2020-2120 ("the Koltko-Rivera American models")**	**91**
4-3	Projections for the rest of the American Christian religious scene, 2020-2120 (membership in millions)	93
5-1	Per-decade actual LDS growth rate, 1830-1910	99

(continued)

5-2	Per-decade LDS membership, actual versus "projected" from the vantage point of 1912	100
5-3	Assemblies of God & LDS in the USA	123
7-1	Per-decade LDS growth rates for selected countries in Central & South America and Africa, 1999-2009	140
7-2	Religious origins of American LDS converts compared to American population (2007)	145
7-3	Per-decade LDS growth rates for selected European countries, 1999-2009	156
10-1	LDS membership in the world, the U.S., the Intermountain West, and Utah: 1980 & 2010	239
B-1	Annual Mormon Growth, 1978-2011	297
B-2	LDS Convert Baptisms, 1977-2011	299
B-3	Means, standard deviations, and intercorrelations for annual LDS convert baptisms and predictor variables, 1977-1990	302
B-4	Regression analysis summary for variables predicting annual LDS convert baptisms, 1977-1990	302
B-5	Means, standard deviations, and intercorrelations for annual LDS convert baptisms and predictor variables, 1991-2011	307
B-6	Regression analysis summary for variables predicting annual LDS convert baptisms, 1991-2011	307

Important! How to Read This Book

Different people might read this book differently:

- I suggest that everyone read the Preface. It describes the questions that this book answers, and the sub-questions that each chapter answers.

- Readers who are not familiar with Latter-day Saint beliefs, practices, or history will find a helpful overview in the Introduction. I recommend that everyone read the first three pages of the Introduction (where I explain what is at stake for different groups of people, regarding Mormon growth) and the last three pages (where I describe the terminology used in the book).

- **Some readers just cannot stand statistics.** No problem. If you are one of these readers, I suggest that you begin with Chapter 1, where you will learn about the history of Mormon growth through 2011. You may wish to glance at Figures 3-2 and 4-3, to get a sense of my projections for LDS membership in the world and in the United States, respectively. However, the heart of this book for you likely will be:

  - ➢ Chapter 8 (the psychological forces at work in culture and society that will drive future Mormon growth);

  - ➢ Chapter 9 (the way that the Church will bring its message to the world, online);

- ➢ Chapter 10 (what a future 'more Mormon' world would look like); and,
- ➢ the Afterword (what Mormon growth really means, in the great grand scheme of things—especially from the point of view of those who are not Mormons themselves).

- Those who are more comfortable with light statistics will find the other chapters quite accessible. Most of the statistics in this book are counts and percentages (including proportions and change rates).

- Appendices A and B will be of most interest to statistical specialists. Appendix A gives my sources for data and my methods for making my projections. Appendix B reports two multiple regressions.

- Appendix C presents evidence that it is actually the attraction of Mormon beliefs, along with personal spiritual experiences, that move people to make the final step of conversion to Mormonism—rather than social forces, as some social science theories of religious conversion would have it.

- Appendix D provides a chart that readers may complete, to compare my projections against actual Mormon growth annually for the period 2012-2040.

There is something here for everyone who is interested in the Latter-day Saint faith and its growth, past, present, and future. Enjoy.

Preface

This book answers three questions:

1. How did The Church of Jesus Christ of Latter-day Saints—popularly referred to as 'the Mormons'—become as large as it is now, with well over 14 million members in a little over 180 years?

2. Just how large will the Mormons become over the next century or so?

3. What will the world be like with that many more Mormons in it?

In the course of answering these three questions, we will consider a number of sub-questions about the rise of the Mormons, as well:

- Just who are the Mormons, and what is the LDS religion? (See the Introduction.)

- How did the Latter-day Saints grow from a tiny group in upstate New York in 1830 to become the fourth-largest church in America by late 2012? (See Chapter 1.)

- What is the current status of the Mormon people, in terms of its preparation for growth, in late 2012? (Chapter 2.)

- Just how much will the Mormons grow during the 21st century, in the world generally and in the United States in particular? (Chapters 3 and 4.)

- Why should we believe predictions of immense Mormon growth, and what will the mechanisms of this huge growth be? (Chapters 5 through 9.)
    - ➤ In particular, what large-scale psychological forces in society will drive Mormon growth? (See Chapter 8—which, for many readers, will be the heart of this book).
- If indeed the LDS faith will grow as hugely in adherents as I predict it will, what will that 'more Mormon' world be like? (Chapter 10.)
- What should the Mormons do about the predictions of huge growth that I make here? What about people who are *not* Latter-day Saints? What does "Mormon growth" mean in the great, grand scheme of things, anyway? (See the Afterword.)

I think this book will appeal to two very different groups of readers. One will be the Mormons themselves (more properly called the Latter-day Saints), who are deeply interested in their future as a religious people. The other group will be readers who are *not* Latter-day Saints (LDS), but who nonetheless want to know what all the fuss is about regarding the predictions of enormous Mormon growth that one hears about in the media with greater frequency these days. These readers may not know much about Mormon history, lifestyle, or beliefs. In the Introduction, I give a whirlwind tour of Mormonism. However, the reader interested in a more in-depth understanding of things Mormon should see two other books in this series: *What Mormons Believe* and *Mormon Controversies*, which are scheduled to appear in the Fall of 2012.

Who am I to be writing about all this? As far as my Mormon credentials are concerned, I am a Latter-day Saint convert, baptized during my college years in Pennsylvania. I completed a two-year full-time LDS mission in Japan. I have served as a bishop's counselor (like an associate pastor in other Christian churches) in two LDS "wards" (the Mormon term for congregations) in Manhattan, and on a stake high council in New Jersey (somewhat like a diocesan council in the Episcopal Church). I regularly attend the LDS Manhattan Temple. I currently serve as a home teacher and a family history consultant in my ward in Manhattan. (For the sake of those who are not familiar with the Mormon argot, this all means that I am "for real" and in good standing as a Mormon.) I have published several articles in the independent LDS publications, *Sunstone* magazine and *Dialogue: A Journal of Mormon Thought*. I blog as the author of *The Manhattan Mormon*™ [1] and *LDS 101*™,[2] and I post occasional videos about the LDS faith on my YouTube channel.[3]

In terms of social science credentials, I hold a doctoral degree in psychology from New York University. I have taught dozens of sections of statistics and research design, and so I am qualified to perform the statistical analyses upon which much of this book depends. Among my scholarly writings are two award-winning articles in the *Review of General Psychology*, as well as other articles in the *Journal of Humanistic Psychology* and *Psychotherapy*. I am an elected

---

[1] http://themormonldsblog.blogspot.com/
[2] http://lds101mormonism.blogspot.com/
[3] http://www.youtube.com/user/koltkorivera

Fellow of the American Psychological Association. I also write *The Psychological Blog*™.[4]

No doubt some will say that my account of the LDS faith is immediately suspect because it *is* my own faith. These are the same people who would not blink at, say, Thomas Merton giving an account of his Catholic faith in *The Seven Storey Mountain*, or Herman Wouk describing his Jewish faith in *This Is My God*, or Reza Aslan explaining his Islamic faith in *No god but God*. To people who consider a Mormon's account of the LDS faith to be suspect, no rational response is possible.

I had planned to publish a version of *What Mormons Believe*, *Mormon Controversies*, and *The Rise of the Mormons* as a single book through a trade publisher. I am still interested in doing this, and I invite communication from literary agents and editors at trade publishers. I may be reached (by readers and news organizations, as well) at the e-mail address below.

One sometimes detects, especially in the more recent anti-Mormon literature written by evangelical authors, a note of something very much like fear. Consider the tone of the following passage:

> But two things, perhaps, mark Mormonism's success more than anything else: the LDS Church's growth from 6 members at its founding in 1830 to over 11 million today [over 14 million in 2012], and the massive missionary force it fields around the world,

---

[4] http://thepsychologicalblog.blogspot.com/

making Mormonism continually visible to outsiders.

Evangelicals have often underestimated the challenge Mormonism's success poses to evangelism and world missions, if they have considered it at all.[5]

To me, this sounds more than a little like the words of people who feel threatened by the thought of Mormon growth. Even the title of the book where the quoted essay appears—*The New Mormon Challenge: Responding to the Latest Defenses of a Fast-Growing Movement*—is reminiscent of books about military or political threats to the nation; it calls to mind the panic of earlier generations about 'the Red Scare' and 'the Yellow Peril.'

Very well, then. I would appreciate it if someone would please pass on a message for me to people who fear that the Latter-day Saints are going to grow very, very numerous, so numerous that they will have real and substantial impact on the world at large:

They are entirely correct.

—Mark Koltko-Rivera, Ph.D.
September 25, 2012
New York City

www.MarkKoltkoRivera.com *and*
www.MarkKoltko-Rivera.com

E-mail: authorMEKR@yahoo.com

---

[5] Mosser (2002) p. 60.

Acknowledgements

I am deeply indebted to a special group of people, each of whom read an earlier manuscript of this book in its entirety (some more than one), and provided thoughtful reflections on what I had written. This group includes: Bonnie Ballif-Spanvill, Dwight Blazin, Paul R. Gunther, James W. Lucas, Glen Nelson, and Peter A. Rivera. My thanks to you all, who have made this a much better book than it otherwise would have been. I also am very grateful for the encouragement of Lynda Gunther regarding my writing.

My special thanks are due to two people who go by the designations "Ms. M.S." (always my first and best reader) and "Magic Dragon Who Strikes Like Lightning" (the only martial arts *sensei* who ever had the courage to put a *katana* in my hands) for their indispensable moral support and counsel.

Of course, I bear sole responsibility for any errors of fact or interpretation in this book.

The Rise of the Mormons

Introduction

The future growth of the Latter-day Saint (LDS, or "Mormon") people will affect your life, whatever your religious tastes.

In this book, I show how the Saints may well become at least the second-largest church in the United States, and the second-largest religious group overall in the world, over the next century or so. Now consider in what position such a development would put these groups of people:

- **People who are committed to some other religion.** These people will find that some of their friends and family members become Latter-day Saints. People in leadership positions in other faith traditions—priests, ministers, imams, rabbis, other religious teachers—will be faced with substantial attrition from their congregations and groups. This will confront people with questions about what they really believe, and why.

- **Seekers.** People who seek for greater spiritual insight and truth will be put in an interesting position by Mormon growth. As the Mormons become more numerous, their actual beliefs (as opposed to the distortions of them that appear in popular entertainment and today's news media) will become better known. LDS beliefs offer very specific answers to questions that thinking people have had for thousands of years: Where do I come from—*me*, that is, the personality, the very consciousness that I identify with? Why am I here on earth? What is the purpose of human life in general, and of my life in particular? If a good God exists, then why is there evil in the world? What will happen to me when I die? Mormon growth will confront many people with the need to make a personal decision about Mormon teachings and the faith itself.

- **The atheist community.** Atheists see the spread of religion generally as an increase in superstition, so of course atheists will see the growth of the LDS faith as a negative. However, as Mormons become more numerous, it will become better known that the Saints strongly emphasize secular education, that Mormon scriptures teach that "the glory of God is intelligence," and that the Latter-day Saint faith is very friendly to science in general and the scientific method in particular. Thus, atheists will find that the Mormons break many stereotyped beliefs about religion and religious people. This may necessitate some adjustment in atheists' thinking.

- **Everyone** will see a lot more "Mormon" around the everyday world. Mormon meetinghouses and even temples will be much more common. More importantly, Mormon concepts about the meaning and purpose of life will appear more frequently in culture, art, and popular entertainment—as real points of departure, not just as objects of ridicule. Latter-day Saint points of view will appear in public discourse. The person on the street is going to wonder what sort of stance to take towards all this.

- Finally, Mormon growth has important implications for **the Saints themselves.** The Saints feel that their growth is something prophesied. The Mormon people as a whole have sacrificed through their missionary efforts for over 180 years (and counting) to further this growth. However, the kind of growth I write about in this book carries a weighty obligation. I show that immense Mormon growth is *possible*, but this growth is far from *inevitable*; it will require an equally immense effort on the part of the Mormon people to bring this growth about.

All of this means that, *whoever* you are, you have a stake in understanding the whys and hows of Mormon growth. That is what this book will convey to you.

To understand Mormon growth, it will help to have some knowledge of the Latter-day Saint faith, a religion that is remarkably poorly understood by the general American public.[6] My hope is that this chapter will give enough background about this faith to put the rest of the book into proper context.

LATTER-DAY SAINT LIFESTYLE AND RELIGIOUS PRACTICE

As with any faith, Mormons vary in the degree to which they practice their religion. The LDS faith has distinctive standards and expectations of conduct. Observant Latter-day Saints follow these practices:

- They pray and study the scriptures, both daily.
- They abstain from sexual relationships outside of heterosexual marriage.

---

[6] In a study sponsored by the Brookings Institution, 82% of surveyed American adults said that they knew little or nothing about Mormon beliefs and practices (Chingos & Henderson, 2012, p. 2).

- They give service to the poor and needy.
- They donate ten percent of their income—a biblical tithe—to the church, in addition to other offerings (for example, for the relief of the poor).
- They dress modestly.
- They each have a "calling" (a 'church job,' unpaid) where they give some sort of service on a regular basis (such as teaching a church class on Sundays).
- As "home teachers" or "visiting teachers," adult Latter-day Saints visit other Mormons monthly, and see to their welfare.
- They abstain from alcohol, tobacco, and 'recreational' drugs (as well as coffee and tea).
- They abstain from profanity in their speech.
- They abstain from shopping or very active recreation on Sunday, the Latter-day Saint Sabbath, preferring to use the day for worship at church, rest, quiet family activities, service to others, and spiritual development.

Further points of distinction include the following:
- Eighteen- or nineteen-year-old LDS men are expected to devote the next two years of their lives to missionary service, at their own expense; nineteen-year-old LDS women are welcome to contribute 18 months of service in this fashion, as are retired married couples and singles. Applicants for missionary service do not indicate preferences for where they would serve; they are about as likely to be assigned to Manila as to Manhattan.

- The Saints—both men and women—are encouraged to obtain as much education as possible.

- In addition to regular public worship on Sunday at thousands of LDS meetinghouses worldwide, observant Mormon adults attend special worship at the Latter-day Saint temples (of which 136 were operating around the world at the end of 2011).

- Observant Saints marry in these temples, under an authority that they believe permits these marriages to last throughout all eternity. Although some Mormons do divorce, LDS marriages as a group tend to be more stable than those of the surrounding culture, and produce about one more child than the typical marriage in that culture.

- LDS high school students attend the Seminary program for four years, daily before or after school classes, to study the scriptures. They also attend youth activities, one evening a week, and regularly contribute labor to service projects.

- The Saints support humanitarian aid and disaster relief projects around the world. This includes personally volunteering for local relief projects.

This all puts the Latter-day Saint lifestyle at odds with, for example, the hedonistic, materialistic, self-obsessed lifestyle that is celebrated in much popular entertainment in early twenty-first century American culture.[7]

---

[7] For example, the lifestyle of observant Mormons rarely if ever provides material for television shows or websites such as *TMZ*, *E!*, or *MTV News*.

LATTER-DAY SAINT BELIEFS

Distinctive as the Mormon lifestyle is, this is just an external expression of LDS *belief*, which is, if anything, even more distinctive than the lifestyle.[8] Especially important aspects of LDS belief include the following:

- God the Father, Jesus the Christ, and the Holy Spirit are three separate beings united in purpose in one Godhead.

- God the Father wants each human being to possess all the joy, powers, and capacities of God Himself; this is "eternal life," that is, the kind of life enjoyed by God, the Eternal One. (The process by which we come to have eternal life is called "exaltation.") There are implications of this belief that are not, strictly speaking, officially declared LDS doctrinal positions, including the following:

  - God the Father once was a mortal human on some other world, and ultimately received the gift of eternal life, which He now wishes to make available to us, on condition of our worthiness, that is, our obedience to Him.

  - As the 19th century Latter-day Saint aphorism goes, "As man now is, God once was; as God is now man may be."[9]

---

[8] See my *What Mormons Believe*. For brief online expositions of central LDS beliefs, see mormon.org and Oaks (2011); a longer description, also online and authoritative, is *Gospel Principles* (2009). A recent encyclopedic work is Millet, Olson, Skinner, & Top (2011).

[9] "Lorenzo Snow" (2004). "Man" here means "humankind."

- ➢ God the Father is eternally married to our Heavenly Mother.

- We all lived as spirits with God in heaven before the world was created, and accepted God and Christ's plan for our future happiness and exaltation. A crucial element of this plan is moral free agency, the human capacity to choose behavior.

- The atonement of Jesus Christ, in which Christ took upon himself the penalty for all the sins of humanity, has two great effects:

  - ➢ All human beings who have ever lived shall be physically resurrected.

  - ➢ Those who are obedient to Christ will partake of exaltation and eternal life.

- God communicates with humanity now, as anciently, through revelation given to prophets.

- The canon of scripture includes, in addition to the Bible: the Book of Mormon (the record of ancient prophets in the Americas), the Doctrine and Covenants (selected revelations from the 19th century on), and the Pearl of Great Price (ancient and modern sacred histories).

- God communicates with individuals through direct personal revelation. This is available to anyone willing to seek after God in humility and sincerity.

- "The Priesthood in general is the authority given to man to act for God."[10] Priesthood authority is necessary to direct church work and to perform any reli-

---

[10] *Teachings of Presidents of the Church: Joseph F. Smith* (1998), p. 141.

gious ritual, such as baptism, or to bless the sacrament of the Lord's Supper. Latter-day Saint priesthood holders trace their authority back through the ancient apostles to Jesus Christ Himself.

- Latter-day Saint temples are places where the Saints prepare for exaltation after this life, and where marriages are performed that can last not only through time, but eternity.

  > People who die without receiving baptism under proper priesthood authority may accept the gospel in the spirit world after death. On earth, in LDS temples, people may be baptized as proxies for those who died earlier. Only if the deceased individual actually accepts the gospel in the spirit world does this proxy baptism take effect.

Thus, there are points of overlap between LDS belief and the beliefs of other Christian churches, and important points of difference. The LDS faith involves a serious commitment, and an encompassing lifestyle.

LATTER-DAY SAINT HISTORY

As with individuals, the growth of a religion involves change over time. To put LDS growth into context, it will help to have a basic understanding of Mormon history.[11]

---

[11] Recent histories for the general reader include those by Bowman (2012) and C. L. Bushman & R. L. Bushman (2001); see also Allen & Leonard (1992) and Arrington & Bitton (1992). A brief history produced by the Church of Jesus Christ, available online, is *Our Heritage* (1996).

In the Spring of 1820, Joseph Smith, Jr., was a poor 14-year-old farm boy in upstate New York.[12] At a time of religious revivalism, when various Christian churches were competing for members, Joseph went off to pray in a grove of trees to know which church to join. He later reported that he was visited by God the Father and the Son, who told him to join none of the churches then in existence.

In the Fall of 1823, again at prayer, as Joseph reported, he was visited by a heavenly messenger who announced himself as the angel Moroni, sent by God. Over the next four years, Moroni taught Joseph, and prepared him for the responsibilities that Joseph would have in restoring the ancient Christian church. Joseph reported that this ancient church had fallen into a state of apostasy not long after the death of the original apostles in the late first century A.D.

In 1827, Moroni gave Joseph a record of ancient prophets who were descended from people led by God from Jerusalem to the Americas, circa 600 B.C. This record was titled *The Book of Mormon* after one of these prophets. Joseph translated the Book of Mormon by inspiration, and published it in 1830, the year in which he formally organized the Church of Jesus Christ. Not long before, he received the priesthood of God through angelic messengers.

The early Latter-day Saints were persecuted and so left New York and Pennsylvania to gather in Ohio and Missouri. The Saints established a headquarters in Kirtland, Ohio, where they built their first temple. Internal apostasy forced the faithful to abandon the Ohio community and its temple. At the same time, external persecution in Missouri became intense and violent. The Saints moved on to Illi

---

[12] For LDS history, 1820-1829, see the account in the LDS Standard Works: the Pearl of Great Price, Joseph Smith—History, chapter 1. The definitive biography of Joseph Smith is R. L. Bushman (2005).

nois, where they built up a village into the city Nauvoo, then the second-largest city in Illinois. The Saints' second temple was built in Nauvoo, and it was here that Joseph instituted distinctive temple ceremonies involving exaltation and proxy baptism for the dead.

Violent persecution continued. Ultimately, in June 1844, Joseph Smith was assassinated by an armed mob of anti-Mormons. The Saints split into several groups at this point. The largest group followed Brigham Young,[13] the President of the Quorum of the Twelve Apostles, and used wagon trains to head out to what is now called Utah, then a part of Mexico (although soon annexed by the United States). This over-1,000-mile exodus was the largest overland migration accomplished by a single sizeable group of people at one time until, perhaps, the Long March of the Chinese Red Army a century later.

The Saints had what they called the Territory of Deseret largely to themselves until the coming of the transcontinental railroad in 1869. Falsely accused of treason in the late 1850s, the Saints had to endure the presence of an occupying U.S. army before the Civil War. The headquarters of the church remains in Salt Lake City, Utah, although it has regional administrators and local congregations throughout the world.

The Saints publicly practiced plural marriage (the marriage of one man to more than one woman at a time) from 1852 to 1890, after which the Church banned the practice. That ban is still in force today, the practice being punishable by immediate excommunication from the Church.

Missionary work began even before the formal organization of the Church in 1830. The Latter-day Saints sent

---

[13] The definitive biography of Young remains Arrington (1985/2012).

missionaries to many regions in the United States and Canada, as well as to Europe and distant locations around the world, almost from their earliest days. This missionary work has resulted in the membership of the church growing from a few hundred by the end of 1830 to well over 14 million by the end of 2011.

ORGANIZATION

The LDS priesthood is held by males. The Church is directed at the top by the First Presidency (the President of the church—also known as the Prophet—and his two counselors), and the Quorum of the Twelve Apostles. These individuals are given a formal sustaining vote at semiannual Church-wide conferences, where the membership supports them as "prophets, seers, and revelators."[14] These officers, along with others (notably the members of the Quorums of Seventy and the Presiding Bishopric) comprise what the Saints call the "General Authorities" of the Church. These and other administrators (such as the female Presidency of the women's Relief Society) direct the work of the Church of Jesus Christ worldwide.

A local LDS congregation is called a *ward*. It is directed by a *bishop* (equivalent to a pastor in other Christian congregations), who is assisted by two *counselors*. (Very small congregations are called *branches*, directed by a *branch president* and two counselors.) In a given geographic area, the local wards and branches are grouped into a *stake* (much like a diocese in other Christian churches), presided over by a *stake president* and two counselors.

Church meetings are held during a three-hour block of time; coordination of schedules allows up to three congre-

---

[14] E.g., "The Sustaining of Church Officers" (2012).

gations to share a building without serious overcrowding. One hour of the "meeting block" is devoted to Sacrament Meeting, which involves the Sacrament of the Lord's Supper (that is, communion) and talks by members of the congregation. One hour is given to Sunday School, where every member of the congregation is enrolled in some class grouped by age. One hour is dedicated to Priesthood Meeting and Relief Society (for males and females, respectively). Smaller children attend Primary during the Sunday School and Relief Society/Priesthood hours. (During the week, there are additional meetings for adolescent youth, in the Young Men and Young Women organizations.) Within each ward, there are separate presidencies for each of several priesthood groups, the Relief Society, and the Young Women and Young Men organizations.

At the ward and stake levels, all officers in the Church are unpaid. Given the need to staff the various presidencies and the many classes that are taught at LDS church meetings, at any given time, most observant Saints will have the responsibilities of one or more church offices throughout their lives, from early adolescence on.

A few words on terminology and notation:

- The official name of the church under consideration here is The Church of Jesus Christ of Latter-day Saints. I shall refer to it hereafter as "the Church of Jesus Christ" (sometimes just "the Church") to save space.[15] I do *not* use the term popular in American media, "the Mormon Church," because that term

---

[15] This is in keeping with current practice within The Church of Jesus Christ of Latter-day Saints itself (Ballard, 2011).

falsely gives the impression that the Church worships the prophet Mormon; readers will note that the word "Mormon" does not appear anywhere in the Church's official name.

- The abbreviation "LDS" stands for "Latter-day Saint" as an adjective (as in "LDS beliefs") or as a plural noun (as in "the LDS believe").

- I often refer to the *people* of the Church as "the Saints," as they do themselves. In the ancient Christian church, a "saint" was simply a baptized member, who had made covenants to live a sacred life. Today's Latter-day Saints see themselves as a restoration of ancient Christianity, and they have taken upon themselves the ancient designation.

- "Mormon" is the name of an ancient prophet that occurs in the distinctive LDS scripture, *The Book of Mormon*. Early on, members of the Church of Jesus Christ were referred to by their neighbors derisively as "Mormonites," and later as "Mormons." (Similarly, in ancient times, the followers of Christ were referred to as "Christians," although the term had never been used by Jesus during his mortal ministry[16]). For the sake of variety, I use the word "Mormons" as a synonym for "Latter-day Saints."

- Just as the word "Christianity" does not occur in the Bible, there is no word in the LDS scriptures to describe the Latter-day Saints' religion as distinct from the Church of Jesus Christ itself. When referring to

---

[16] LDS Standard Works: Bible, New Testament, Acts, chapter 11, verse 26.

the religion, I use the terms "LDS faith," "LDS religion," or, for variety, "Mormonism."

- Sources in footnotes given with dates in parentheses (such as "Koltko-Rivera (2004)" will have full citation information given in the References. Sources in footnotes given with dates in square brackets (often films or television shows, such as "*Independence Day* [1996]") do <u>not</u> have entries in the References.

The reader now has had the nickel tour of Mormonism, as it were. We shall now focus on Mormon growth—although, as we shall see, that subject is inextricably bound up with matters of LDS belief, practice, and history.

Chapter 1

Mormon Growth and Why It Happened, 1830-2011

Why did the Church of Jesus Christ grow so quickly after its founding in 1830? Why did the LDS growth rate increase after 1973? Why did it drop after 1990? These are the questions that this chapter answers. As the reader will discover, the answers to these questions say a great deal about the prospects for Mormon growth in the 21st century.

We first consider the most basic question involving LDS growth: why? We then inspect the simple count of Latter-day Saints, and how that number has changed, especially over the course of recent years.

WHY PEOPLE BECOME LATTER-DAY SAINTS

In early 19th century America, many Americans were 'seekers,' interested in the beliefs, practices, and forms of so-called primitive Christianity—the religion practiced in the generation of Jesus' original apostles, which religion, many of these Americans believed, had become corrupted in ancient times.[17] When these people came into contact with Mormon missionaries, typically they became interested in some aspect of the Mormon message related to the idea of a *restoration* of ancient Christianity. This might involve the exercise of spiritual gifts, or manifestations of the Holy Spirit, as well as practices and beliefs associated with

---

[17] Harper (2000); Vogel (1988). See also Shipps (1985) chapt. 4.

ancient Christianity. One historian has described the situation of some early Mormon converts this way:

> All along the way, they considered themselves quite rational, and clearly they approached ... Mormonism rationally, if also with hope of finding the primitive gospel, which they could identify empirically by its manifestation of the Holy Ghost, which would be manifest according to certain prescribed patterns set down in the Bible. ... [C]onverts relied heavily on scriptural precedent [that is, the precedents found in the Christian Bible] as proof. Those who became Mormons were almost always first contemplative Bible believers who were skeptical of false prophets. They considered it reasonable that signs would follow true believers, and they held out for empirical confirmation. Dozens of primary accounts of early Mormon conversions emphasize this pattern.[18]

Other characteristics of the new faith that appealed to early Mormon converts included the following:

- The ancient Christian church featured living apostles and prophets.[19] From its beginnings in the 1830s, the Church of Jesus Christ has proclaimed that God spoke through a living prophet in modern times, Joseph Smith being the first prophet of the

---

[18] Harper (2000) p. 104, reference omitted.

[19] LDS Standard Works: Bible, New Testament, 1 Corinthians, chapters 12 and 14 (especially chapter 12: verse 28, and chapt. 14, vv. 1-6).

restoration of ancient Christianity.[20] In 1829, Joseph Smith described a revelation in which God promised the designation of twelve modern apostles, and laid out the procedures by which the first such apostles were to be selected.[21] This modern restoration of an ancient Christian institution appealed to many Mormon converts.

- The Book of Mormon brought forth by Joseph Smith contained teachings that addressed many Christian disputes through the ages, such as the true nature of Jesus Christ and his atonement for the sins of humanity; the nature of baptism and the Lord's Supper; the meaning of faith; the availability of personal revelation to ordinary people; the "last days" before the second coming of Christ; the spirit world, and the nature of the resurrection. Early Mormon converts were impressed with these teachings.

- The Book of Mormon contains a promise that any person, interested in investigating the legitimacy of that scripture, may simply approach God in prayer with humility and real intent—and then God will respond to that person through the Holy Spirit.[22] This promise concludes with the words, "And by the power of the Holy Ghost ye may know the truth

---

[20] This is widely stated throughout the Doctrine & Covenants, an LDS book of scripture that records revelations received by Joseph Smith and his successors. In the Doctrine & Covenants (D&C), Joseph Smith's appointment as a prophet is indicated through designation as a special "servant" of God with prophetic responsibilities (e.g., D&C 1:17-18, 29; 5:1, 9-10). The LDS position on prophets, ancient and modern, is available in *Gospel Principles* (2009), chapter 9.

[21] LDS Standard Works, Doctrine & Covenants, Section 18, vv. 26-39.

[22] LDS Standard Works: Book of Mormon, Moroni, chapt. 10, vv. 3-5.

of all things." This concept was appealing to many American Christians at the time, who were comfortable in churches that emphasized spiritual gifts and prophecy.[23] It continues to be appealing to converts today, who have a way to religious truth that does not rely upon tradition or external authority.

Additional points of attraction from the 19th century onward include the following:

- The Book of Mormon relates detailed teachings regarding the state of the human soul between death and resurrection,[24] and the nature of the physical resurrection promised to all.[25] In 1832, Joseph Smith received a vision that related a detailed account of the final destinies of different types of people after the resurrection, depending upon how they had lived on earth.[26] These teachings were a great comfort to the earliest Mormons, whose early 19th century American frontier environment was filled with untimely death to an extent difficult to imagine today[27]; these teachings remain a comfort to potential converts today.[28]

---

[23] This is well-documented for "Methodists and many other evangelicals in early America" (C. Jones, 2012, p. 84; see pp. 83-84 for sources).

[24] LDS Standard Works: Book of Mormon, Alma, chapter 40, verses 11-14. See also *Gospel Principles* (2009) chapter 41.

[25] LDS Standard Works: Book of Mormon, Alma, chapter 40, verses 1-10, 16-26, and chapter 41.

[26] LDS Standard Works: Doctrine & Covenants, Section 76. See also *Gospel Principles* (2009), chapter 46.

[27] Brown (2012).

[28] E.g., Boyé (2012).

- In 1841, Joseph Smith reported a revelation in which he was commanded to build a temple in Nauvoo, Illinois, where special blessings could be conveyed to the Saints.[29] This temple was built over the next few years, and was the site of many "temple sealings," or wedding ceremonies performed under priesthood authority that permits the marriages to last eternally.[30] The idea of "forever families" continues to be very attractive to many contemporary Mormon converts today.

- Joseph Smith reported revelations in which the Saints were commanded to be baptized as proxies for those who had died without a knowledge of the gospel.[31] In the 19th century mainstream Christian world, the received teaching was that those who died without authoritative baptism were damned to hell. The LDS teaching, by contrast, offered salvation to the entire population of the world throughout human history, in line with what the Saints (and some other scholars today) believe were ancient Christian practices.[32]

The importance of these issues for conversion is confirmed by survey data. In 2011, 59% of surveyed American Mormon converts said that they became Latter-day Saints because of the beliefs of the Church; another 23% said that

---

[29] LDS Standard Works, Doctrine & Covenants, Section 124, vv. 25-28.

[30] LDS Standard Works, Doctrine & Covenants, Section 132, verse 19. See also *Gospel Principles* (2009) chapters 36 and 38.

[31] LDS Standard Works: Doctrine & Covenants, Section 124, vv. 26-36; Sect. 127:5-9; Sect. 128:1-18. See also *Gospel Principles* (2009) ch. 40.

[32] LDS Standard Works: Bible, New Testament, 1 Corinthians, chapter 15, verse 29. See also Trumbower (2001), especially pp. 35-41.

this choice resulted from personal spiritual experiences of one sort or another, including 17% who said that they had been called of God, or 'received a testimony.'[33]

The primacy of LDS teachings and personal spiritual experience in conversion to the faith is borne out in reading converts' narratives. For example:

- Alex Boyé, now known as a pop singer of Nigerian ancestry, was a teenage boy when he first met LDS missionaries in London. What first attracted him to the LDS faith was the testimony of a missionary that, because of Jesus Christ's atoning sacrifice, all people would be resurrected bodily after death.[34]

- Jason Chaffetz, now a Congressperson representing Utah, "grew up in California, Arizona, and Colorado in an agnostic household."[35] He was a college student when he prayed while reading a copy of the Book of Mormon that his roommate had given him. He later wrote, "I got down on my knees, and I prayed, and I felt that same warmth and comfort that I had felt when I was five years old" and had first prayed.[36]

- Peggy Cowherd, currently the CFO of global business travel at American Express in New York, was baptized after a long career at IBM. As she wrote, "I joined this Church because I felt the confirmation of the Spirit that it was the right choice for me."[37]

---

[33] *Mormons in America* (2012) p. 48.
[34] Boyé (2012).
[35] Chaffetz (2012) p. 48.
[36] Chaffetz (2012) p. 51.
[37] Cowherd (2012) p. 90.

Chapter 1: Mormon Growth, 1830-2011   21

- Reeve Nield, a professional golf coach on the Ladies European Tour, described how her parents reacted upon first meeting the Mormon missionaries when she was a child in Zimbabwe (then Rhodesia). "The missionaries' message that day was: 'Where do we come from? What is our purpose here on earth? and Where [will we] go when we die?' At the end of the lesson my parents were overjoyed, and my father told the missionaries, 'You have taught me more in one night than I have known my whole life!'"[38]

These, then, are the main reasons that people convert to the LDS faith: its teachings are attractive to the potential converts, and they have spiritual experiences that mark these teachings and the Church as having divine approval.[39] (We consider these ideas further in Appendix C.)

This will be an important point to keep in mind throughout this book. Because I will be presenting statistical data, of course I will be relating the number of convert baptisms to the number of missionaries serving at any given time, and to historical events. Statistics, by their very nature, deal with groups not individuals. To understand the LDS faith, it is crucial to understand that, on the level of the individual potential convert, missionaries teach but do not convert; they teach potential converts to seek for

---

[38] Nield (2012) p. 251.

[39] Of course, the presence of personal connections between potential converts and the Saints eases the decision to convert, as predicted by Stark (2005) ch. 3, and Stark & Finke (2000) ch. 5. However, LDS annals are replete with accounts of people who contacted Church headquarters to request baptism after they had simply read missionary literature, such as the "fifteen thousand unbaptized converts who were waiting for the Church to come to them" in Nigeria in 1961 (E.L. Kimball, 2008, p. 23).

counsel directly from God about accepting the LDS faith, rather than to accept the word of anyone else—including the LDS missionaries themselves.

People tend to stick with Mormonism because they perceive that they receive a great deal of value from their membership.[40] This is why Mormons make sacrifices for their religion, and sacrifice they do. Observant Mormons sacrifice to go on missions, they sacrifice to attend the LDS temple, they sacrifice time and effort to serve in their church responsibilities (the Church having no paid clergy or officers at the local level), and they sacrifice financially to pay a full tithe.[41] This high degree of sacrifice and commitment both results from the faith of the Saints, and strengthens that very faith.[42]

Now we approach the question: How have these points of attraction affected Mormon growth to date?

MORMON MEMBERSHIP, 1830-2011

One can hardly read a press article about the Mormons without a mention of the high growth rate of their church (see Table 1-1 and Figures 1-1 and 1-2). However, as we shall see, the forces affecting Mormon growth are complex.

As the reader can see in Fig. 1-1, LDS increase has been geometric and fast. The logarithmic chart in Fig. 1-2 shows

---

[40] See data presented by Stark (2005) chapter 4, especially pp. 92-93. See also Stark (2008) chapter 3.

[41] Hinckley (1993), Monson (2011a), Oaks (2012).

[42] An evangelical Christian blogger wrote that the dedication shown by observant Mormons to their church work, and the lower degree of selfishness that this demonstrates, relative to others, are two of the reasons "why Mormons are beating Baptists (in church growth)" (French, 2012).

that, past 1860, this increase is simply the result of a steady growth rate, with acceleration of growth between 1950 and 1990—after which the rate of growth slowed. How could growth like this occur? What could slow it?

Decade Ending in Year	LDS Members Worldwide	Per-Decade Growth Rate
1830	280	—
1840	16,865	5923.2%
1850	51,839	207.4%
1860	61,082	17.8%
1870	90,130	47.6%
1880	133,628	48.3%
1890	188,263	40.9%
1900	283,765	50.7%
1910	398,478	40.4%
1920	525,987	32.0%
1930	670,017	27.4%
1940	862,664	28.8%
1950	1,111,314	28.8%
1960	1,693,180	52.4%
1970	2,930,810	73.1%
1980	4,639,822	58.3%
1990	7,761,207	67.3%
2000	11,068,861	42.6%
2010	14,131,467	27.7%

Table 1-1. Global LDS membership and growth rate by decade, 1830-2010

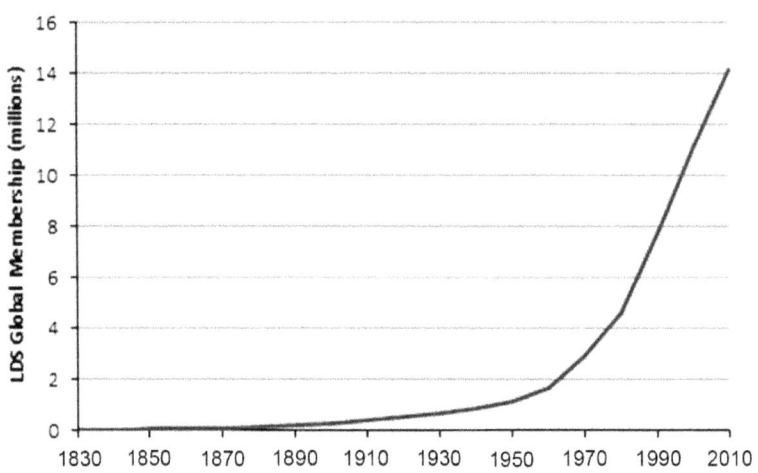

Figure 1-1. **Global LDS membership, 1830-2010**

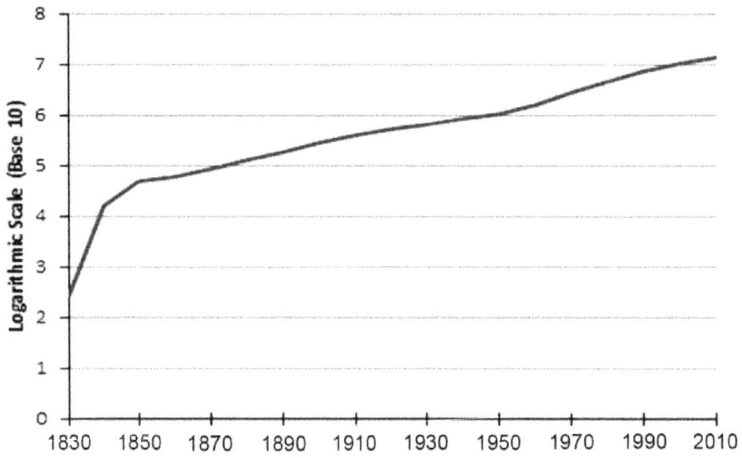

Figure 1-2. **LDS growth, 1830-2010, on a logarithmic scale**

*   *   *

By the early 1980s, Rodney Stark had established himself as one of the most prominent sociologists of religion in the history of the discipline.[43] Unattached to a church himself, as a graduate student at Berkeley, he had been friends

---

[43] For his background, see the preface and introduction to Stark (2005).

with fellow student Armand Mauss, a Latter-day Saint who discussed with him the dynamics of LDS growth.

In the early 1980s, as a minor project, Stark used statistics printed in the official LDS annual *Deseret News Church Almanac* to extrapolate Mormon growth over the following century; his purpose was to explore the dynamics of a successful new religion, to elucidate discussions of new religious movements in general. He was "not prepared" for the sheer magnitude of Mormon growth that his statistical models projected.[44]

In his 1984 article, "The Rise of a New World Faith,"[45] Stark made low and high estimates of LDS growth, decade by decade through 2080. His low estimate, based on an annual growth rate of 2.658% (or 30% per decade), projected almost 64 million Latter-day Saints in the world by 2080. Stark's high estimate, based on an annual growth rate of 4.138% (50% per decade), placed about 265 million Mormons on earth by 2080. Either of these robust growth rates were defensible on the basis of historical data. Stark concluded that the Mormons "stand on the threshold of becoming the first major faith to appear on earth since the Prophet Mohammed rode out of the desert,"[46] and in his easy-to-follow statistical analysis he attempted "to demonstrate that the Church of Jesus Christ of Latter-Day Saints, the Mormons, will soon achieve a worldwide following comparable to that of Islam, Buddhism, Christianity, Hinduism, and the other dominant world faiths."[47] Revisiting

---

[44] Stark (2005) p. ix.
[45] Stark (1984).
[46] Stark (1984) p. 19.
[47] Stark, 1984, p. 18. Stark considers Mormonism as "a *new* religion" distinct from Christianity (Stark, 2005, pp. 140-141), but he says this as a sociologist, not a theologian. In the sociology of religion, "new

the issue in 2005, Stark wrote, "I am absolutely astonished that two decades later it is the high estimate that best approximates what has taken place."[48]

Indeed, the actual growth rate of their church caught even the Mormons by surprise. In 1975, when the church had 3.6 million members, church statisticians estimated that, by 1990, global LDS membership would be 6.5 million.[49] That figure wound up underestimating the actual number reached in 1990—7.76 million—by over 1.2 million members (see Table 1-1). Put another way, the Mormons underestimated their own future growth, over only a 15-year period, by 30%.

However, after 1990, the Mormon annual growth rate slowed considerably. The median annual LDS growth rate worldwide from 1963 through 1982, the two decades before Stark wrote "The Rise of a New World Faith," was 5%; however, the church's median annual growth rate from 1991 through 2010 was only 3%, and the growth rate in the last decade of that period dropped to 2.4%.[50] As of 2011, LDS annual growth was too low to sustain even Stark's "low estimate" of future LDS population, let alone his high estimate. How could this have happened?

---

religions" or "new religious movements" are defined as movements on the periphery of a dominant religious culture (Introvigne, 2001), which certainly describes Mormonism. However, movements on the periphery have been known to move to the center of a culture, and vice versa, a very real possibility when it comes to Mormonism and the mainstream of Christianity, as we shall see.

[48] Stark (2005) p. ix.
[49] *Deseret News 1975 Church Almanac*, table on p. A50.
[50] Author's calculations from data in *Deseret News 2012 Church Almanac*, p. 205.

It is crucial to understand that, by a large margin, Mormon growth means convert baptisms rather than natural growth (that is, the birth or baptism of "children of record," the LDS term for children born to Mormon families). Converts have comprised an increasing share of overall Mormon growth for over half a century. In 1951, convert baptisms comprised 30% of overall annual Mormon growth; by 1981, the converts' share was 67%, by 1997 it was 81%,[51] and by 2011 it was slightly over 90%.[52]

Thus, *by a large margin, most new Mormons are converts*, rather than being born into the faith. For the most part, people choose the LDS faith, rather than inherit it. I doubt that this can be said for any other of the five largest religious organizations, either in the U.S. or the world.

So, for Mormon growth to slow substantially, this would have to involve a reduction in the growth rate of convert baptisms—the growth *rate*, not the absolute number of converts—which is the situation depicted in Figure 1-3 for the years 1990 through about 2011.

From the mid-1970s through 1990, the Church of Jesus Christ not only gained converts, but the number of new converts itself grew from year to year, from 79,603 in 1973 to 330,877 in 1990.[53] Thereafter, although the Church has

---

[51] *Deseret News 1999-2000 Church Almanac*, pp. 6, 111.

[52] Author's calculations, based on data in "Statistical Report, 2011" (2012). The increasing share of Mormon growth comprised of convert baptisms seems largely lost on both the popular and the academic press, where it is often reported that LDS growth is largely a matter of the Saints having large families.

[53] Reported in "Statistical Report" articles, published from 1974 through 1991. I am ignoring the decrease in baptisms from 1981 to 1983, which resulted from the temporary reduction of the term of missionary service for males from 24 to 18 months during this period.

continued to gain many converts, the number of annual new converts slipped, down to 272,814 in the year 2010.[54]

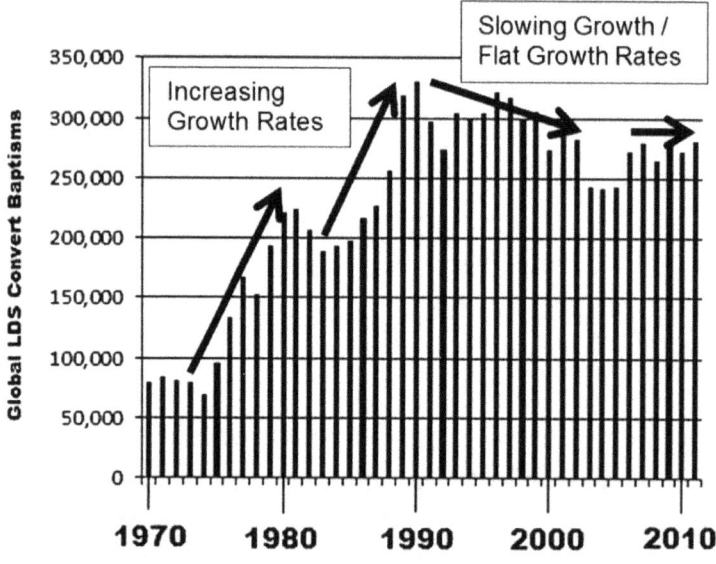

Figure 1-3. Annual LDS Convert Baptisms Worldwide, 1970-2011

All of this gives rise to three questions: (1) What happened after 1973 to raise the number of convert baptisms so dramatically? (2) What happened after 1990 to cause growth rates to drop and stall? (3) What do these developments mean for the Mormon future?

---

[54] Data in "Statistical Report" articles, published from 1992 through 2011.

Chapter 1: Mormon Growth, 1830-2011 29

WHY THE DRAMATIC RISE IN LDS CONVERTS AFTER 1973?

The years 1973-1975 were a watershed, both for American society and for the Church of Jesus Christ, about two-thirds of whose members were American citizens at that time.[55] In part, this had to do with a dramatic development in American history; in very large part, it resulted from a major shift in the way that Mormons looked upon the obligations of missionary work; finally, it had to do with an improvement in LDS missionary preparation.

The end of the Vietnam War-era draft

Millions of American men were drafted into the military during the war in Vietnam. In January of 1973, the Secretary of Defense announced that the draft was ended.

The end of the draft permitted many young LDS men who otherwise would have been drafted into the American military to volunteer for LDS missionary service instead. In 1973, the number of LDS missionaries called to service increased by 20% over the previous year (to a total of 9,471 called to serve). Two years later—with Saigon fallen, the Vietnam War conclusively ended, and many American military personnel discharged from the armed services—the number of LDS missionaries called to service increased by 47% over the preceding year, for a total of 14,446 called to serve. Only rarely since that time has the Church ever called fewer missionaries to service within a given year.

Thus, one reason LDS convert baptisms skyrocketed beginning in 1973 was that the pool of young men available for missionary service went up precipitously. However,

---

[55] In 1974, 67% of all LDS were in the United States; author's calculations on figures in *Deseret News 1976 Church Almanac*, pp. E17, E21.

it is one thing to have a pool of *potential* missionaries, and another altogether to have actual missionaries in the field. As it happens, the proportion of potential LDS missionaries who became actual proselytizing missionaries underwent a significant change during this time period, as well.

"Every young man should serve a mission"

The growth of convert baptisms in the Church was downright staggering during the period 1974-1990 (Figure 1-3). This is largely because, at the beginning of that period, an exceptional LDS leader made presentations to Church leadership and general membership that had far-reaching effects.

Spencer W. Kimball was an extraordinary man even among the presidents of the Church of Jesus Christ.[56] An executive in a family-run insurance business in Depression-era Arizona, he was 48 years old when he was ordained one of the LDS Quorum of the Twelve Apostles in 1943. In 1957, throat cancer left him with only one-half of a working vocal cord, and a hoarse whisper of a voice. In 1972, he survived open heart surgery. When the church's then-president Harold B. Lee died unexpectedly, and Kimball became the LDS President in December 1973 at the advanced age of 78, Kimball had been widely expected to be a sort of caretaker. Many thought that he would serve quietly and without special distinction until his death, which some predicted would follow soon after his appointment as Church president. The reality could not have been more different from these expectations.

---

[56] For his life, see: E.L. Kimball & A.E. Kimball (1977), E.L. Kimball (2005).

On April 4, 1974, a little over three months after being 'set apart' as Church president, Kimball addressed a seminar of regional representatives, then a middle level of Church leadership. The gathering was held in the Church Office Building, a 420-foot-tall, clean-lined structure completed just two years earlier, which consolidated a variety of church administrative functions for the first time in generations. The lobby of this new building was dominated by a work then still in progress, a mural 16 feet high and 66 feet long of the New Testament scene known traditionally as "the Great Commission," that moment when the resurrected Jesus Christ commanded his ancient apostles to "teach all nations, baptizing them in the name of the Father, and of the Son, and of the Holy Ghost: Teaching them to observe all things whatsoever I have commanded you."[57] This turned out to be quite the appropriate setting for President Kimball's presentation.

President Kimball outlined his ideas for the expansion of LDS missionary work, the scope of his ideas being clear from his title: "'When the World Will Be Converted.'"[58] He opened by making reference to the Great Commission:

> I ask you, what did he mean when the Lord took his Twelve Apostles to the top of the Mount of Olives and said: "… And ye shall be witnesses unto me both in Jerusalem, and in all Judea, and in Samaria, and unto the uttermost part of the earth." (Acts 1:8.)
>
> What is the significance of the phrase "uttermost part of the earth"? …. Was it the

---

[57] LDS Standard Works: Bible, New Testament, Matthew, ch. 28, vv. 19-20.

[58] Kimball (1974).

people in Judea? .... Or did he mean all the living people of all the world and those spirits assigned to this world to come in centuries ahead? Have we underestimated his language or its meaning? How [can] we be satisfied with 100,000 converts out of nearly four billion people in the world who need the gospel?

The preceding year, from a world population of 3.9 billion, the Church had baptized 79,603 converts. From his podium, President Kimball raspily quoted a number of LDS scriptures to make a point: God had commanded that every human being was to hear the gospel as the Saints understood it. He continued:

My brethren, I wonder if we are doing all we can. Are we complacent in our approach to teaching all the world? We have been proselyting now 144 years. Are we prepared to lengthen our stride? To enlarge our vision?

He made clear that *his* vision involved sending missionaries to far more countries, including states that were then politically inaccessible. The key, he said, was to have many more missionaries, and to have the countries in which the Saints then preached supply missionaries for their own countries and others besides; this would free up American members of the missionary corps to preach in more countries. Aided by a short film that used maps and arrows to show the future movements of missionaries into country after country, Kimball continued, sometimes using language that would have been appropriate to planning the great troop movements of World War II:

Suppose that South Korea with its 37,000,000 people and its 7,500 members were to [supply their own missionaries and so] take care of its own proselyting needs and thus release to go into North Korea and possibly to Russia the hundreds who now go from the [United] States to Korea.

If Japan could furnish its own 1,000 missionaries and then eventually 10,000 more for Mongolia and [mainland] China, if Taiwan could furnish its own needed missionaries plus 500 for [mainland] China and Vietnam and Cambodia, then we would begin to fulfill the vision. Suppose that Hong Kong could furnish its needed missionaries and another 1,000 to go to both of the Chinas [i.e., mainland China and Taiwan]; suppose the Philippines could fill its own needs and then provide an additional 1,000 for the limitless islands of southeast Asia; suppose the South Seas and the islands therein and the New Zealanders and the Australians could furnish their own and another several thousand for the numerous islands of south Asia and for Vietnam, Cambodia, Thailand, Burma, Bangladesh, and India.

With this movement of missionaries who would be traveling north and west, the lands of the world could begin to be covered with the gospel as the lowlands of the world are covered with the oceans.[59]

---

[59] President Kimball referred here to Isaiah's biblical prophecy: "the earth shall be full of the knowledge of the LORD, as the waters cover

....

> Great Britain, with seven missions and 14 stakes now but numerous others later, should join that army and all together the army of the west would move across western Europe and central Europe and Arab [sic] lands, and in a great pincer movement join their efforts with the missionary army from the east to bring the gospel to millions in [mainland] China and India and other populous countries of the world. ....
>
> Using all the latest inventions and equipment and paraphernalia already developed and that which will follow, can you see that perhaps the day may come when the world will be converted and covered?

To say this plan was ambitious would be a monument to understatement. Russia at this time was the major state in the Soviet Union, an aggressively atheistic communist super-state. The People's Republic of China on the mainland was the most heavily populated atheistic communist state in a world with many such states. Vietnam, Cambodia, Mongolia? Along with Russia and China, all were atheistic communist states that did not permit Mormon missionaries to enter their countries.

But ambitious or not, this was the agenda that their Prophet had set, and the Mormon people adopted it as their own. Kimball's phrase, "lengthen our stride," imme-

---

the sea" (Isaiah 11:9), a prophecy also quoted in the Book of Mormon (2 Nephi 21:9). The seminar audience would have been familiar with these scriptures, which by 1974 had been quoted for over 140 years in LDS teaching as prophecies of LDS missionary work.

diately entered into the Mormon popular vernacular, as shorthand for working *that* much harder, not just in missionary work, but in all manner of Church service.

Key to President Kimball's plan was a vast increase in the LDS missionary corps. Up until this time, the missionary service of young LDS men was seen by many Mormons as optional. President Kimball had different ideas. He talked about this, not only in his regional representative seminar, but in a presentation to the priesthood of the Church that was presented by satellite link in stake centers around the United States and abroad. Some LDS friends of mine, in the audience at their stake center in suburban Philadelphia, sat and listened to President Kimball as he asked, during his live broadcast presentation, "should *every* young man serve a mission?" As several of my friends later told me, they were at least mentally shaking their heads *no* as they heard this, musing that lots of young men had other things to do. But then they heard President Kimball answer the question he had just posed:

> And the answer has been given by the Lord. It is "Yes." Every young man should fill a mission. He [that is, the Lord] said: "Send forth the elders of my church unto the nations which are afar off ...; unto the islands of the sea; send forth unto foreign lands; call upon all nations ...." (D&C 133:8.) He did not limit it.[60]

Several of my Philadelphia-area friends, hearing this talk, decided then and there to serve a mission. For example, Jack Itri was an accountant in his late twenties as he sat listening in the congregation—well past the age when

---

[60] Kimball (1974).

most young Mormon men served missions. (My guess is that, being one of two sons of a Mormon mother of pioneer stock, on the one hand, and a non-Mormon Italian-American father, on the other, Jack just thought that his duty was to stick close to home.) However, as Jack later explained it to me, President Kimball's exhortation was a call to action for Jack personally. Soon after hearing Kimball's talk, Jack's older brother Nick left on a mission (to Italy, as it happened), and Jack left not long afterward on his own mission (being assigned to the same mission in Japan to which I was later assigned myself.)[61]

Like Nick and Jack, the overall membership of the Church responded to President Kimball's call for missionaries. In 1973, the year before Kimball's seminar address, the Church had issued calls of service to 9,471 new missionaries. In 1975, the year after, the Church issued 14,446 such calls, an increase of 53%.

With minor fluctuations, the number of new missionaries called in a given year continued to rise until 2003 (when a drop occurred, described below). A total of 30,563 new missionaries were called in 2010. Because each missionary serves for either 24 months (males) or 18 months (females and retired couples), the total number of missionaries *serving* in any year is much larger than the number *called* during that year. At year-end 2011, a total of 55,410 LDS missionaries served full-time worldwide.[62]

---

[61] John Kyle "Jack" Itri has passed on now, but he was quietly proud of his missionary service for the rest of his life.

[62] "Statistical Report, 2011," p. 30. One of these missionaries happened to be Elder Viktor Koltko—my son.

Missionary preparation: standardized teaching plans

Mormon missionaries have used a variety of approaches to teach 'investigators'—the Mormon term for non-LDS people who express some interest in the Church of Jesus Christ—since the beginning of Mormon missionary work in 1830. During the first century or so of the Church's existence, missionary work was built around street meetings (essentially 'soapbox'-type presentations) and door-to-door "tracting," in which "the object was to leave a religious tract at every home, hoping for a possible discussion later if individuals had any questions from their reading."[63] Through the 1940s, here and there one could find individual missionary leaders who devised some plan or other for LDS missionaries to use in teaching potential converts. Some of these teaching plans were remarkably effective; one created by a missionary sent to Oregon resulted in the number of baptisms in that mission increasing from 48 to 225, comparing the first quarter of 1948 to the same period in 1949,[64] an increase of 369%.

However, it was only beginning in 1952 that a standardized, Church-wide method for missionary teaching was developed (titled *A Systematic Program for Teaching the Gospel*), and this method was only implemented on a voluntary basis. In 1961, another lesson plan (titled *A Uniform System for Teaching Investigators*) was made mandatory across all LDS missions, as was another plan, *The Uniform System for Teaching Families*, in 1973.[65]

---

[63] Cowan (2000) p. 105.
[64] Cowan (2000) pp. 110-111.
[65] See Duffy (2005) about five systematic plans for LDS missionaries to use in their teaching, rolled out from 1952 to 2004. See also Cowan (2000).

The positive effect of these teaching methods on missionary effectiveness was noticeable—even despite a temporary drop in the missionary force. In 1951 and 1952, the number of LDS missionaries called to serve dropped precipitously because of the mandatory military draft for the Korean War. (In 1950, the Church of Jesus Christ called 3,015 missionaries to service; in 1952, that number was 872.) Despite the drop in the strength of the missionary corps, the Church of Jesus Christ not only grew, but its rate of growth increased substantially through this period. In 1950, the Church grew by 3.03%, and in 1951, by 3.13% (an increase of growth *rate* of only 3.33%, comparing annual percentages of growth). However, in 1952, the year that the *Systematic Program* was introduced, the Church grew by 3.65% (an increase of 37.3% in growth rate over 1951).

Another major increase in convert baptisms was seen with the introduction of the *Uniform System for Teaching Investigators* in 1961. In 1960, the Church of Jesus Christ had grown by 4.77%, but in 1962, it grew by 7.79% (an increase in growth rate of a notable 63.3% over the course of just two years). This happened even though the actual number of missionaries grew by only 19.6% from 1960 to 1962.

Unfortunately, the effect of introducing the *Uniform System for Teaching Families* in 1973 is harder to tease out of the data.[66] However, the introduction of a new teaching plan in 1986 (*The Uniform System for Teaching the Gospel*) clearly increased the growth rate in LDS convert baptisms.

---

[66] This is because of the near-simultaneous effect of President Kimball's 1974 proclamation that every young man should serve a mission, a proclamation that by itself increased the size of the missionary corps—and thus the number of converts—substantially.

Chapter 1: Mormon Growth, 1830-2011   39

In 1985, the year before the *Uniform System for Teaching the Gospel* was introduced, the number of LDS converts grew by 2.4% over the previous year. In 1986, the year this teaching system was introduced, the number of LDS converts itself grew by 9.4% compared to the preceding year, even though the number of LDS missionaries grew only 5.8% that year. In 1988, the number of converts grew by almost 13% compared to the previous year, even though the number of missionaries grew by only 4% that year. Stunningly, in 1989, the number of LDS converts grew by **24.3%** over the preceding year, even though the number of missionaries grew by only 10% that year.

In the early 21st century, the Church made a serious change in the way that missionaries were to approach their teaching. As reported in LDS media:

> Missionaries no longer are to teach the gospel by a memorized recitation of the standard missionary discussions, the First Presidency and Quorum of the Twelve announced in a "Statement on Missionary Work," dated Dec. 11, 2002. **Missionaries should learn the concepts of the discussions and then teach from the heart,** according to the statement, using their own words as prompted by the Spirit, rather than by rote presentation.[67]

This represented a sea-change in the approach to teaching that Mormon missionaries had used. Over the preceding 40 years, LDS missionaries had used memorized lessons ("discussions"), in part, perhaps, to ensure the correct use of vocabulary in foreign languages. Now mission-

---

[67] *Deseret Morning News 2004 Church Almanac* (2004) p. 7, boldface in original.

aries would teach a standard sequence of concepts, but use their own words, "as prompted by the Spirit."

The most recently developed standardized missionary lessons, the *Preach My Gospel* program, were released in 2004. Before that release, in 2003, the number of converts dropped by 14.2% from the previous year, paralleling the 15.8% drop in the number of missionaries called to service that year compared to 2002 (as described below). In 2006, two years after the release of *Preach My Gospel*, the number of annual converts grew by 12.2% compared to the previous year, even though the number of missionaries serving increased only 2.1% over the previous year.

The lesson to be learned from these figures is both important and clear. Introduction of improved methods of missionary teaching—essentially, better missionary preparation—makes for an increase in the number of LDS convert baptisms. As we shall see, the factor of missionary preparation plays an important part in my predictions for future Mormon growth.

All other things being equal, more—and better prepared—missionaries lead to more convert baptisms. In 1973 (pre-President Kimball's seminar), there were 79,603 convert baptisms; in 1975 (post-seminar), there were 95,412, and in 1976, there were 133,959. For many years, annual convert baptisms continued to rise, reaching an all-time high of 330,877 during 1990.

And then things changed. After 1990, the number of annual convert baptisms began to drop even as the number of LDS missionaries serving continued to rise through 2002. The search for the reasons behind this drop leads us to the third question with which we began this chapter.

Chapter 1: Mormon Growth, 1830-2011　　41

WHY THE SLOWING OF GROWTH AFTER 1990?

The first thing to say about the slowing of LDS growth after 1990 is that it was precisely that: a *slowing of growth*, and no more. To read some authors tell the story, it almost seems as if they were claiming that the Church of Jesus Christ was *shrinking*, and that most certainly is not the case. No, the Church of Jesus Christ is still growing, and by quite a bit annually. However, it is incontrovertible that the *rate* of that growth from year to year has indeed declined since 1990. The reasons for that decline, and the meaning attributed to it, have been the subject of dispute.

Ironically, one major reason that the number of LDS convert baptisms dropped after 1990 was an *increase* in LDS missionary work itself—that is, an increase in its *scope*. Here, too, important historical forces played a major part in shaping the Mormon growth curve. Another major reason is that the number of LDS missionaries fell—because of a desire for better-qualified missionaries.

Changes in the scope of LDS missionary work

In the most important political developments of the later 20th century, the so-called Revolutions of 1989 ended the rule of communist regimes in several Eastern Bloc nations allied with the Soviet Union, including Poland, East Germany, Hungary, Bulgaria, Czechoslovakia, and Romania. This was an important milestone in a process that culminated in the formal dissolution of the Soviet Union on Christmas Day of 1991, an event that left fifteen republics of the former USSR as independent sovereign states, from the immensity that is Russia to smaller states like Belarus, Estonia, Latvia, and Lithuania. Over the next few years, political communism was abandoned by Albania and Yugoslavia in Europe, as well as by Cambodia and Mongolia in Asia. The response of the LDS leadership to these developments was to expand the geographical scope of LDS missionary work immensely.

Two years previous to the Revolutions of 1989, the incoming president of the LDS Finland Helsinki Mission, Steven Ray Mecham, was "set apart" for his new office by one of the LDS Quorum of the Twelve Apostles, Elder Russell M. Nelson. It is customary among the Saints, upon taking a new office or church responsibility, for the new appointee to receive the laying on of hands from the presiding authority, who then "sets apart" the appointee for the office, and pronounces impromptu words of blessing. In this instance, "in the blessing Elder Nelson stated that President Mecham would open missionary work in the Baltic States and Russia."[68] Events unfolded:

> Two years later, in October 1989,[69] Elder Nelson attended a mission presidents' seminar for Europe ... in Budapest, ...[70] and so [did] President Mecham.... Elder Nelson took him aside ... and said, "President, the time has come for you to begin missionary work in Estonia and in Russia." President Mecham promptly sent two missionaries from Finland into Estonia on month-long visas. By Decem-

---

[68] Hilbig (2005/2008) p. 61. The Baltic States include Estonia, Latvia, and Lithuania.

[69] This would be about twenty six months before the formal dissolution of the Soviet Union.

[70] Some seminar attendees observed, from a window, the dismantling of the Red Star from atop the parliamentary building in Budapest itself—quite the cinematic moment (Hilbig, 2005/2008, pp. 62-63).

ber 1989 four Estonians had been baptized. They were the first citizens of the Soviet Union baptized in this era. Between December 1989 and April 1990, one hundred people had been baptized in Estonia.[71]

Taking advantage of the greater religious freedom in Eastern Europe that followed the Revolutions of 1989, the Church's leadership established formal missions in short order in the formerly communist nations of Poland, Hungary, and what is now the Czech Republic (all 1990), Bulgaria (1991), Romania (1993), and later on in Albania (1996) and what are now Croatia and Slovenia (both 1999). Within the component states of the former USSR, the Church formed missions in Russia[72] (1990) and Ukraine (1992); the Baltic states of Latvia, Lithuania, and Estonia, as well as Belarus (all 1993); and Armenia (1999).

At the same time, the Church of Jesus Christ continued to expand its preaching into new areas of Africa and Asia. In sub-Saharan Africa, the Church already had missions in South Africa (back in 1903), Nigeria (1980), Ghana (1985), Zimbabwe and what is now the Democratic Republic of the Congo (both 1987), and Liberia (1988). In the post-Soviet era, the Church established new missions in Kenya (1991), Ivory Coast (1993), Madagascar (1998), the former Soviet client states Uganda and Mozambique (both 2005), and Sierra Leone (2007).

In Asia, the Church already had missions in Hong Kong (1955), South Korea (1962), Japan (1968), Singapore (1969), Taiwan (1971), and Thailand (1973). In the post-

---

[71] Hilbig (2005/2008) p. 61.

[72] The establishment of the first permanent LDS mission in Russia is described by the former mission president, Gary Browning (1997). For the current status of the Church in Russia, see Cranney (2012).

Soviet era, the Church established new missions in India (1993), Indonesia (1995), and formerly communist Mongolia[73] (1995) and Cambodia (1997). The church did all this without neglecting their numerous and very busy missions in Central and South America, and while sustaining many other missions in Europe and North America.

Such expansion, however, came with a price.

For over a generation before 1990, most new LDS missions had been formed by divisions of already-existing missions; this is how California alone wound up with 16 LDS missions by late 2011. In most such areas, a potential convert faces a large community of Latter-day Saints in local congregations with whom to form social ties, a process that makes it more likely that a potential convert will actually be baptized.

Take New York State, for example. At the end of 2010, there were four LDS missions in New York State, where 78,031 Latter-day Saints lived among a total population of 19.5 million. On average, one New York State resident in every 257 was a Mormon.[74]

In Manhattan, congregations of the Church of Jesus Christ are large and well-attended; even the Canal Street Branch in Chinatown, a Chinese-language congregation that meets in rented quarters in an office building, has a full chapel on Sunday mornings. Where I regularly attend church meetings, in a building near Lincoln Center, my LDS congregation, the Manhattan First Ward, has hundreds of people in attendance on any given Sunday, as do

---

[73] Yes, as a Latter-day Saint missionary, one really *can* be sent to Outer Mongolia—that is, the Mongolia Ulaanbaatar Mission.

[74] *Deseret News 2012 Church Almanac*, p. 377.

the other two wards that share the building with us in staggered meeting schedules. Non-LDS visitors to the 14 Manhattan wards and branches comprising the LDS New York New York Stake—including those in Chinatown, Harlem, Inwood, Lincoln Center, Morningside Heights, Union Square, and the Upper East Side—likely will find someone to whom they can relate among the regular congregants: another young or middle-aged married couple with or without children, another single parent, another aspiring writer, artist, or actor, another interracial couple, another student studying *xyz*, and so on.

But it is another story altogether in someplace like Latvia or Mozambique. In Latvia, the 1,102 Saints at the end of 2010 were sprinkled lightly among a population of 2.2 million, leaving one Mormon for every 2,426 Latvians. Even that is twice the concentration of Saints in Mozambique, where, in 2010, the 5,392 LDS were sifted into a population of 21.7 million, a ratio of one Mormon for every 4,467 Mozambicans. Yet either of these places is practically Provo, Utah, compared to Poland, where 1,648 members were tucked into a country of 38.5 million, meaning there was but one Saint for every 24,796 Poles at the end of 2010.[75] The LDS congregations are not so large in these nations; there is not yet the kind of variety among members that makes social integration of potential converts easier. Nor could there be: the Church is simply too young there.

Rodney Stark developed a model of religious conversion that sheds light on this phenomenon, a model in which two concepts play a central part: *networks of faith* and *religious capital*.[76] Stark points out that people are much more likely to convert to a different religion if people they

---

[75] *Deseret News 2012 Church Almanac*, pp. 508, 525, 547.
[76] Stark & Finke (2000) ch. 5; Stark (2005) ch. 3.

know are already involved in that faith: if potential converts have—or form—a social network that extends into that different religion, they are much more likely to actually convert than if they are going it alone, as it were. The application to post-1990 Mormon missionary work in the new LDS missions of Eastern Europe, Africa, and Asia is clear: the typical potential convert had little or nothing in the way of pre-existing social networks that included Mormons. The networks available within LDS congregations in those nations were tiny in the generation or so following 1990; overall, social integration and conversion were simply much less likely.

For Stark, a potential convert's investment in his or her current religion's culture—the personal experiences with and knowledge of the beliefs and practices of the current faith—defines that person's religious capital. The more that a potential convert can retain that religious capital when converting to a different faith, the more likely a conversion is.

In the religious capital department, the newer, post-1990 LDS missions posed a special challenge. Several states of Eastern Europe had populations that were very attached to Roman Catholicism or the Orthodox Churches, in a context where these churches were refuges from totalitarian communism. In such countries, religious experience in traditional churches was bound up with the generations-long struggle for personal and political freedom. Thus, potential converts to Mormonism in Warsaw, Poland, or Moscow, Russia, might feel that they had more to lose in the way of religious capital than potential converts in Warsaw, Indiana, or Moscow, Idaho.

In the newer missions of Africa and Asia, on the other hand, a fair amount of the population's religious capital is invested in non-Christian religions altogether. In Madagascar, for example, about 40% of the population is affiliated with tribal religions; LDS conversion for these people involves a complete break with the religion they have known from birth. In 2010, over half of Mongolians were affiliated with Tibetan Buddhism. The potential loss of religious capital faced by a Buddhist who is thinking of converting to Mormonism in Ulaanbaatar—the tantric practices of Vajrayana, the Diamond Vehicle of Buddhism; the thousand-year-old legacy of Tibetan Buddhist scripture and tradition—is much higher than the potential loss in religious capital faced by, say, Methodists in Milwaukee, Wisconsin, who would read from the same Bible in LDS Sunday School as they did in their Methodist congregations (albeit in the King James translation).

Mormon growth slowed after 1990, all right, but it did so in large part because, from that year on, more LDS missionaries were being assigned to places where LDS missionary work was simply harder to do. In places like Eastern Europe, Asia, and Africa, it is simply harder for people to convert to Mormonism, either because so many of the population are not Christian to start with (the case in Africa and Asia), or because Mormonism is still very small (the case in all three areas).

Analyzing LDS membership data from 1977 to 2011, we find an interesting set of facts. For every missionary added to the LDS corps during 1977-1990, on average, an additional 7.8 converts entered the fold. However, the story was very different when we consider each additional *country* added to the list of countries where the Church of Jesus Christ had organized congregations. During the period 1977-1990, adding a country to that list had no statistically significant effect on the number of new converts. However, during the period 1991-2011 (essentially, the post-Soviet era), for each additional country added to the list, over 1,300 *fewer* converts joined the Church.[77]

This is the price that the Church has paid for expanding into previously uncharted territory on multiple fronts around the world simultaneously: a slowing of growth in the number of converts, at least in the short term. However, this is all in keeping with the Great Commission depicted in that huge mural at the Church Office Building in Salt Lake City.

"Raising the bar" for missionary service

Another factor in the slowing of LDS growth involves the effort to improve missionary quality, as distinct from quantity. President Kimball had mentioned this matter in his "lengthen our stride" presentation in 1974, but in late 2002, the church emphasized this issue more than it ever had before. During the October 2002 General Conference of the church, in a session directed specifically to holders of the LDS priesthood and broadcast throughout the LDS world, Elder M. Russell Ballard of the Quorum of the Twelve Apostles spoke about a change in expectations in a talk that thereafter was referred to in LDS circles by one of its key phrases: "raising the bar."[78] In his presentation, Elder Ballard at first acknowledged that an appreciable minority of missionaries had gone out into the field without a full commitment to their faith:

---

[77] See multiple regression analyses in Appendix B.
[78] Ballard (2002).

We don't need you to just fill a position; we need your whole heart and soul. We need vibrant, thinking, passionate missionaries who know how to listen to and respond to the whisperings of the Holy Spirit. ... We cannot send you on a mission to be reactivated, reformed, or to receive a testimony. We just don't have time for that....

As I heard this presentation (as a live broadcast to my LDS congregation in Florida, where I then resided), I certainly knew, from my own experience as a missionary in the late 1970s, that some of my fellows had gone on missions because their parents or local church leaders thought that mission service would be 'just the thing' to set straight the life of a young man who had been on an eccentric course. The missionaries I served with were mostly upstanding young men. But a certain minority had had alcohol or drug problems until a rather brief time before their missions; a few had not even read the Book of Mormon before their missions, had been relatively inactive in the church before their mission service, and did not really have a personal conviction of the faith that they were now preaching. By contrast, in his 2002 presentation (essentially a message to prospective missionaries), Elder Ballard was saying that the use of mission service as a sort of spiritual reform school would no longer be tolerated.

As Elder Ballard continued:

As an Apostle of the Lord Jesus Christ, I call upon you to begin right now—tonight—to be fully and completely worthy. Resolve and commit to yourselves and to God that from this moment forward you will strive diligently to keep your hearts, hands, and minds pure and unsullied from any kind of moral transgression. Resolve to avoid pornography as you would avoid the most insidious disease, for that is precisely what it is. Resolve to completely abstain from tobacco, alcohol, and illegal drugs....

And that is not all we expect of you, my young brethren. We expect you to have an understanding and a solid testimony of the restored gospel of Jesus Christ....

Now these are high standards. We understand that, but we do not apologize for them.... There's nothing new in them, nothing you haven't heard before. But tonight we call upon you, our young brethren ..., to rise up, to measure up, and to be fully prepared to serve the Lord....

Please understand this: the bar that is the standard for missionary service is being raised. The day of the "repent and go" missionary is over. You know what I'm talking about, don't you, my young brothers? Some young men have the mistaken idea that they can be involved in sinful behavior and then repent when they're 18 1/2 so they can go on their mission at 19. While it is true that you can repent of sins, you may or you may not qualify to serve.[79]

The response of the Church as a whole was immediate and dramatic. Missionary preparation programs had exist-

---

[79] Ballard (2002).

Chapter 1: Mormon Growth, 1830-2011 51

ed in some LDS congregations since at least as early as 1932,[80] but such programs were lacking in many congregations by 2001. After Elder Ballard's talk, many LDS congregations around the world implemented or reinvigorated their missionary preparation programs. (Certainly the Church's preparation of my own son for missionary service—he being among the missionaries called in 2010—was much more rigorous than in the late 1970s, when I was getting ready to serve.)

Higher standards for missionary service had a striking effect on the number of missionaries serving. The total number of new missionaries called to service in 2002, the year of Elder Ballard's October talk, was an all-time high of 36,196. The following year, the number of new missionaries called dropped by 16% to 30,467, with that number flattening out for years thereafter. From 2003 through 2010, the annual number of new missionaries called never varied by more than ±4% from an average of 30,210. The church was quite serious about raising the bar for missionary service, even at the cost of sending significantly fewer missionaries into the field.

A plateau in the quantity of missionaries had consequences. Because the number of LDS convert baptisms is highly correlated with the number of LDS missionaries serving in the field,[81] a drop in the number of missionaries

---

[80] *Deseret News 1982 Church Almanac*, p. 57.

[81] Spearman's rho = +.881 (n = 14, p < .001), correlating the number of convert baptisms in the period 1977 through 1990 with the number of missionaries serving during that period. Given the highly skewed distributions of the two variables, a non-parametric measure of association was preferable to Pearson's r; given the small sample size, Spearman's rho was preferable to Kendall's tau (Xu et al., 2010). The number of missionaries serving in the field, and the

in the field would slow the rate of growth in the number of convert baptisms. This explains at least some of the slowing of LDS growth since 1990, at least for the period 2003 and thereafter.

Thus, the drop in LDS growth seems largely due to two factors: the shift of missionary focus to more difficult fields of labor, and the 'raising of the bar' for qualification as a missionary, with a consequent drop in both missionary numbers and, further downstream, convert baptisms. What implications does each of these factors have for the future of LDS missionary work? The answer to this question will occupy us throughout the following chapter.

---

number of convert baptisms, may be found in the "Statistical Report" articles for the respective years.

Chapter 2

The Matrix of Future Mormon Growth: The Mormon World in 2012

The preceding chapter's review of selected aspects of Mormon history since about 1973 demonstrates three especially relevant factors involving Mormon growth:

1. **All other things being equal, *more* LDS missionaries leads to a greater number of converts to the LDS faith.** This point is firmly established by the data reported in Chapter 1, and the analysis reported in Appendix B for the period 1977-1990.

2. **All other things being equal, *better prepared* LDS missionaries leads to a greater number of converts to the LDS faith.** This point is also sustained by the analyses discussed in the preceding chapter, in which I establish that phenomenal increases in the rate of LDS convert baptisms have occurred because of developments in teaching methods.

3. **All else being equal, the greater the number of Latter-day Saints there already are in a given area, the greater the number of future converts.** This much is clear from the multiple regression presented in Appendix B, for the period 1991-2011. The reader will recall that, for each additional nation added during this period to the list of countries where the Church of Jesus Christ had organized

congregations, 1,300 *fewer* converts joined the Church. This finding is certainly in accord with Rodney Stark's notion of networks of faith: the idea that religious conversion is facilitated to the extent that a potential convert has, or can easily form, a network of associates in the new faith. A new country added to the mix will, at first, have next to no Saints for the potential convert to form a network with. Once a critical mass of Saints develops, potential converts have an easier time finding points of connection in the community of the Saints.

The future growth of the Church of Jesus Christ depends, then, on at least these three factors: the size of the missionary force, the preparation of that missionary force, and the availability of Church members in any given area for potential new converts to connect to. I contend that, in each of these areas, the Church of Jesus Christ is poised to experience explosive growth—and the evidence of this is already available.

The size of the LDS missionary force

As I write these words in 2012, the LDS community has been preparing its young people for almost a decade to meet the higher standards for missionary service outlined by Elder Ballard. These efforts are beginning to bear fruit. It now appears that the LDS missionary corps is growing considerably.

The number of missionaries serving at year-end 2011 was 55,410—a full 6% increase over the preceding year, and the largest one-year increase in the LDS missionary corps since 1997, fourteen years earlier. This is also the

Chapter 2: The Matrix of Future Mormon Growth   55

largest number of missionaries serving since 2003, the year after Elder Ballard's "raising the bar" presentation, which began a drop in the number of missionaries serving. No doubt at least in part as a consequence of this increase in the number of missionaries, the number of LDS converts in 2011 was 283,312,[82] an increase of over 3% in the number of converts compared to 2010, and the fifth-highest percentage increase in the annual number of converts since 1990.

The LDS missionary force will only get larger in the near future—much larger. Recent LDS policy changes, and Mormon demographics, dictate this.

Changes in Missionary Eligibility Policy

For many years, the age of eligibility for missionary service was set as 19 years of age for males (for whom missionary service is a priesthood duty), and 21 years of age for females (for whom missionary service is optional). This changed as this book was going to press, in a way that will alter the face of the LDS missionary force permanently.

In the first session of the Church's fall conference, on October 6, 2012, LDS President and Prophet Thomas S. Monson announced that, effective immediately, eligibility for missionary service would change as follows:

- Males now have the option to serve as missionaries as early as 18 instead of 19 years of age, if they have graduated high school.

- Females are now welcome to serve as missionaries as early as 19 instead of 21 years of age, if they have graduated high school.

In making this announcement, President Monson emphasized that missionary work remained "a priesthood re-

---

[82] "Statistical Report, 2011" (2012), p. 30.

sponsibility." Thus, missionary service remains optional for women. However, in practice, this policy change is likely to significantly increase the number of both men and women serving missions.

For young men, the policy change makes missionary service less disruptive to educational pursuits. For the most part, young men now have the option of going on missions directly or soon after graduating high school. Then, following their missionary service, they may pursue their college studies or technical training without interruption. This will make the opportunity to serve as a missionary more attractive to young men who otherwise might be dissuaded from missionary service.

For young women, the picture is a bit more complicated. Missionary service has always been only optional for women. However, the lowering of the required age for missionary service doubtless means that at least some of the women who would otherwise marry during the period of 19 to 21 years of age (which, anecdotally, it appears that a number do) will instead choose to serve as missionaries and marry a little later. This has the potential to increase the missionary force by a large factor.

We can only speculate on the effect that this policy change will have on the size of the LDS missionary force. Conservatively, I estimate that this change will result in a 20% increase in the number of LDS missionaries serving in 2013 and 2014 alone. Over the long run, I would expect even larger increases, as young men and women adjust their plans for their personal futures in reaction to this development.

Demographics

Worldwide, most Mormons are first-generation converts. However, most Mormon *missionaries* seem to be individuals raised in LDS homes. These people are referred to as "children of record" on Church records. Thus, one would expect the number of children of record baptized at the age of 8 in 1999 to roughly parallel the number of missionaries called at the age of 19 in 2010. In fact, the correlation of the baptism of children of record in one year with the number of missionaries called 11 years later is high.[83]

Many of the missionaries called to serve in 2010 were baptized as 8-year-old children of record in 1999, when 84,118 such baptisms occurred. In 2007, 93,698 children of record were baptized, an increase of 11.4% over 8 years. One might expect an increase of at least 5% in the LDS missionary force over the next 8 years, and possibly much more, just on the basis of this demographic factor.

However, I believe that a larger *proportion* of this age cohort will volunteer for missionary service than earlier cohorts. This is because the "raising the bar" for missionary service substantially raised the profile of that service in the mental economy of the typical young Latter-day Saint, through the additional local sermons and Church-wide conference addresses devoted to the higher bar, as well as

---

[83] Spearman's rho = +.762 (n = 27, p < .001), correlating the number of children of record baptized in the period 1973 through 1999 with the number of missionaries called during 1984 through 2010. Given the non-normal distributions of the two variables, a non-parametric measure of association was preferable to Pearson's r; given the small sample size, Spearman's rho was preferable to Kendall's tau (Xu et al., 2010). The number of missionaries serving in the field, and the number of baptisms of children of record, may be found in the "Statistical Report" articles for the respective years.

the missionary preparation classes. Emphasize missionary work to a generation of children, as the Mormons have increasingly done, first with President Kimball's 1974 seminar and again with Elder Ballard's "raising the bar" talk in 2002, and you will have a generation of missionaries.

In addition, the Church's current top leadership has issued a clear call for more missionaries. President Monson issued a direct call for more missionaries at the General Conference of the Church in October 2010.[84] He backed this up in 2011 with a message on this topic printed at the beginning of an issue of the Church's magazine for adults.[85] In the following issue of that magazine, there appeared a brief review of the teachings of many earlier Presidents of the Church regarding missionary service.[86]

Because of all these factors, I suspect that a larger portion of the currently-below-19 age cohorts will serve as missionaries than was the case with earlier age cohorts. If that happens, we will see increases in the size of the missionary corps on the order of, not 5%, but 20% to 30% or more over current levels, just based on the service of those baptized as children of record.

Of course, not all missionaries were baptized as children of record. This author, for example, served as an LDS missionary (Japan Okayama Mission, 1978-1980) even though I was baptized, not as a child of record, but as a convert myself in college. Thus, we should expect that, as convert baptisms rise, so too will the number of missionaries rise, leading to yet more convert baptisms, and so on.

---

[84] Monson (2010)
[85] Monson (2011b).
[86] "A Call for Missionaries" (2011).

Chapter 2: The Matrix of Future Mormon Growth

The preparation of LDS missionaries

The "raising the bar" regimen also comes into play when it comes to the overall preparation of LDS missionaries. The major point of the missionary training given to LDS youth is to help these youth be better prepared—intellectually, physically, and especially spiritually and morally—to serve as missionaries. So much can be seen from the manual[87] currently used in LDS missionary preparation classes, both at BYU and in many congregations.

Of the fourteen chapters of this 123-page manual, only one is focused on the Saint's obligation to serve as a missionary. The rest of the chapters involve other aspects of preparation for that service: personal morality (one chapter, prominently placed near the beginning of the manual); spiritual preparation (such as being worthy of the companionship of the Holy Spirit in one's daily life; four chapters); intellectual preparation (one chapter); physical and emotional preparation (one chapter); time management (one chapter); and aids to preparing investigators for baptism and confirmation (one chapter). In addition, four chapters lead the missionary through some basic gospel doctrines.

This might seem elementary, but it is light-years beyond the formal preparation given to prospective missionaries in, say, the late 1970s, when this author was preparing for a mission. In that era, missionary preparation before entering the Missionary Training Center was largely a do-it-yourself affair, and anecdotal evidence suggests that some prospective missionaries prepared themselves far better than others.

Does all this formal preparation make a difference? Statistical analysis suggests that it does.

---

[87] *Missionary Preparation Student Manual: Religion 130* (2005).

The *Missionary Preparation Student Manual* was published in 2005. The median number of convert baptisms per missionary, during the five-year period before this publication (2000-2004) was 4.59. By contrast, the median number of convert baptisms per missionary during the five most recent calendar years (2007-2011) is 5.22, or an increase of 13.7%.[88] One explanation for this change is improved missionary preparation.

In sum, it seems that improved missionary preparation has resulted in double-digit percentage increases in the number of convert baptisms per missionary, compared with prior history. There is every reason to expect that this improvement will be sustained in the foreseeable future.

"LDS networks of faith"

I have made the case that one of the major factors in the slowing of LDS growth after 1990 was the expansion of the Church into areas where there were very few or no Latter-day Saints already in residence (such as Russia, Latvia, Kenya, and Mongolia). I have stated that ultimately Latter-day Saints would build up sufficiently large "networks of faith" (in Rodney Stark's phrase) to present a potential convert with an adequately sized community with which to identify and connect. Potential converts will find Mormons among their acquaintances at work or school, or in their neighborhoods; their social networks will have some extensions into the Mormon network of faith. In addition, potential converts will find people in the local LDS wards to whom they can relate.

---

[88] Author's calculations using data in the "Statistical Reports" published for the noted years.

Chapter 2: The Matrix of Future Mormon Growth   61

How far is the Church from reaching that position today? As it happens, in some of the Church's frontier areas, it has already reached this position, albeit fairly recently.

In this connection, it is worthwhile to look at the number of stakes that the Church of Jesus Christ is organizing in its 'frontier' areas, including Africa, Eastern Europe, and Asia. An LDS stake is a multi-congregational unit, roughly equivalent to a Catholic or Episcopal diocese. A stake may have four to a dozen or so wards (the LDS term for fully functional congregations), each of which has 100 to 400 church members. The formation of an LDS stake is a sign that church membership, activity, and the depth of leadership in a given area have reached a caliber that can sustain the Church organization at the level of both single and multiple congregations. Stake formation, in other words, is an indirect measure of the maturation of an area of the church into a more self-sustaining form. It is thus a sort of measure of the maturity and extent of the Mormon social networks to which converts might attach themselves.

Of the 72 stakes formed by the Church from October 1971 through September 1973, only 3 stakes (4%) were formed on the LDS frontier, all in Eastern Asia; these included the first stakes each within Korea and the Philippines, and the second stake in Japan.[89] By contrast, of the 88 stakes formed from October 2009 through September 2011, 14 stakes (16%) were formed on the LDS frontier, including 9 in Africa, 4 in Asia, and 1 in Eastern Europe. Overall, this is a four-fold increase in the stakes formed on the LDS frontier, on a percentage basis. These included the first stakes each within Indonesia, Russia, and Uganda, the second in Madagascar, the fourth in Côte d'Ivoire (Ivory

---

[89] *Deseret News 1974 Church Almanac* (1974), pp. 175-177.

Coast), the seventh in Ghana, the tenth and eleventh stakes in the Democratic Republic of the Congo, the eleventh in Taiwan, the twelfth in South Africa, the 17th in Nigeria, and the 78th through 80th stakes in the Philippines.[90] Subsequently, the first LDS stake in India was formed.[91] Thus, there are indications that the Church on its frontier is already achieving the kind of critical mass needed for the rate of convert baptisms to increase, even substantially.

The number of LDS missionaries is increasing, and is likely to show significant increases in the next decade (I estimate by 40%-50%, taking all factors into account). The preparation of missionaries has improved, and this preparation has already had a significant impact on the number of converts baptized per missionary in the field (on the order of 14%). The Church has recently developed stable communities of faith in Asia, Africa, and Eastern Europe, to add to the communities it already has in North, Central, and South America (improving the relative strength of its communities of faith here by at least a factor of four).

The slowing of LDS growth is poised to end, and soon.[92] All the ingredients for major increase in LDS growth are in place. In the next two chapters, I describe just how far that growth shall extend, in the world in general, and in the United States in particular.

---

[90] *Deseret News 2011 Church Almanac* (2011), p. 5, and *Deseret News 2012 Church Almanac* (2012), p. 5.

[91] "Apostle creates" (2012); "Elder Oaks establishes" (2012), p. 20.

[92] Indeed, the number of LDS convert baptisms in 2011 (281,312) was the highest number in nine years, representing a modest 3% increase over the number in 2010 (272,814). If this trend continues, it may well be that the slowdown in Mormon growth is already over.

Chapter 3

Future Mormon Growth Worldwide through 2120

What will Mormon growth look like in the future? In this chapter, I consider projections for LDS growth in the world at large. After describing the global context for LDS growth—the membership of the world's major Christian churches, and then other major religions, as these stand at present—I describe three projections for LDS growth. Using these projections, I compare the potential size of the future Church of Jesus Christ to these other global religious organizations. I conclude with a comparison between my projections and other projections of LDS growth.

THE GLOBAL CONTEXT

In Table 3-1, I show the membership of selected religious groups on the global scene, along with my calculations for their median annual growth rates for the years 1991-2011. These data are presented graphically in Figure 3-1.

Religious Group	2011 Global Membership (est.)	Median Annual Growth[a], 2001-2011
Christians[b]		
Roman Catholics	1,184,358,000	0.94%
Protestants[c]	426,065,000	1.61%
Independents[d]	348,511,000	1.62%
Orthodox[e]	275,808,000	0.56%
Anglican	87,925,000	1.25%
Latter-day Saints	14,441,346	2.38%
Subtotal: Christians	2,337,108,346	
Muslims	1,560,391,300	2.06%
Hindus	959,941,000	1.10%
Chinese folk religionists[f]	468,451,000	0.71%
Buddhists	467,546,000	0.90%
New Religionists[g]	63,201,000	0.43%
Sikhs	24,285,000	1.98%
Jews	14,875,000	0.34%
Total membership:	5,895,798,646	

Table 3-1. **Major Religious Groups Worldwide, 2011**

Notes to Table 3-1:
Sources: The LDS membership data are from *Deseret News 2012 Church Almanac*, p. 205, and "Statistical Report, 2011" (2012). Membership data for the other religious groups

was found in the 2011 Annual Megacensus of Religions (2011) and previous Annual Megacensuses, found in the *Encyclopedia Britannica Books of the Year*, 1991-2010. The Annual Megacensus does not report data regarding all categories of religious involvement or uninvolvement, and so the total figure does not add to the total population of the world in 2011 (est. 7 billion).

[a] "Growth" includes both converts and births of those raised in the faith.

[b] Does not include Christians unaffiliated with any specific church, or most groups that the Annual Megacensus considers "on the margins of organized mainstream Christianity," such as "Unitarians, ... Jehovah's Witnesses, Christian Science, and Religious Science."[93]

[c] Anglicans, technically Protestants, are counted separately in the Annual Megacensus.

[d] The Annual Megacensus' term for groups, primarily in Africa and Asia, that are "postdenominational and neoapostolic and thus independent of historical, mainstream, ... denominationalist Christianity."

[e] E.g., the Greek Orthodox and Russian Orthodox Churches.

[f] The Annual Megacensus' term for followers of a religion that combines elements of Confucianism, Taoism, folk religion, and the worship of household and local gods and ancestors.

[g] The Annual Megacensus' term for "followers of Asian 20th–century neoreligions, ... radical new crisis religions, and non-Christian syncretistic mass religions."

---

[93] Barrett, Johnson, & Crossing (2007), p. 292.

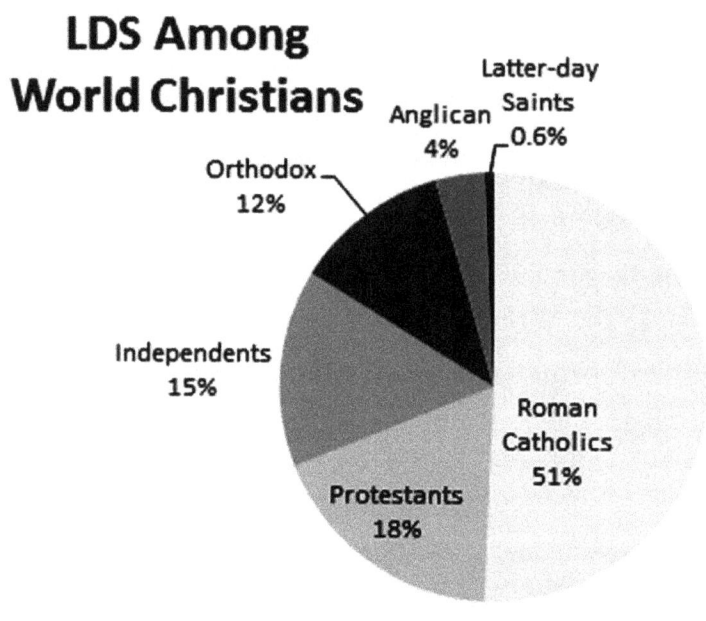

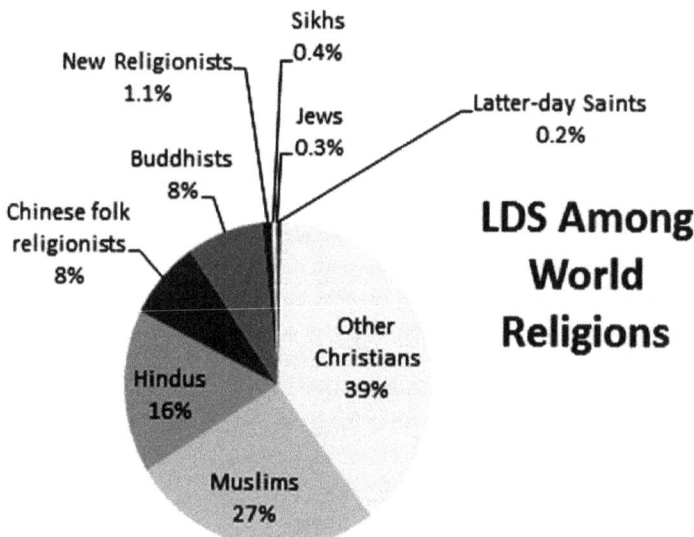

2011: LDS have a tiny global presence ...

Figure 3-1. LDS Global Presence and Growth Rate, 2011

Chapter 3: Future Mormon Global Growth

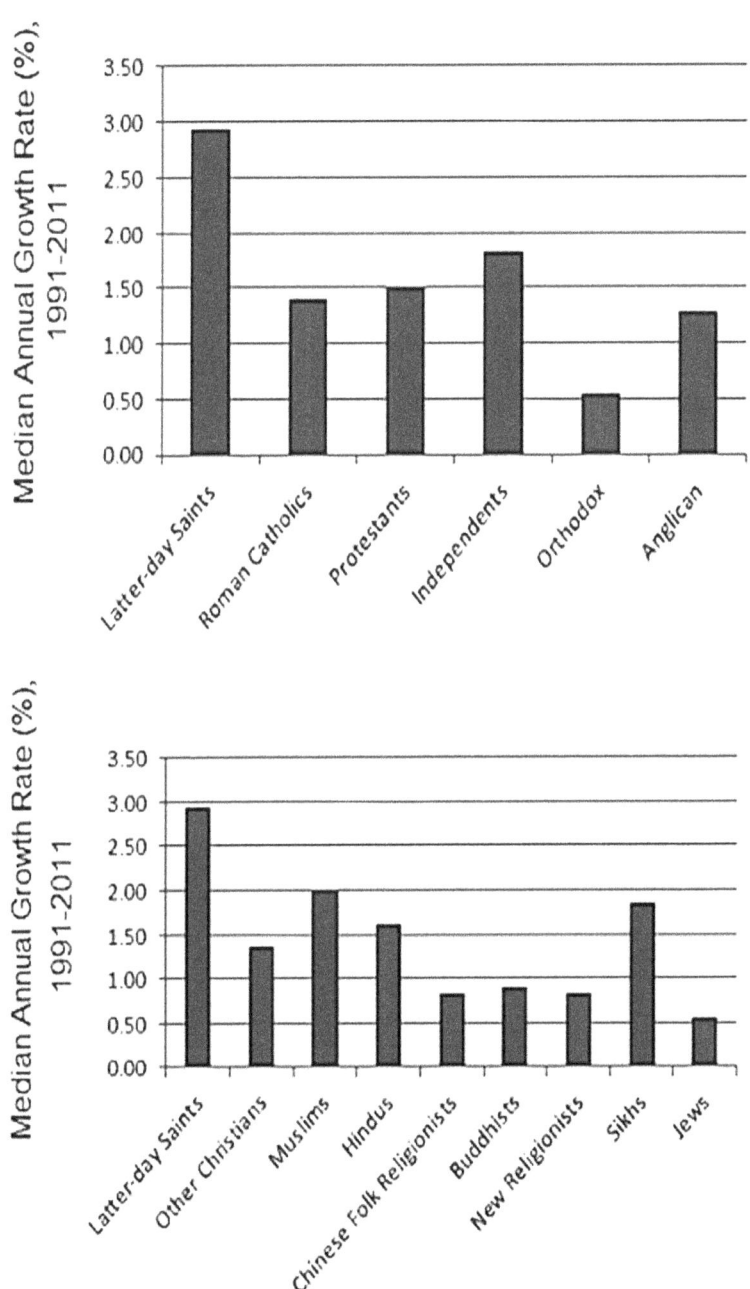

... but they also have a high growth rate.

Table 3-1 and Figure 3-1 highlight several noteworthy aspects of the contemporary world religious scene, and the LDS place within it:

- On a global scale, the Latter-day Saints comprise a tiny presence, but they have a higher growth rate than groups that are numerically dominant at present.
- Just the three groups of Christians, Muslims, and Hindus combined account for over 4.8 billion of the approximately 7 billion inhabitants of the planet in 2011.
- Although a little over half of the world's Christians are accounted for by Roman Catholics, most of the rest are accounted for by groups that are not as well known in the United States as they are in the rest of the world, including the Orthodox and the so-called Independents.
- Similarly, there are huge non-Christian religious groups in the world that are relatively scarce in the United States, including Muslims, Hindus, Chinese folk religionists, and Buddhists.
- Although there are currently more Christians than Muslims in the world, the median annual growth rate for Muslims is much larger than most of the Christian groups (except for the Latter-day Saints), reflecting relatively higher overall Muslim fertility.

MODELS OF FUTURE GLOBAL LDS GROWTH

To project global Mormon growth over the next century, I created three different growth models. In all of them, I

Chapter 3: Future Mormon Global Growth   69

assume that the annual Mormon growth rate continues to fall after 2011, reaching 2% by the end of 2013. It is in what happens after 2013 that the models diverge.

The Low-Growth Global Model: The low-growth model assumes that the case I have made for LDS growth rebounding in the near future amounts to nothing: once reaching 2% in 2013, the annual growth rate stays at that figure for the next century, reaching a stable per-decade growth rate of 21.9% from 2022 on. Given that the *minimum* per-decade growth rate since 1910 has been 27.4% (median: 40%), the low-growth model is the most conservative model that is at all plausible. (It even may be within the "unrealistically conservative" range, but one must consider limiting cases.)

The Moderate-Growth Global Model The moderate-growth model assumes that LDS growth bounces back slowly: the annual growth rate increases after 2013 by an additional 0.05% per annum, reaching 4% in 2053, and then staying there. The per-decade growth rate would rise from 27.7% in 2010 to 48% by 2062, and hold there from then on. This would bring the LDS growth rate back to what it was in the early 1950s (well before the high growth seen from 1960 through 1989).

The High-Growth Global Model: The high-growth model assumes that LDS growth bounces back more quickly, and to a higher level, than the moderate-growth model: the annual growth rate begins to rise after 2012 at the rate of an additional 0.1% per annum, reaching a ceiling of 5.5% in 2048, and staying at that level thereafter. The per-decade growth rate would thus rise from 27.7% in 2010 to 70.8% by 2057, and hold at that level from then on. High as this rate is, it is still less than the per-decade growth rate actually seen in the 1960s (73.1%), and is not that much higher than the growth rate actually seen in the 1980s (67.3%).

The results that arise from the differing assumptions of these three models are shown in Table 3-2 and Figure 3-2. The reader may use the first chart in Appendix D to track these projections against actual global LDS membership figures, on a year-by-year basis, during the period 2012 through 2040.

Year	Low-Growth	Moderate-Growth	High-Growth
2020	17,275,666	17,514,123	17,755,278
2030	21,058,940	22,694,251	24,446,196
2040	25,670,730	30,871,040	37,064,269
2050	31,292,477	44,075,020	61,649,041
2060	38,145,355	65,147,728	105,305,467
2070	46,498,975	96,434,552	179,876,950
2080	56,681,991	142,746,695	307,255,816
2090	69,095,031	211,299,979	524,837,319
2100	84,226,457	312,775,587	896,497,958
2110	102,671,581	462,984,275	1,531,348,019
2120	125,156,084	685,329,827	2,615,763,633

Table 3-2. **Three Models of Projected LDS Growth Worldwide, 2020-2120 ("the Koltko-Rivera global models")**

Chapter 3: Future Mormon Global Growth 71

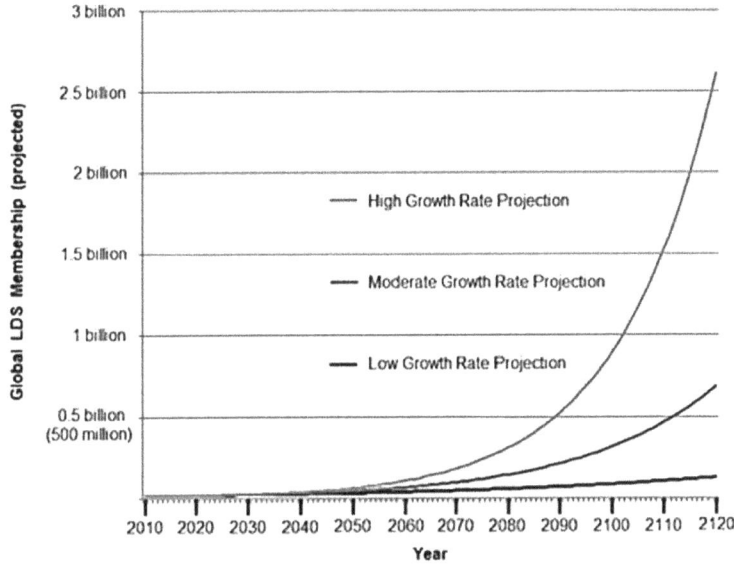

Figure 3-2. **Projected Global LDS Membership, 2010-2120, according to the Koltko-Rivera global models**

It is noteworthy that, in the beginning, the models are very close in their predictions for LDS membership. At the end of 2020, LDS membership under the high-growth model is only 2.8% larger than that under the low-growth model. It is only from about 2030 onwards that differences among the three projections become truly noticeable. Later on, of course, those differences become pronounced.

But really, now: *over two billion Mormons?!?* Is the high-growth projection for 2120 so much as *sane*, let alone possible? Even allowing for the likelihood that world population in 2120 may reach 10.2 to 18.4 billion,[94] the number

---

[94] I am extrapolating here from the medium-growth and high-growth variants of the United Nations projections for world population (Population Division, 2010). I do not extrapolate the low-growth variant, which I believe is unrealistically low, nor the constant-

of Saints predicted by this model just seems astronomical. However, a closer look at the numbers reveals that this prediction is more plausible than it might at first appear. (I consider other objections to these projections in Chapter 5.)

The high-growth model depends on a sustained annual growth rate of 5.5%, or about 71% per decade. It is important to note that Mormons *already achieved* this sustained growth rate, during the "Mormon go-go years" of the 1960s; in addition, the per-decade growth rate of the 1980s, just before the recent slowing of LDS growth, was not far behind. (In Table 1-1, see the per-decade growth rates for the decades ending in 1970 and 1990, respectively.) These periods saw an explosion of LDS growth in the United States, Central and South America and elsewhere. The Mormons showed the world that they could grow at this rate, especially after the Saints refocused themselves on missionary work when President Kimball advised the Saints to "lengthen our stride" in his 1974 presentation.

Yes, after 1990, the sudden expansion into many new mission areas slowed LDS growth. However, this slowdown seems likely to be temporary. As Stark himself pointed out, even two world wars and a global depression in the twentieth century had only a temporary effect on Mormon growth.[95] Five percent per annum is a reachable annual growth rate for the Mormons to attain (again), once Stark's "networks of faith" effect kicks in, in places like sub-Saharan Africa, Eastern Asia, and Eastern Europe.

My hunch is that what we will observe in reality is the high-growth model. I cannot help but see a resemblance

---

fertility variant, which—predicting a world population of 26.8 billion in 2100—I simply consider too terrifying to contemplate.

[95] Stark, (1996) p. 177, (2005) pp. 143-144.

between the historical growth curve of the Mormons and the projected future high-growth curve, comparing Figures 1-1 and 3-2 (the vertical axes, of course, differ in scale by a factor of about 200). In essence, the high-growth projection argues that future Mormon growth will be much like past Mormon growth. In Chapters 6 through 9, I give a more detailed rationale for the idea that the high-growth model is the most likely of my three projections.

However, Mormon growth will not occur in isolation. Although the leadership of the Church of Jesus Christ does not publish comparisons with other faiths, certainly some readers will wonder how Mormons jostle up against other religions under my three projections for growth. I shall make these comparisons from two angles: the Church as compared against other facets of global Christianity, and Mormonism as compared against other world faiths. In all my projections for the growth of other groups, I anticipate that their growth will occur as it does now: primarily through natural increase.

THE LDS COMPARED TO OTHER GLOBAL CHRISTIAN CHURCHES

To project the growth rate of other (that is, non-LDS) Christian religious groups worldwide, I used the median annual growth rates for these groups for the period 1991-2011 (Table 3-1), progressively discounted for falling fertility, and extended those growth rates through the year 2120 (see Appendix A for details). The comparison of these other Christian groups with my three LDS projections is shown in Table 3-3 and Figures 3-3, 3-4, and 3-5.

	RC	Prt.	In.	Or.	An.	LDS		
Yr.						Lo	M.	Hi
2020	1,284	489	401	289	98	17	18	18
2030	1,396	564	462	304	109	21	23	24
2040	1,507	643	527	318	121	26	31	37
2050	1,615	724	594	332	133	31	44	62
2060	1,719	805	661	345	144	38	65	105
2070	1,817	885	728	356	155	46	96	180
2080	1,908	962	791	367	166	57	143	307
2090	1,988	1,032	849	376	175	69	211	525
2100	2,058	1,095	901	383	183	84	313	896
2110	2,115	1,147	944	390	190	103	463	1,531
2120	2,158	1,188	977	395	195	125	685	2,616

Table 3-3. Projections for the Global Christian Religious Scene, 2020-2120 (membership in millions)

Notes. "Yr." = "Year"; "RC" = Roman Catholics; "Prt." = Protestants (not including Anglicans); "In." = Independents; "Or." = Orthodox; "An." = Anglicans. (See Table 3-1, notes *c* and *d*).

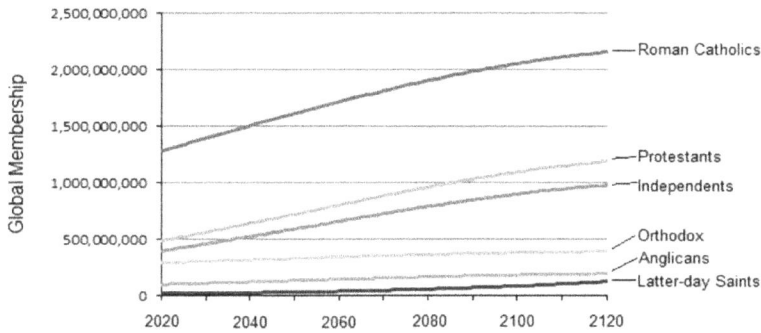

Figure 3-3. LDS low-growth projection and other global Christian groups, 2010-2120

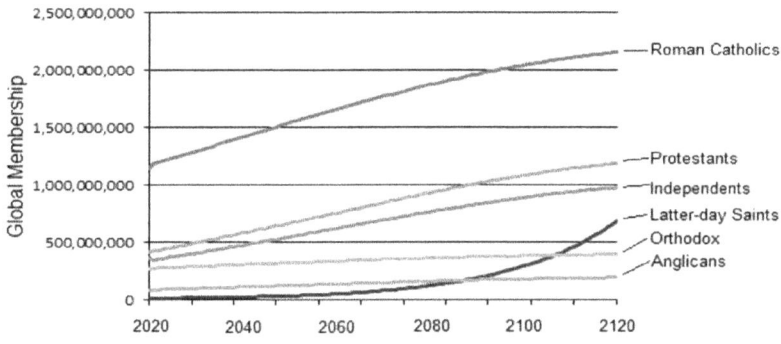

Figure 3-4. LDS moderate-growth projection and other global Christian groups, 2020-2120

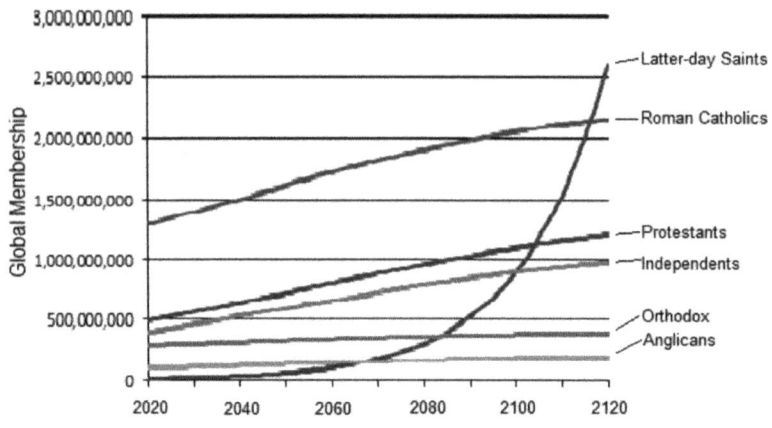

Figure 3-5. **LDS high-growth projection and other global Christian groups, 2020-2120**

Working from Table 3-3 and Figures 3-3, 3-4, and 3-5, we can say several things about the LDS faith in comparison with other groups within global Christianity in the century ahead:

- In the low-growth scenario, Mormonism never becomes a major global presence. The major components of global Christianity in 2011 would be in the same order of numerical precedence in 2120.

- In the moderate-growth scenario, the Latter-day Saints take the position of a major component of global Christianity, actually becoming the second-largest Christian church in the world, behind only the Roman Catholic Church. This is so, in part, because of the fractured nature of Christianity.[96] This

---

[96] The 849 million Independent Christians in 2090 will be in churches that do not affiliate with the traditional denominations; perhaps

Chapter 3: Future Mormon Global Growth 77

could occur as early as 2090, when the LDS would outnumber the combined Anglican communions.

- **In the high-growth scenario, the Church of Jesus Christ becomes the largest Christian church on Earth by 2120.**

LDS COMPARED TO OTHER WORLD RELIGIONS

To project the growth rate of global non-Christian religions, I used median annual growth rates for 1991-2011 (Table 3-1), progressively discounted for falling fertility, and extended those growth rates through the year 2120. (See Appendix A for precise description of method.) The comparison of these religions with my LDS projections is shown in Table 3-4, and in Figures 3-6, 3-7, and 3-8.

Jews and Sikhs are omitted from Table 3-4 and the accompanying figures for reasons of space. However, in all three scenarios for LDS growth, Mormons come to outnumber Jews by year-end 2013[97]; indeed, the Mormons may already outnumber the Jews worldwide.[98] The LDS

---

none will be larger than the Church of Jesus Christ at that time. In 2090, the world's one billion Protestants will be divided, as now, among several different churches, possibly none as large as the Church of Jesus Christ. The Orthodox community is split among several churches as well. Even if we consider the Orthodox Christian community as a single group, by 2110, the Church of Jesus Christ would outnumber the Orthodox under this scenario.

[97] Or not. Jewish demographics are in flux. In particular, growth in the Orthodox sub-population is increasing the number of Jews overall in many places, such as New York City (J. Berger, 2012).

[98] Using figures from the Jewish People Policy Institute, *The Economist* reported a worldwide Jewish population of 13,580,000 for the year 2010 ("Alive and well," 2012, p. 3)—a year in which there were 14,131,467 Mormons worldwide (*Deseret News 2012 Church Almanac*, 2012, p. 205).

grow larger than the Sikhs by the end of either 2043 (LDS high-growth scenario), 2053 (moderate-growth scenario), or 2094 (low-growth scenario).

Yr.	Mus.	Hin.	Bd.	CFR	NR	LDS		
						Lo	M.	Hi
2020	1,862	1,055	505	498	66	17	18	18
2030	2,233	1,164	547	530	68	21	23	24
2040	2,639	1,272	589	562	71	26	31	37
2050	3,071	1,380	629	592	73	31	44	62
2060	3,519	1,484	668	621	75	38	65	105
2070	3,972	1,584	705	648	77	46	96	180
2080	4,415	1,676	738	672	79	57	143	307
2090	4,833	1,759	768	693	80	69	211	525
2100	5,210	1,832	793	711	81	84	313	896
2110	5,532	1,891	815	726	82	103	463	1,531
2120	5,783	1,937	831	737	83	125	685	2,616

Table 3-4. Projections for the Global Non-Christian and LDS Religious Scene, 2020-2120 (membership in millions)

Note. "Mus." = Muslims; "Hin." = Hindus; "Bd." = Buddhists; "CFR" = Chinese Folk Religionists; "NR" = New Religionists (see Table 3-1, notes *f* and *g*).

Chapter 3: Future Mormon Global Growth

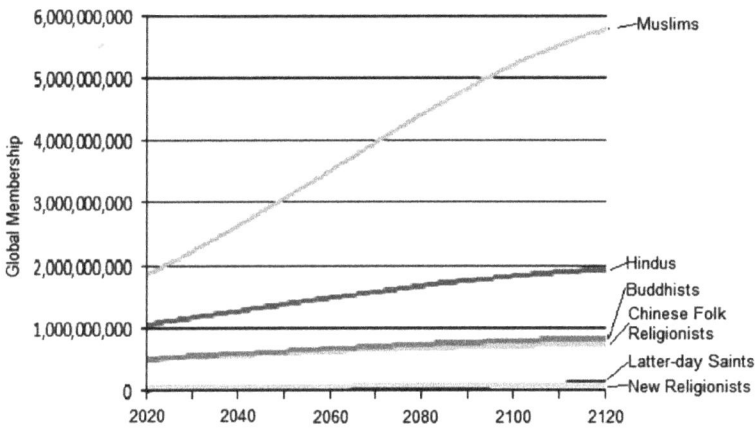

Figure 3-6. LDS low-growth projection and global non-Christian groups, 2020-2120

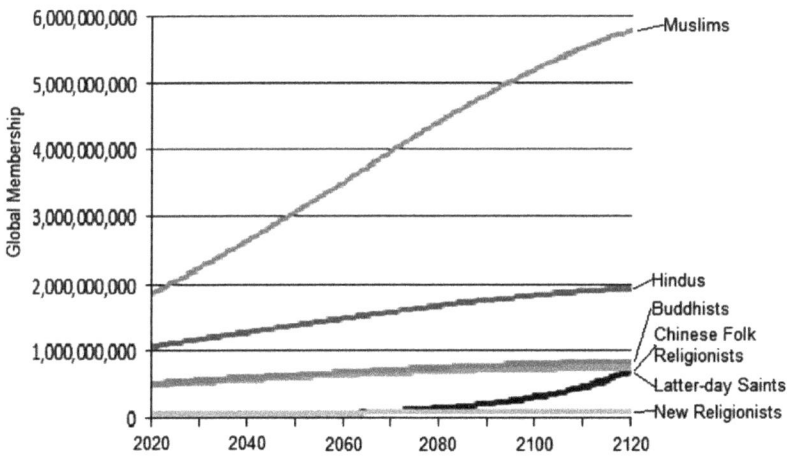

Figure 3-7. LDS moderate-growth projection and global non-Christian groups, 2020-2120

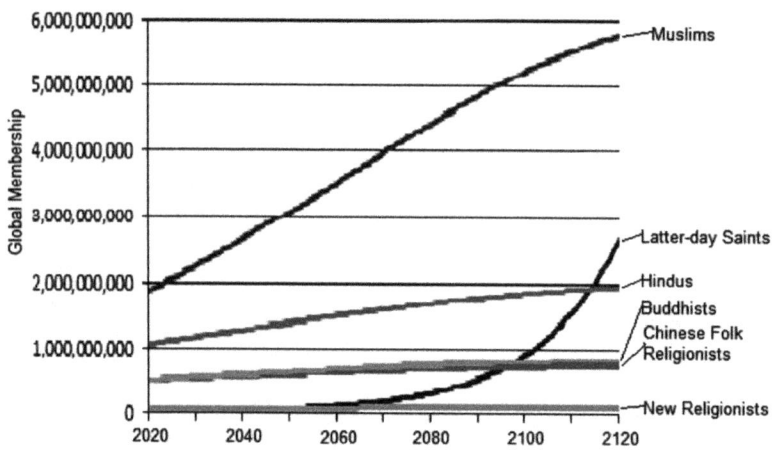

Figure 3-8. LDS high-growth projection and global non-Christian groups, 2020-2120

Working from Table 3-4 and Figures 3-6, 3-7, and 3-8, we can say the following about the LDS faith in comparison with global non-Christian religions by 2120:

- In the low-growth scenario, the LDS barely make a numerical dent on the global scene, although they do come to outnumber the so-called New Religionists by about 2100.

- In the moderate-growth scenario, Mormons have a major presence on the global religious landscape, as their membership approaches in size that of the world's Buddhists or Chinese folk religionists.

- **In the high-growth scenario, the Church of Jesus Christ becomes the second-largest religious body on the planet, behind only the Muslims.**

Comparing Projections for Global LDS Growth

It is of interest to compare our projections with those of both Rodney Stark and the Church of Jesus Christ itself, as the latter were expressed in the *Deseret News Church Almanac*. However, there are some problems in doing this.

Stark's updated projections in 2005 were extrapolated from 2003 membership figures. However, the *Deseret News Church Almanac* projections were extrapolated from 2000 membership figures. Both sets of projections are out of date, and each is based on a different membership figure. Meanwhile, the important question is, which growth rate winds up being correct?

To put all models on an equal footing, I took the per-decade growth rates used in Stark's low estimate model (30% growth per decade), Stark's high estimate model (50% growth per decade), the *Almanac* model (45% growth per decade[99]), and my own low-growth, moderate-growth, and high-growth models (each with variable growth per decade), and applied each of these to the 2010 LDS membership figure as a base.

The resulting projections are compared in Table 3-5 and Figure 3-9, which can be used going forward to compare the accuracy of the Stark and *Almanac* models, as well as my own, all working from the same base. The reader will note that my low-growth projection predicts the least LDS growth of any of the models, while my high-growth projection predicts, by a very large margin, the greatest amount of LDS growth of any of the models. In Chapters 6 through 9, I explain why it is that my high-growth projection is actually the most likely of any of the models presented here.

---

[99] Calculated from *Deseret News 2001-2002 Church Almanac*, p. 151.

	K-R Low	Stark Low	K-R Mod.	Al.	Stark High	K-R High
	Per-Decade Growth Rate					
Yr.	21.9%	30%	up to 48%	45%	50%	up to 70.8%
2020	17	18	18	20	21	18
2030	21	24	23	30	32	24
2040	26	31	31	43	48	37
2050	31	40	44	63	72	62
2060	38	52	65	91	107	105
2070	46	68	96	131	161	180
2080	57	89	143	190	241	307
2090	69	115	211	276	362	525
2100	84	150	313	400	543	896
2110	103	195	463	581	815	1,531
2120	125	253	685	842	1,222	2,616

Table 3-5. Comparison of Projections for LDS World Membership, 2020-2120 (membership in millions)

Note. "K-R" = Koltko-Rivera; "Mod." = Moderate; "*Al*" = *Almanac*; "Yr." = Year.

Chapter 3: Future Mormon Global Growth

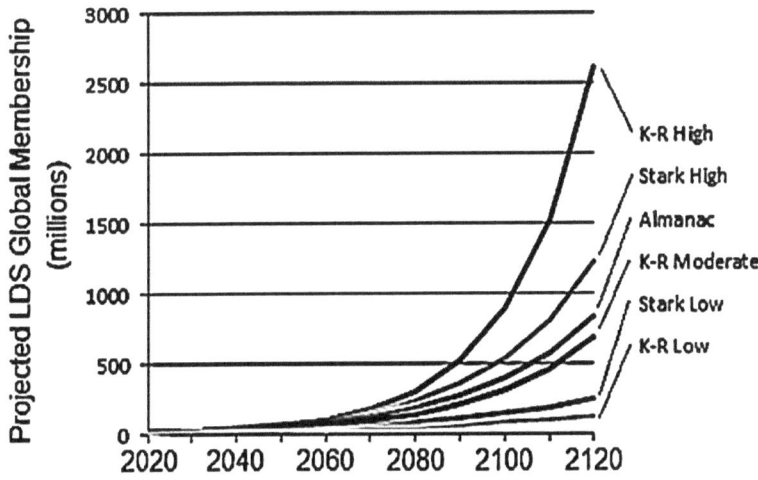

Figure 3-9. Comparison: Projections of Global Mormon Membership, 2020-2120

Note. "K-R" = Koltko-Rivera.

Chapter 4

Future Mormon Growth in the United States through 2120

In this chapter, I consider projections for LDS growth in the United States. After describing the national context for LDS growth—the nation's major Christian churches—I describe three projections for LDS growth, and compare the potential size of the future Church of Jesus Christ against these other American Christian churches.

THE AMERICAN CONTEXT

It is important to place American LDS growth within the context of the nation's largest religions. In Table 4-1, I display the 2010 membership of selected large Christian churches, their most recent change rates, and my calculations for their median annual change rates for the years 1991-2010.[100] (Statistics are shown for the largest churches in the nation for which annual statistics were available in the *Yearbook of American and Canadian Churches*.) I also illustrate these data in Figures 4-1 and 4-2.

---

[100] The greater volatility in religious membership changes to be seen in an individual nation compared to the world at large suggested that, in the American projections, I use a longer period over which to calculate the median annual change rates, compared to the global projections.

Church	2010 Membership (USA)	Change from 2009	Median annual change, 1991-2010
Roman Catholic Ch.	68,202,492	-0.44%	+0.75%
Southern Baptist Cnv.	16,136,044	-0.15%	+0.35%
United Methodist Ch.	7,679,850	-1.22%	-0.75%
(Combined Luth.) [a]	6,553,441	-4.40%	-0.60%
Church of Jesus Christ (LDS)	6,144,582	+1.41%	+1.87%
Evangelical Lutheran Church in America	4,274,855	-5.90%	-0.53%
Assemblies of God	3,030,944	+3.99%	+1.69%
Presbyterian C. (USA)	2,675,873	-3.42%	-1.50%
Lutheran Church — Missouri Synod	2,278,586	-1.45%	-0.74%
Episcopal Church	1,951,907	-2.71%	-0.66%

Table 4-1. **Membership and Change Rates in Major American Christian Churches (2010)**

Notes:
Sources: The U.S. LDS membership data are from editions of the *Deseret News Church Almanac* dating from 1988-2012. Membership data for the other churches were found in the *Yearbook of American and Canadian Churches* for the years 1988-2012.

[a] Combination of the Evangelical Lutheran Church in America and the Lutheran Church — Missouri Synod.

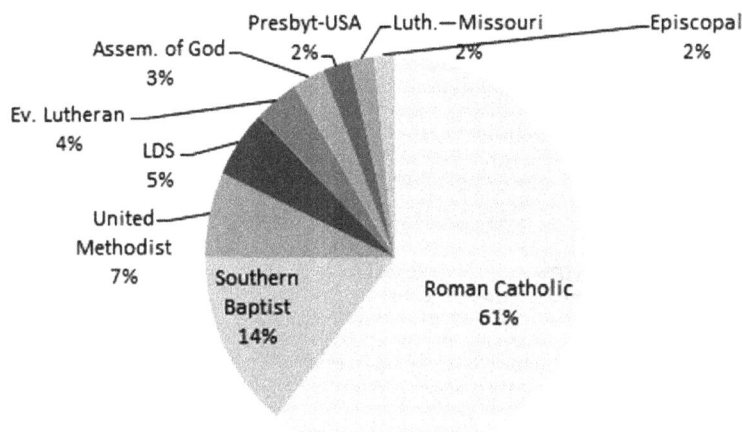

Figure 4-1. 2010 Membership Distribution Across Major American Churches

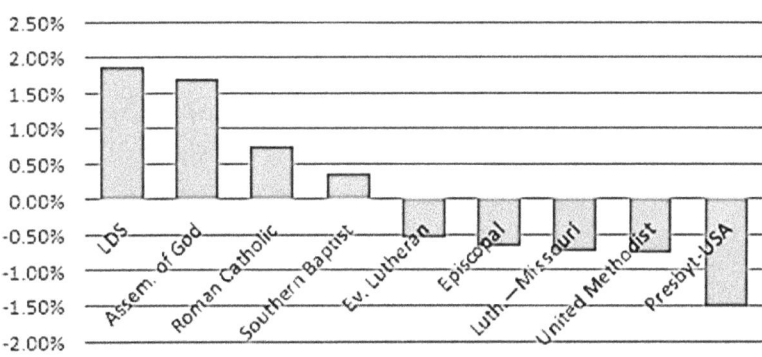

Figure 4-2. Median Annual Change Rates, 1991-2010, Major American Churches

In Table 4-1 and Figures 4-1 and 4-2, we see:

- The American religious landscape is dominated by a few large denominations. Just the top five groups listed in Table 4-1 accounted for 105.3 million Americans in 2009, or just over one-third the entire U.S. population that year (about 308 million).

- Many major Protestant groups are in decline, including Methodist, Lutheran, Presbyterian, and Episcopal denominations. Although Southern Baptists have shown modest annual growth overall from 1991, they showed a decline in membership in 2010 (as they had in 2009, 2008, and 2007[101]).

- The Assemblies of God showed a higher annual growth rate than the Latter-day Saints in 2010, although the LDS median annual growth rate for 1991-2010 was higher. Since 1990, the LDS have had a higher yearly growth rate than the Assemblies of God on 12 occasions, and the Assemblies of God have had a higher yearly growth rate on nine occasions. Of the nine largest churches for which the National Council of the Churches of Christ has received regular annual membership figures over the last few years, depending on the year, either the Assemblies of God or the Latter-day Saints may be called the "fastest growing church in America"—at least in terms of percentage growth rate.

- For most groups, 2010 was a punishing year, where rates of growth were down and rates of decline were up, relative to the preceding quarter-century.

---

[101] *Yearbook of American & Canadian Churches* (2012).

This may be attributable to the effect of the global Great Recession, in its third full year in 2010.[102]

It may surprise some readers to learn that in 2010 the Church of Jesus Christ was already the fourth-largest church in the United States (fifth-largest if one counts the combined Lutheran group instead of its constituent denominations). The Church of Jesus Christ grew larger than the Presbyterian Church (U.S.A.), the Episcopal Church, and the Lutheran Church—Missouri Synod, all sometime before 1980[103]; Mormon membership became larger than the Evangelical Lutheran Church in America in 2000.[104] As Rodney Stark put it, "[the fact] that the Latter-day Saints have overtaken such prominent and 'traditional' faiths as the Congregationalists, Presbyterians, Episcopalians, and even the Lutherans must be one of the most unremarked cultural watersheds in U.S. history."[105]

Models of Future LDS Growth in the USA and Comparison to American Churches

For the Church of Jesus Christ, I prepared low-growth, moderate-growth, and high-growth projections for American membership. All projections started from the base of 6,144,582 American Mormons in 2010 (when the American Mormon growth rate for the year was 1.41%). All projections assume that the American Mormon growth rate rises

---

[102] Stark (1996, p. 177; 2005, pp. 143-144) showed that the Great Depression of the 1920s had a negative, albeit temporary, impact on Mormon growth. Similarly, the Great Recession of 2007+ seems to have similar effects across religious bodies that accept converts.

[103] *Deseret News 1982 Church Almanac*, p. 229.

[104] *Yearbook of American & Canadian Churches: 2002* (2002) pp. 10-11.

[105] Stark (2005) p. 140.

after 2010, the difference between models consisting of how quickly the growth rate rises, and to what level.

The Low-Growth American Model: In this model, the annual growth rate increases from 1.41% by an additional 0.01% per annum, until reaching a maximum of 1.67% in 2036. The per-decade growth rate thus rises from 17.96% in 2010 to 18.01% in 2045 and thereafter. (The median annual American Mormon growth rate from 2001 through 2010 was 1.67%; it seems reasonable to expect U.S. Mormon growth to return at least to that level.)

The Moderate-Growth American Model: In this model, the annual growth rate increases from 1.41% by an additional 0.02% per annum, until reaching a maximum of 3.43% in 2111. The per-decade growth rate thus rises from 17.96% in 2010 to 40.11% in 2120. (This represents a maximum annual growth rate about mid-way between that of the low-growth and high-growth American models.)

The High-Growth American Model: In this model, the annual growth rate increases from 1.41% by an additional 0.04% per annum, until reaching a maximum of 5.18% in 2105. The per-decade growth rate thus rises from 17.96% in 2010 to 65.70% in 2114 and thereafter. (The estimated median American Mormon annual growth rate from 1981 through 1990 was 5.18%; it seems at least possible that U.S. Mormon growth might return to that level.)

I illustrate these projections for LDS growth in the U.S. in Table 4-2 and Figure 4-3. (The reader may find it of interest to compare these with projections for LDS growth globally, in Table 3-2 and Figure 3-2.) The reader may use the second chart in Appendix D to track these projections against actual LDS membership figures for the United States, on a year-by-year basis, for 2011 through 2040.

Chapter 4: Future Mormon Growth in the U.S.

Year	Low-Growth	Moderate-Growth	High-Growth
2020	7,106,484	7,145,091	7,222,854
2030	8,300,329	8,473,651	8,830,493
2040	9,780,987	10,248,588	11,226,747
2050	11,542,794	12,640,708	14,840,536
2060	13,621,947	15,899,228	20,394,176
2070	16,075,608	20,392,070	29,131,207
2080	18,971,237	26,669,247	43,245,589
2090	22,388,442	35,563,774	66,710,157
2100	26,421,174	48,354,424	106,916,618
2110	31,180,304	67,031,590	176,693,348
2120	36,796,676	93,917,120	292,787,051

Table 4-2. **Three Models of Projected LDS Growth in the U.S.A., 2020-2120 ("the Koltko-Rivera American models")**

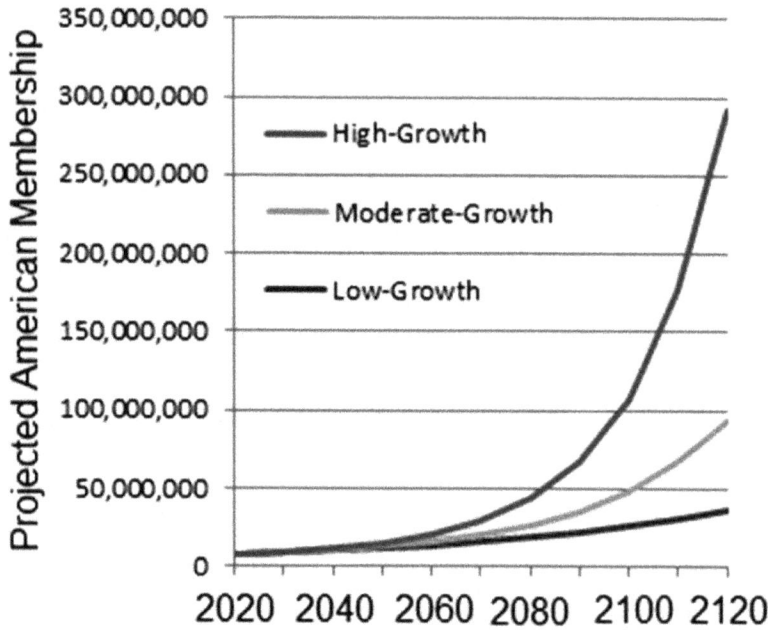

Figure 4-3. **Projected LDS Membership in U.S.A., 2020-2120, according to the Koltko-Rivera American models**

For the purpose of future projections of other American Christian churches, I used a moderate model of membership change for the non-LDS groups to provide a basis for comparison with the Mormons (which is to say, I did not focus on the recent, sharper rates of membership decline). I extrapolated the membership change for the non-LDS groups through 2120, using the median annual membership change rate for the period 1991-2010, as found in Table 4-1. (This procedure assumes that the higher rates of decline and lower rates of growth that most groups saw in 2010 are merely temporary.)

Chapter 4: Future Mormon Growth in the U.S.

The results of these projections through 2120 are found in Table 4-3. The comparison of American Christian groups with the three models of projected LDS growth in America may be found in Figures 4-4, 4-5, and 4-6.

Year	RC	So. Bp.	Un. Mt.	Co. Lt.	Asm. G-d	Pr.	Ep.
2020	73	17	7.1	6.2	3.6	2.3	1.8
2030	79	17	6.6	5.8	4.2	2.0	1.7
2040	85	18	6.1	5.5	5.0	1.7	1.6
2050	92	19	5.7	5.2	5.9	1.5	1.5
2060	99	19	5.3	4.8	7.0	1.3	1.4
2070	107	20	4.9	4.6	8.3	1.1	1.3
2080	115	21	4.5	4.3	9.8	0.9	1.2
2090	124	21	4.2	4.0	11.6	0.8	1.1
2100	134	22	3.9	3.8	13.7	0.7	1.1
2110	144	23	3.6	3.6	16.2	0.6	1.0
2120	155	24	3.4	3.4	19.2	0.5	0.9

Table 4-3. **Projections for the rest of the American Christian religious scene, 2020-2120 (membership figures in millions)**

Notes. "RC." = Roman Catholic; "So. Bp." = Southern Baptist; "Un. Mt." = United Methodist; "Co. Lt." = Collected Lutheran; "Asm. G-d" = Assemblies of God; "Pr." = Presbyterian (U.S.A.); "Ep." = Episcopalian.

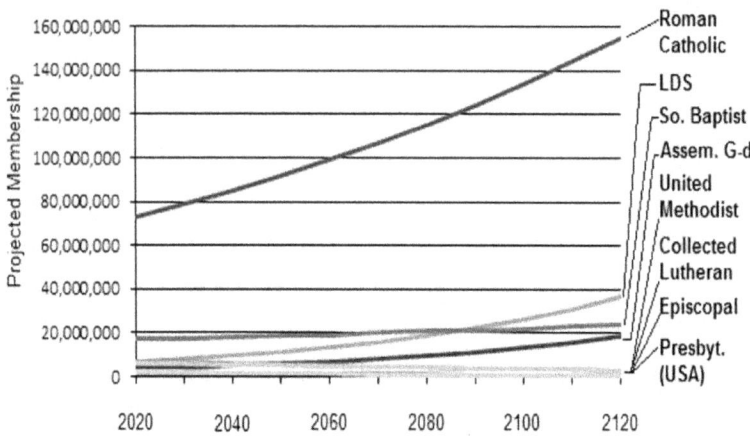

Figure 4-4. LDS low-growth projection and other American Christian groups membership, 2020-2120

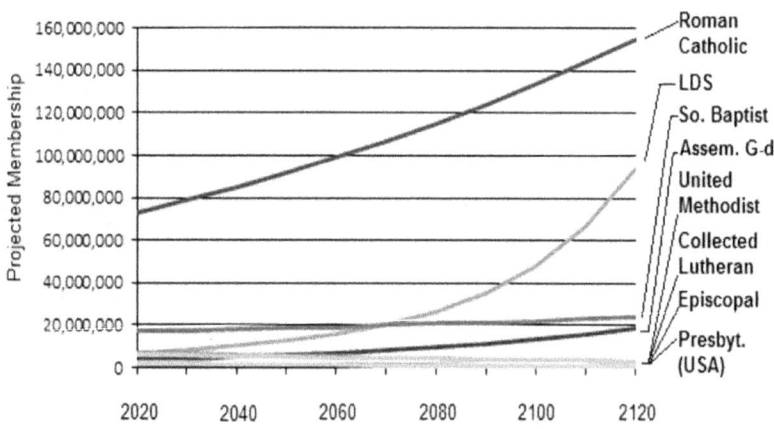

Figure 4-5. LDS moderate-growth projection and other American Christian groups membership, 2020-2120

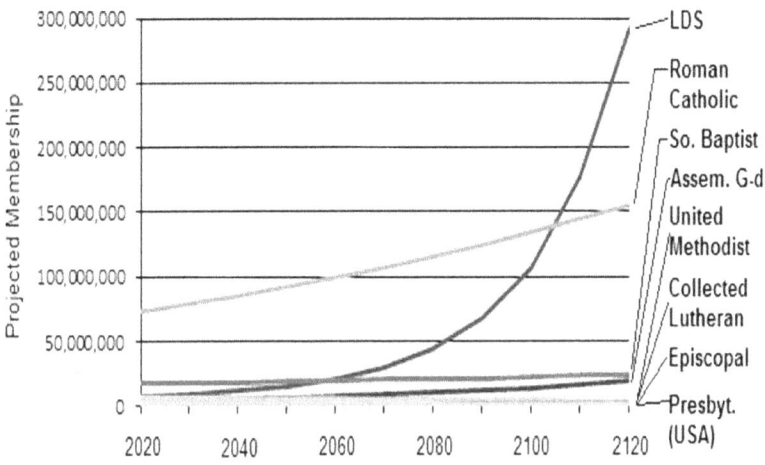

Figure 4-6. **LDS high-growth projection and other American Christian groups membership, 2020-2120**

The three growth projections agree that the Church of Jesus Christ will surpass the size of the Combined Lutheran group by the end of 2014. In addition, the three projections agree that Mormons will outnumber the members of the United Methodist denomination by the end of 2020 or 2021, with the Church of Jesus Christ thus becoming the third-largest church in the nation at that time.

Perhaps more surprising, the three growth projections agree that, sometime during the contemplated time period, the Latter-day Saints will become more numerous than the Southern Baptists, currently the second-largest American church. In the low-growth model, the Church of Jesus Christ becomes the second-largest church in the country by the end of 2087; in the moderate-growth projection, this occurs by 2075, and in the high-growth model, by 2059—or roughly just before the time that my first two grandchildren, born in 2011, begin to enjoy *their* first grandchildren.

Most provocatively of all, **the high-growth projection indicates that the Latter-day Saints will outnumber the Roman Catholics in the U.S. as of 2106, thus becoming the largest Christian church in America at that time.**

That is the American picture for the 21st and early 22nd centuries: Mormons galore. However, there comes a time in every discussion when one must ask what I have come to think of as the quintessential New Yorker's question: *So what?* What does it matter that there will be millions upon millions of Mormons in the United States (and more in the world at large, if the preceding two chapters are to be believed)?

As it happens, a future with that many Mormons in it will be a somewhat different place than today's world. That is the issue I address in Chapter 10. But before we get to that, I address some of the many objections and critiques that could be made of my projections (Chapter 5), and why I think my large-growth projection is actually the most likely (Chapters 6 through 9).

Chapter 5
Objections and Responses

Of course, as with any projections into the future, one may raise legitimate objections to the projections I have made regarding future Mormon growth. I respond to several such objections below, including the following:
- "How valid can projections be, so far into the future?"
- "All sorts of things could upset your predictions!"
- "The pitfalls of straight-line projections" and the effects of organized opposition to Mormonism.
- "How could the LDS grow so large so quickly?"
- Issues related to modernization and secularization.
- "An American church like the LDS will be less appealing in a post-American world."
- "The Mormons will run out of money first."
- "The Pentecostals will outgrow the Mormons."
- "There won't be enough people on the Earth to accommodate these projections."
- "There won't be enough people in America."
- "So many Mormons—in Protestant America?"
- "But more Mormons than *Catholics?!?*"
- "The Mormons are falling away in droves."
- "But the LDS scriptures say the future Church will be 'few' and its dominions 'small'!"

"How Valid Can Projections Be, So Far into the Future?"

In this book, I project Mormon growth to the year 2120, which is over a century in the future as I write these words in the year 2012. How presumptuous of me!

How can projections so far into the future be valid? Just think what would it have been like to try to predict life in the year 2012 from the perspective of a century earlier. The intervening years have seen an almost incredible degree of technological innovation. Transcontinental travel, a weeks- to months-long affair in 1912, is accomplished within hours in the year 2012. Computational technology has gone from mechanical adding machines to experiments with quantum computing. Entire fields of endeavor, like nanotechnology, have developed just over the last few decades. Given the likelihood that the next century promises to be at least as full of technological marvels,[106] how dare I think century-forward predictions could be valid?

Human religion is older than human technology.[107] Humanity's psychological composition changes much more slowly than its technology, so religious trends tend to be more durable than technological ones. This allows long-

---

[106] For a survey of likely technological developments over the course of the next century, see Brockman (2002) and Kaku (2011/2012).

[107] Evidence of the use of controlled fire, the first known purely human technology, became widespread in the period between 50,000 and 100,000 years ago. However, evidence of human burial rites, which suggest the existence of religious belief, date back into the Middle Paleolithic era, as early as 300,000 years before the present, considering evidence from Atapuerca in Spain (O'Neil, 2012; Smithsonian Institution, n.d.). At the very least, there is evidence of ritual burial conducted by Neanderthals, 90,000 years ago (O'Neil, 2012).

Chapter 5: Objections and Responses 99

term predictions about religion to be more reliable than, say, a prediction of future digital storage formats.

This can be demonstrated by a simple thought experiment. How well would my great-grandfather, Emil Koltko, have done in 1912, in predicting Mormon growth over the following century?[108]

The data available in 1912 to Emil would have included Mormon membership figures for the years 1830 (the year the Church of Jesus Christ was organized by Joseph Smith, Jr.) through 1910. As shown in Table 5-1, the per-decade growth rates for the Church become reasonable to work with from the decades ending 1860 and onwards.

Decade Ending in Year	Global LDS Membership	Per-Decade Growth Rate
1830	280	
1840	16,865	5923.21%
1850	51,839	207.38%
1860	61,082	17.83%
1870	90,130	47.56%
1880	133,628	48.26%
1890	188,263	40.89%
1900	283,765	50.73%
1910	398,478	40.43%

Table 5-1. **Per-Decade Actual LDS Growth Rate, 1830-1910**

---

[108] Emil Koltko was born in Poland and immigrated to America, where his son, my maternal grandfather Zygmunt, was born in Waterbury, Connecticut, in 1902. Emil was a plumber by trade, so the simple mathematics required to make these projections probably would have been well within his grasp.

The average of the per-decade growth rates for the decades ending 1860 through 1910, the last decade for which data were available to Emil, was 40.95%. Thus, Emil could have used a per-decade growth rate of 40.95% to predict Mormon membership figures from 1920 through 2010, as shown in Table 5-2 and Figure 5-1. In the table and figure, the actual LDS membership for the decade is also shown, as is the error made by the projection, in either overestimating actual LDS membership (shown by a positive percentage of error) or underestimating (shown by a negative percentage).

Decade Ending in Year	Actual LDS Membership	"Projected" LDS Membership	Error
1920	525,987	561,655	6.8%
1930	670,017	791,652	18.2%
1940	862,664	1,115,834	29.3%
1950	1,111,314	1,572,768	41.5%
1960	1,693,180	2,216,817	30.9%
1970	2,930,810	3,124,603	6.6%
1980	4,639,822	4,404,128	-5.1%
1990	7,761,207	6,207,618	-20.0%
2000	11,068,861	8,749,638	-21.0%
2010	14,131,467	12,332,614	-12.7%

Table 5-2. Per-Decade LDS Membership, Actual versus "Projected" from the Vantage Point of 1912

As Table 5-2 and Figure 5-1 illustrate, this simple method of projection actually would have performed pretty well. Sure, a projection made this way in 1912 would overestimate Mormon growth during the then-unseen years of the First World War and its aftermath (the decades ending in 1920 and 1930), the Great Depression (the decade ending in 1940), the Second World War (the decade ending in 1950) and the Korean War (the decade ending in 1960) — none of which events could have been predicted in 1912. However, the projection would also *underestimate* Mormon growth in the aftermaths of Pres. Kimball's "lengthen our stride" presentation (the decade ending in 1980 and all subsequent decades) and Elder Ballard's "raising the bar" talk (the decade ending in 2010).

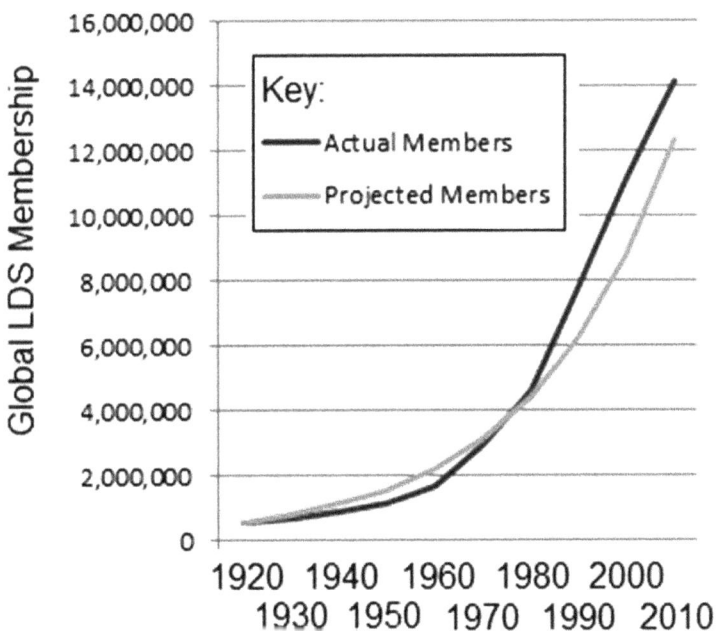

Figure 5-1. Global LDS Membership,
Actual versus "Projected" from the Vantage Point of 1912

Despite six decades of overestimating versus only four of underestimating, the model overall performs admirably, ending the century in 2010 with a 12.7% *under*estimation of actual LDS membership. Thus, in 1912, someone starting from only six data points (Mormon membership by decade, 1860-1910), and using nothing more sophisticated than a pencil, some paper, and knowledge of percents and multiplication, could have estimated Mormon membership by straight-line extrapolation *a full century out* within an error of only 13%.

How is this any different from what I do in this book in terms of projecting Mormon growth? Well, to summarize: (1) I add a great deal of detail and perspective, by bringing in the global and national religious landscapes; (2) I consider different scenarios for growth, with my low-, moderate-, and high-growth projections; and (3) within each scenario, I consider growth rates changing over time. However, the foundation of the method—projections based on historical data—is the same, both for me and for my great-grandpa, hypothetically working this out with a pencil on the back of old plumbing invoices. I would like to think that the modifications to the method that I have added enable me to be at least as accurate as great-grandfather Koltko would have been.

Sociologist Rodney Stark, who conducted his own version of this exercise on a different set of years, put it well:

> The fact is that straight-line projections will be accurate unless or until something basic changes in the process involved. That is, unless there is a really dramatic shift in the basis

Chapter 5: Objections and Responses 103

on which current Mormon growth rests, the past does reveal the future.[109]

"ALL SORTS OF THINGS COULD UPSET YOUR PREDICTIONS!"

One might object that any one of a variety of unforeseen events would change the world enough to invalidate my predictions. This is certainly true. There could be large-scale warfare[110]; global catastrophes[111]; hyper-disruptive technological change, such as the development of the technological Singularity[112]; the discovery of extraterrestrial life[113]; even archaeological discoveries.[114] Western civilization itself could collapse, as the fossil fuels that power it run out.[115] In addition, there is nothing to rule out the possibility that some other religion—either one already in existence, or a new one yet to form—might grow so large as to overwhelm the world, or substantial regions of it.

Yes, any of these events *might* happen. However, I must respond to this possibility as I have earlier to another, although more emphatically: *So WHAT?*

It is in the very nature of any prediction—forecasts of tomorrow's weather, farm production, the stock market, or

---

[109] Stark (1996) p. 177.
[110] Friedman (2009/2010).
[111] Casti (2012).
[112] Kurzweil (2005). We should prevent this (Koltko-Rivera, 2011b).
[113] Paul Davies (2003).
[114] One can imagine archaeological discoveries that would strongly favor one religious position over another, with consequent shifts in religious allegiances that could make the religious world unrecognizable compared to 2012. Obvious examples would be discoveries of heretofore-unknown teachings by the authors of the Upanishads, or by Moses, Buddha, Confucius, Jesus, or Mohammed.
[115] Kunstler (2005).

socio-technological conditions—that there is always an unavoidable degree of uncertainty at the heart of every prediction. No one will ever be able to eliminate this existential fact of mortal human life: the universe, the world, and life are all uncertain to some degree.

In the face of existential uncertainty, then, do we just give up making predictions? Of course not; life would be unlivable. All human action is based on assumptions and predictions. In the face of uncertainty, we do what smart humans have done for centuries, and practice principles of what the financial world calls "risk management": (1) we try to reduce the uncertainty in a given situation (for example, we look at satellite data to find out whether it might rain); (2) we hedge our positions (and put that mini-umbrella in the bag or briefcase); and, in the absence of compelling information to the contrary, (3) we project that the future will be an extension of past and present trends.

Rodney Stark found that people took issue with his projections on the basis of similar objections that he called "pointless."[116] I hope that my comprehensive treatment here will forestall such ultimately useless objections.

"THE PITFALLS OF STRAIGHT-LINE PROJECTIONS" AND THE EFFECTS OF ORGANIZED OPPOSITION TO MORMONISM

Some may criticize my projections as supposedly being mere products of 'the mindless use of straight-line extrapolation from past data.' No doubt, like Rodney Stark before me, I am destined to be "given the benefit of ... counselling

---

[116] Stark (1996) p. 177, (2005) p. 144.

concerning the pitfalls of straight-line projections."[117] Let us take a closer look at some of those pitfalls.

Economists have dealt with the problems inherent in linear projections for a very long time. Management professor Roger Martin[118] has argued that, although linear projections work well for predicting trends in the nonhuman world, the behavior of humans—beings who work in what they perceive to be their own best interest—is not modeled well by straight-line projections. Economist Robert Lucas, author of the so-called Lucas critique of economic modeling, won the Nobel Prize for pointing out that changes in government policy change the playing field, as it were, such that citizens and corporations will change their behavior to adapt to new policy environments, especially to avoid future perceived economic harm (for example, from taxes); future behavior thus might *not* resemble the past.[119] Economist Thomas Sargent won the Nobel Prize, largely for developing tools to incorporate people's changing expectations into economic models.[120]

What impact do these critiques have on my models? As the Church of Jesus Christ grows, some organizations may perceive the LDS as some kind of threat, and take action in self-defense. Might not some religious organizations, sensing themselves threatened by Mormon growth, start preaching against the Latter-day Saints? Might not some governments, under the influence of more traditional religious bodies, close their borders to LDS missionaries? And would not such developments have a negative impact on Mormon growth?

---

[117] Stark (1996), p. 175.
[118] R. Martin (2011).
[119] Thoma (2011).
[120] Thoma (2011).

The problem with this critique is that such things have happened before, but ultimately have had little effect on Mormon growth. Consider governmental opposition:

- In 1838, misled by false reports of Mormon rebellion, Governor Boggs of Missouri issued his infamous "extermination order" against Mormons, resulting in more persecution and death, and the total expulsion of the remaining Saints from the state.[121] Much antipathy against the Saints remained among Missourians for generations. The Saints organized a small congregation in Missouri in 1911, the first such branch to be permanently organized since the extermination order.[122] As of the beginning of 2011, there were over 66,000 Latter-day Saints in Missouri, amounting to over 1% of the state's population, divided into 14 stakes; there were two LDS missions in Missouri, and LDS temples in St. Louis and Kansas City.[123] News accounts noted that "Missouri's governor, Jay Nixon, attended the [public] open house for the [Kansas City] temple and referred to that event and the dedication as 'a time of healing.'"[124]

---

[121] Missouri was a slave state. Many Missourians were convinced that the Saints (largely Northerners) were trying to interfere with Missouri slavery, as well as recruit among free people of color; R.W. Walker, Turley, & Leonard (2008) pp. 8-9. This goes a long way toward describing the roots of the bad feeling of mid-19th century Missourians towards the Mormons. See also Kinney (2011); B. H. Roberts (1900/2001).

[122] *Deseret News 2012 Church Almanac* (2012) p. 368.

[123] *Deseret News 2012 Church Almanac* (2012), pp. 246, 283, 295, 367-369; "Kansas City Missouri Temple Dedicated" (2012).

[124] "Kansas City Missouri Temple Dedicated" (2012) p. 78.

- In June 1989, also due to misinformation about the church, the government of Ghana expelled all Mormon missionaries and forbade all LDS operations; church meetings had to be held in private homes. "The Freeze," as it became known among the Ghanaian Saints, lasted 17 months before it was lifted, after the Ghanaian government "expressed satisfaction that the [LDS] Church taught members to be obedient to government laws and promoted racial harmony."[125] A decade later, in 2001, then-president of Ghana, John Ageykum Kufuor, told one of the Church's apostles that the Church of Jesus Christ was "a part of Ghana."[126] In 2011, after 30 years of missionary work in Ghana, there were over 45,000 Saints there, divided among eight stakes, along with two missions and one temple.[127]

Examples could be multiplied, but no doubt the reader will see where I am headed. Government policies—even governments themselves—change. Anti-Mormon governmental opposition only seems to last for a limited period of time—even extreme opposition, or general opposition to religion itself. (Consider Russia, where, in 2012, Moscow itself, the former capital of the atheistic Soviet superstate, was the site of an LDS stake and the headquarters of two separate LDS missions.) In short, my projections are likely to stand up in the face of potential future governmental opposition to Mormonism precisely because such opposition would be just another instance of the future being like the past.

---

[125] *Deseret News 2012 Church Almanac* (2012) p. 485. See also Allen & Leonard (1992) and Searle (1996).
[126] *Deseret News 2012 Church Almanac* (2012) p. 485.
[127] *Deseret News 2012 Church Almanac*, pp. 485-486.

But what about *religious* opposition? Could not a major religious group in some nation, or a transnational religious body, mobilize its people in opposition to the Mormons?

In principle, yes, such a thing could happen. However, here again, much of this has happened before. Religious leaders preaching against the Mormons would simply reenact, perhaps on a larger scale, the opposition that Mormon missionaries received from Protestant preachers in Europe in the 19th century; the missionaries in some cases were withdrawn from different areas for a period, sometime for years, but over the long run the representatives of the LDS faith simply outlasted the opposition.

The Church of Jesus Christ has not faced a coordinated international anti-Mormon campaign run by a transnational religious organization. Perhaps such a campaign would have an impact on LDS missionary work. But who would initiate and maintain such a campaign? Certainly no major transnational religious body seems inclined to do that at the present time; with all the other challenges that face various organizations—falling membership numbers in this church, clergy shortages in that one—I simply do not see an international anti-Mormon campaign in the forseeable future.

How about *religiously motivated violence* directed specifically against the Saints, in the international sector? This would be nothing new either. During the mid-19th century, many preachers on the American frontier preached violence against the Saints.[128] However, the Saints are no longer a tiny group in some cultural backwater of a nation, as America was in the mid-19th century. Even in the current

---

[128]Hallwas & Launius (1995); Kinney (2011); Mason (2011); B.H. Roberts (1900/2001).

era of geopolitical uncertainty and transition, the United States is indisputably a global superpower, and it will not stand idly by while its citizens (such as LDS missionaries) are endangered. In the 21st century, religious leaders may incite violence against LDS missionaries, many of whom will be Americans, only at their own peril.

How about the domestic picture? To really interfere with the success of Mormon missionary work in the United States, events would have to take a turn bordering on nightmare. The ascendance of evangelical Christianity to political dominance in the United States—a stated goal in some sectors of the evangelical world[129]—might work out badly for the Mormons, given that (a) many evangelicals consider Mormons to be non-Christians, and (b) some evangelical extremists take the position that "non-Christians" do not have First Amendment rights to freedom of religion.[130] However, so far the American public has retained, however fitfully, the principle of freedom of religion in the United States, and I have every hope that it shall do so in the future.

Surely it is conceivable that denominations that feel threatened by an increasing LDS presence in America might take it upon themselves to counter Mormon growth. Even without going to the lengths of anti-Mormon violence seen in the mid-19th century—an American style of pogrom, if ever there were—there is much that a church

---

[129] E.g., Wagner (2008). See also Linker (2006) and Phillips (2006).

[130] For example, Bryan Fischer of the American Family Association, who claims that the First Amendment only protects freedom of religion for Christian churches, not for those who adhere to non-Christian religions; Fischer specifically claims that the First Amendment does not apply to Mormons, whom he claims are not Christian (Fischer, 2011). See also video from the *Rachel Maddow* show, embedded within Martel (2011).

could do to try to counter LDS growth: educational programs; preaching from the pulpit; ads on billboards, radio, television, and Internet.

There are two problems with such efforts: they do not seem to work that well, and there do not seem to be many churches ready to use them. A variety of evangelical authors and others have been preaching against Mormonism from the pulpit, in print, and lately online, for over a century. The Mormons have still grown. As far as opposition from entire churches is concerned, various other Christian churches have declared that Mormons do not fit in with their sense of what is Christian; again, the Mormons have still grown, in some cases larger than the churches that have labeled Mormons as non-Christian (the Presbyterians being a notable example).

Perhaps some major church will organize an out-and-out anti-Mormon crusade in the future. However, with most mainline American Protestant denominations losing membership (see Table 4-1) and the Roman Catholic Church struggling to deal with the priest shortage,[131] I do not see this as a likely development, even if these churches were so inclined (which they assuredly are not).

The Southern Baptist Convention is a possible exception. Certainly most prominent anti-Mormon authors seem to be affiliated with this group. However, as I noted in Chapter 4, this church has lost membership every year from 2007 to 2010; they may have other more pressing concerns to attend to, rather than taking issue with the Mormons.

---

[131] In 2008, 22.7% of the Roman Catholic parishes in the world were without a single resident priest pastor (calculated from data reported in Center for Applied Research in the Apostolate, 2012).

"How Could the LDS Grow So Large So Quickly?"

My projections involve the Church of Jesus Christ growing from 14 million members to, in my high-growth projection, over 2 *billion* members, in just over a century. This might seem more than a little extreme. How could the LDS grow to such large numbers in such a short period of time? As it happens, on several occasions, religions have shown the capacity to grow extremely large within a relatively short period of time, even with modest growth rates. This is due to what some economists call the miracle of compound interest,[132] but applied to people, not money.

Ancient Christianity itself is a good example of this. Sociologist Rodney Stark has published two extensive studies of the growth of Christianity.[133] As it happens, an annual growth rate of only 3.4% would have been sufficient to carry the Christian community from a size of only 1,000 in the year 40 A.D. to a group numbering over 31.7 million by the year 350; this growth rate produces a growth curve for the early centuries of Christianity that closely fits the information available from the historical record.[134] That is a multiplication by a factor of 31,000, over the course of just over three centuries.

It is noteworthy that, in 350 A.D., a religious group of over 31.7 million people would have amounted to 53% of the total population of the combined Eastern and Western Roman Empire—the Western civilization of its day.

Now consider the Mormons. The median annual LDS growth rate for the years 1961 through 1990—the three decades immediately preceding the disintegration of the

---

[132] E.g., M. Hudson (2012).
[133] Stark (1996; 2011).
[134] Stark (2011) pp. 156-157; see Table 9.1 therein.

Soviet Union—was *5.05%*, much higher than the annual growth rate that converted half the Roman Empire between the times of Christ and Constantine. If such a growth rate or higher were to hold sway—say, the 5.46% growth rate that the Mormons showed for the years 1960 through 1969—then there would be no problem with the Mormons growing to the huge numbers I have predicted.

Of course, this all begs the question of why we should think such high rates of growth *will* hold sway. That is the question that I address in Chapters 6 through 9.

Modernization and Secularization

What about the ongoing modernization of the world? In a line of thought stretching back to the European Enlightenment, generations of philosophers and social scientists have claimed that "modernization necessarily leads to a decline of religion, both in society and in the minds of individuals."[135] As applied to the Saints, Stark observed:

> Many of my colleagues believe the pool of potential new LDS converts is rapidly drying up and soon will be fished out, causing growth rates to plummet. Their reason is that the worldwide trend toward modernization will inevitably result in secularization, and therefore all forms of religion will be relegated to cultural byways and backwaters.[136]

---

[135] P.L. Berger (1999) p. 2. For an overview of the rationale behind the secularization hypothesis, see Mickelthwait & Wooldridge (2009/2010), pp. 9-12, 31-50.

[136] Stark (2005) p. 112.

Chapter 5: Objections and Responses 113

The problem with this argument is that, as Stark found, modernization and secularization are each *positively* correlated with Mormon growth. Based on his quantitative research into the matter, Stark concluded that

> the Latter-day Saints are not recruiting best in the backwaters where magic, mystery, and piety persist .... The Mormons do best, instead, where secularization is greatest.[137]

Peter L. Berger, the sociologist who popularized the secularization hypothesis in the 1970s, gets the penultimate word here, as he wrote in the late 1990s, after a great deal more research had been done:

> ... the assumption that we live in a secularized world is false. The world today, with some exceptions ... is as furiously religious as it ever was, and in some places more so than ever. This means that a whole body of literature by historians and social scientists loosely labeled "secularization theory" is essentially mistaken. In my early work I contributed to this literature. I was in good company ....[138]

Thus, we see two fatal flaws in this objection. First, the notion that the world becomes less religious (and more secular) as it becomes more modern—the secularization hypothesis—is simply false.[139] Second, as Stark's research

---

[137] Stark (2005) p. 106.
[138] P. L. Berger (1999) p. 2.
[139] What about Europe? Research data suggest that Europeans are not so much without religious beliefs as they are *unchurched*, that is, unattached to denominations (Davie, 1999, e.g., p. 68). See also P. Berger, Davie, & Fokas (2008), and Stark (2011).

shows, conversion to the LDS faith is actually *helped* by increasing modernism, and more secular societies are actually more fruitful grounds for LDS missionary work.[140]

"AN AMERICAN CHURCH LIKE THE LDS WILL BE LESS APPEALING IN A POST-AMERICAN WORLD."

Another angle of criticism proceeds along these lines:

The Church of Jesus Christ has spread throughout much of the world, and has attained its present numbers so quickly, because it is an American church. The LDS faith is attractive to those outside the U.S. because it allows those people to identify with something made in America. When the U.S. was an undisputed superpower after World War II, that was one thing, but with the waning of American power in the 21st century, the LDS faith will become much less attractive to those outside the U.S. Thus, the membership of the Church will never attain the size of Koltko-Rivera's moderate- or high-growth projections.

I have several problems with this objection. For one, I believe that the notion of "the decline of America" is heavily oversold.[141] But this is not the main issue.

My major dispute with this objection involves its premise: the idea that it is those American roots that make the LDS faith attractive to potential converts. In this re-

---

[140] Stark 1994, and 2005 ch. 5.

[141] Frank Rich (2012, p. 18) calls the current concern with this issue "declinist panic." My own position is roughly parallel to that of Fareed Zakaria (2011/2012): America will remain immensely powerful, but must recognize the rise of other powers in the world.

spect, I find the activities of the Church's leadership over the last three decades or so to be quite revealing.

Beginning in the late 1980s—when the American share of global Church membership was 60%, but dropping[142]— Church administrators began a sweeping change in the composition of the handbooks and manuals that directed the efforts of LDS local officials and teachers throughout the Church. As two historians put it:

> Texts were to focus on essential gospel principles and avoid illustrations that represented peculiarly American, or Utah, cultural values.... In addition, the international magazines translated and published articles from the *Ensign* and other Church periodicals but also printed articles more specifically directed to people of specific language areas.[143]

The very materials given to missionaries to use in teaching were redesigned to "de-Americanize" missionaries' presentations of the LDS faith. The point was to make their presentations more responsive to local conditions— wherever "local" might be.[144]

---

[142] At year-end 1988, there were 4 million American Mormons out of a global population of 6.65 million Saints (*Deseret News 1989-1990 Church Almanac*, pp. 6, 121), so that 60% of all Mormons were Americans. By comparison, at year-end 2010, the 6.06 million American Mormons comprised only 43% of the world's 14.1 million Latter-day Saints (*Deseret News 2012 Church Almanac*, pp. 4, 324). Put another way, in the space of just 22 years, the American share of global Mormonism has dropped by almost one-third. Mormonism is growing rapidly in America, to be sure—by 50% in that one generation—but it is growing even more rapidly abroad.

[143] Allen & Leonard (1992) p. 647.

[144] Duffy (2005) pp. 38-39.

Beyond that, the effort to replace American mission presidents in non-American countries with native leaders, as well as the effort to increase the percentage of local missionaries, helped avoid misunderstandings and miscommunication.[145]

All of this would be insanity if the Church's leadership were trying to appeal to potential converts on the basis of the Church's American roots. Clearly they are not, and they have a very different idea of the grounds upon which people are attracted to Mormonism, one that seems much more like the factors that I point out in Chapter 1 (see "Why People Become Latter-day Saints") and Appendix C.

"THE MORMONS WILL RUN OUT OF MONEY FIRST"

Yet another critique of my projections focuses on LDS finances. The idea here is that the Saints simply cannot afford, financially, to grow at the rate they have been growing. While the LDS heartland is in prosperous America, this argument goes, much of its growth has been occurring among the poor or financially stressed in Central and South America, Eastern Europe, sub-Saharan Africa, and Northeast Asia (like the Mongolia Ulaanbaatar Mission) and Southeast Asia. At the moment, the American Mormon heartland subsidizes growth in other areas; ultimately, however, the number of less-prosperous Saints will so overwhelm the prosperous that the entire enterprise of Mormon growth will either slow down or collapse.

This objection certainly sounds intriguing. After all, what could be a more down-to-earth criticism than one

---

[145] Allen & Leonard (1992) p. 647.

Chapter 5: Objections and Responses 117

based on sheer economics? However, this critique ignores both the Mormon past and the LDS present.

The Mormons started out dirt-poor, a religion of displaced farmers and craftspeople from rural, small-town America, and later from the lower edges of the working classes of Western Europe. Not only were they poor, they became repeatedly impoverished as they were thrown out of their homes and off of their lands through persecution, particularly the violent persecutions seen in Ohio, Missouri, and Illinois. The later immigrant Saints travelled 1,300 miles west from the banks of the Mississippi River to Salt Lake City, many of them *pulling handcarts on foot*, because they could not afford oxen or horses.

But the Saints are good at building from nothing; that is part of the heritage that they cherish and embrace. All of the material wealth of the Mormon people in the Intermountain West was built from scratch, since the exile to Utah in 1847-8. If the money from the heartland runs out—an iffy proposition, as we shall see—the Church of Jesus Christ throughout the world will carry on as it did in the days of its beginnings. That is part of the Mormon mythos, one might say: building the faith even in poverty. As one journalist who is not especially friendly to the Saints has put it, the Mormons are "a religious sect well scripted for vicissitude"[146]—aye, and one for whom endurance through the worst of trials is a much-admired spiritual virtue.

However, although the Mormon mythos starts in poverty, it does not end there. Mormon industry is legendary; during the Mormon pioneer period, the lowly bee was elevated from a brief mention as *deseret* in a lost language of the Book of Mormon to the status of a unifying symbol of

---

[146] Kunstler (2005) p. 295.

industry and community cooperation. This is why the beehive appears on so many pioneer-era artifacts (including most every doorknob in that flagship of Mormon temples, the LDS Salt Lake Temple); this is why so many Church businesses carry the name "Deseret" (as in the Deseret Books chain of bookstores, the Deseret Industries thrift stores and protected workshops for the needy, and others).

The Saints have long valued education; even Nauvoo and the early Utah settlements had "universities" that enlightened the population, one of which (the University of Deseret) grew into the present-day University of Utah in the public sphere, while another grew into Brigham Young University, one of the two largest private universities in the United States. This is, after all, a religion that proclaims, as doctrine, "the glory of God is intelligence."[147]

Effort and education lead to wealth in the LDS mythos (as in the American). Here is an instance of the mythos affecting reality. Many of the descendants of impoverished, mud-covered pioneers are now manufacturers, professors, scientists, farmers, and bankers themselves.[148] Mormonism teaches its less-prosperous converts to follow in the footsteps of their spiritual ancestors, the Mormon pioneers.

This is no empty platitude, either. In 2001, the Saints established a Perpetual Education Fund (PEF), to loan Church funds to young adult Saints in the developing world for technical, vocational, or professional education;

---

[147] LD Standard Works: Doctrine & Covenants, Section 93, verse 36. For a recently stated LDS position on faith and reason, see "Mormon and Modern" (2012).

[148] These include the authors of some very powerful self-help literature of just the sort to assist motivated individuals rise above their poverty (e.g., C.M. Christensen, Allworth, & Dillon, 2012; Covey, 1989; Covey, Merrill, & Merrill, 1994; Hyrum W. Smith, 1994).

repayments fund new loans.[149] The fund's name echoes that of the Perpetual Emigration Fund, which lent money to 19th century European converts to emigrate to Utah.

The PEF program is opening higher educational opportunities to large numbers of Saints in the developing world. During its first ten years, the PEF assisted over 50,000 Saints in 51 countries.[150] Consider this report about Manaus, an isolated city in northern Brazil:

> When the Perpetual Education Fund was announced in 2001, approximately 30 percent of the 800 institute students in the city [that is, LDS college-age youth in Manaus] were getting an advanced education and/or learning a trade. [A local Church officer] said with the blessing of the fund, now [mid-2012] 80 percent of institute students seek education. "They are getting better jobs and this has helped the growth of the Church," he said.[151]

The PEF promotes financial self-sufficiency. For example, one Saint in the Dominican Republic recently reported that his income increased 400 percent over the course of two years, due to the education he received through the help of the PEF.[152] Although not the purpose of the PEF, improvements in the financial self-sufficiency of the Saints increase the resources of the Church.

Finally, entirely aside from the funds it receives in tithes and offerings from its members, the Church owns

---

[149] Hinckley (2001). See the program's website at http://pef.lds.org/pef/home . See also Atkin (2011), N. Garrett (2011).

[150] Atkin (2011).

[151] Weaver (2012) p. 10.

[152] Bueno (2012).

several profit-generating enterprises, such as "one of the biggest and most profitable cattle operations in the U.S." on 300,000 acres in Central Florida: the Deseret Ranches.[153] The ranch supports the Church's mission to feed the poor and to prepare for emergencies—much beef from Deseret Ranches is given to the poor—and tax-paid profits from the ranches help fund church programs.

Yet the Deseret Ranches are but the tip of the proverbial iceberg when it comes to the Church's profit-producing enterprises. Not only does the Church own many more ranches; several journalists have reported that the Church of Jesus Christ has massive business enterprises in a variety of industries, including agriculture, publishing, and so forth.[154] Such journalists and their publications have often been quite hostile and even mocking towards the Church, as if there were something inherently wrong with a religious group raising funds to further its mission. The Church has often been at pains to explain how the taxed profits of its for-profit ventures are used to fund its spiritual mission, including its missionary efforts,[155] and massive humanitarian relief efforts around the world, for the benefit of people of all faiths or none at all.[156]

So: the church has a near-two-century-long history of helping people move from poverty towards prosperity; the church is currently funding educational projects in the developing world to help improve the socioeconomic status of its membership there; and, the church has massive profit-generating enterprises to help fund its programs. The

---

[153] Barnett (2001), quote on p. 56; "Deseret Ranches" (2012).
[154] Heinerman & Shupe (1985); Ostling & Ostling (2007); Winter (2012).
[155] "The Church and Its Financial Independence" (2012).
[156] "Humanitarian Aid" (2011); "Humanitarian Services" (2012).

Church of Jesus Christ, gone broke? So poor that it cannot sustain its missionary efforts and other operations around the world? I think not.

"THE PENTECOSTALS WILL OUTGROW THE MORMONS"

It could be argued that, if any form of Christianity will expand to immense proportions in the twenty-first century, it would be Pentecostalism. Some neutral observers have claimed that "Pentecostalism is the great religious success story of the twentieth century."[157] Commenting on the "breathtaking" scope of the growth of evangelical Christianity since about 1960, several sociologists have noted the role of Pentecostalism in this growth:

> The most numerous component within the Evangelical upsurge is Pentecostalism, which combines biblical orthodoxy and a rigorous morality with an ecstatic form of worship and an emphasis on spiritual healing.[158]
> ... the main upsurge is not in the older, more staid Evangelicalism but in Pentecostalism. That means we are dealing with movements offering what are called the "gifts of the Spirit" (such as healing, prophecy, speaking in tongues), rather than with what some people label "fundamentalism."[159]

According to the "Pentecostalism triumphant" perspective, the fact that the (Pentecostal) Assemblies of God church in the U.S. registered a 3.99% growth rate from

---

[157] Micklethwait & Wooldridge (2009/2010) p. 217.
[158] P.L. Berger (1999) p. 8.
[159] D. Martin (1999) p. 38.

2009 to 2010—much larger than the LDS growth rate in the U.S. for this period, 1.41%[160]—shows that the Pentecostals are on their way to numerical dominance in America. However, the numbers simply do not bear this out.

There is no question that Pentecostal churches are growing quickly, compared to most forms of American Christianity. However, that one-year growth rate of almost 4% for the Assemblies of God is, to say the least, anomalous. As we see in Table 5-3, the typical annual growth rate of the Assemblies of God over the last two decades and more is much smaller than the 2009-to-2010 rate. In fact, the median annual growth rate for the Assemblies of God for the period 1986-2010 was 1.57%, while for the Latter-day Saints it was 1.88%.[161]

Consider this. Calculating from the data in Table 5-3, the LDS Church went from being 84% larger than the Assemblies of God in 1986, to being 103% larger in 2010. During the 1986 to 2010 period, the Assemblies of God grew by 42%, while the LDS grew by 56%—thus leaving the LDS with a growth rate over one-third larger. Perhaps the Assemblies of God, or another Pentecostal church will grow larger than the Saints. But one could not responsibly predict that from figures such as these.

[Note: The data sources for Table 5-3 are essentially the same as those for Table 4-1.]

---

[160] *Yearbook of American & Canadian Churches: 2012* (2012) p. 12.
[161] Author's calculations.

	Assemblies of God		LDS	
Year	American Members	1-Year Growth	American Members	1-Year Growth
1986	2,135,104	2.51%	3,930,000	1.81%
1987	2,160,667	1.20%	4,000,000	1.78%
1988	2,147,041	-0.63%	4,087,700	2.19%
1989	2,137,890	-0.43%	4,175,400	2.15%
1990	2,181,502	2.04%	4,267,000	2.19%
1991	2,234,708	2.44%	4,336,000	1.62%
1992	2,257,846	1.04%	4,430,000	2.17%
1993	2,271,718	0.61%	4,520,000	2.03%
1994	2,324,615	2.33%	4,613,000	2.06%
1995	2,387,982	2.73%	4,711,500	2.14%
1996	2,467,588	3.33%	4,800,000	1.88%
1997	2,494,574	1.09%	4,923,100	2.56%
1998	2,525,812	1.25%	5,018,255	1.93%
1999	2,574,531	1.93%	5,113,409	1.90%
2000	2,577,560	0.12%	5,208,827	1.87%
2001	2,627,029	1.92%	5,310,598	1.95%
2002	2,687,366	2.30%	5,410,544	1.88%
2003	2,729,562	1.57%	5,503,192	1.71%
2004	2,779,095	1.81%	5,599,177	1.74%
2005	2,830,861	1.86%	5,690,672	1.63%
2006	2,836,174	0.19%	5,779,316	1.56%
2007	2,863,265	0.96%	5,873,408	1.63%
2008	2,899,702	1.27%	5,974,041	1.71%
2009	2,914,669	0.52%	6,058,907	1.42%
2010	3,030,944	3.99%	6,144,582	1.41%

Table 5-3. Assemblies of God & Latter-day Saints in the United States

"There won't be enough people on the Earth to accommodate these projections."

Will we even have a human population on Earth large enough to accommodate my global projections? As we can see from Tables 3-3 and 3-4, by the year 2120, we would need a combined population of about 14.3 billion to accommodate the projections I have made for the world's Muslims, other Christians, Hindus, Chinese folk religionists, Buddhists, and New Religionists, before we even add in the Mormons. That's a lot of people—a bit over twice the 7-billion-strong population of the world in mid-2012, as I write these words.[162]

As it happens, the "high growth" scenario of the most recent United Nations estimate of which I am aware projects a world population of about 15.0 billion in 2120.[163] That would accommodate my projections easily.

But what about adding in the Mormons? Not a problem—given that over 90% of Mormon growth comes from convert baptisms, not natural increase, as I explained in Chapter 1. The Mormon increase thus will come out of the figures projected for the other religious groups, although I do not note that in my projections for these other groups. (I simply have no data on which to project the number of converts from specific global religious groups to the LDS faith.) Yes, there shall be enough population to accommodate my global projections.

---

[162] United States Census Bureau (2012b).
[163] United Nations (2004) p. 13, Figure 6.

Chapter 5: Objections and Responses 125

"THERE WON'T BE ENOUGH PEOPLE IN AMERICA."

But will we have enough *America* to accommodate my projections for LDS growth? As we can see from Table 4-3, by the year 2120, we would need an American population of about 206.4 million to accommodate the projections I have made for the Roman Catholics, Southern Baptists, members of the Assemblies of God, and major Protestant denominations alone. That is less than the total 314 million population of the U.S. in mid-2012.[164] But how will we find room for everybody else, including the 292.8 million Mormons of my high-growth projection (Table 4-2)?

In 2000, the U.S. Census Bureau made projections of United States population for 2100.[165] Their "middle series" (i.e., moderate-growth) projection predicted a U.S. population of over 571 million. Such projections are more than sufficient to accommodate, not only the Catholic and Protestant populations that I have projected, but the Latter-day Saints as well, especially if we recall, again, that 90% or more of the Mormon growth will come from converts from the other religious groups that I have mentioned. There will also be plenty of room for the likely number of non-Christian believers, agnostics, and atheists that will be found in the America of 2120. In sum, there will be more than enough population in the United States to accommodate even my high-growth LDS projection.

"SO MANY MORMONS—IN *PROTESTANT* AMERICA?"

America has a long history of Protestant dominance, with an unbroken Protestant-majority history and an al-

---

[164] United States Census Bureau (2012b).
[165] United States Census Bureau (2000).

most unbroken legacy of Protestant U.S. Presidents over the course of nearly two and a half centuries. Is an America with a religious landscape dominated by Catholics and Mormons conceivable?

Radical changes in the religious composition of America have happened before in American history, and more than once.[166] Churches that once were important forces in American life have become much smaller voices, while groups that once were very small are now very large.

The logic behind the prediction that Saints become at least America's second-largest church seems inescapable. In the low-growth projection, American LDS growth simply continues on the course it established during the first decade of the 21st century. Even with the lowest per-decade growth rate that American Mormonism has seen since at least as far back as 1930, the Church of Jesus Christ under this model still becomes the nation's second-largest church.

"BUT MORE MORMONS THAN *CATHOLICS?!?*"

Short of some nation-sundering catastrophe, I project that the Latter-day Saints will become the largest non-Catholic religious group in America by 2100, and possibly much earlier. But could there ever actually be more Mormons than Catholics in the U.S., as the LDS high-growth projection indicates?

Consider the vagaries of history. Catholics comprised a very small number of people within the English colonies that existed before the War of Independence, from the time that the first successful English colony was founded at Jamestown in 1607. (Of course, there were many more

---

[166] Finke & Stark (2005); e.g., see Fig. 3.1 (p. 56) and Table 7.2 (p. 246).

Catholics in the French and Spanish colonies that were later incorporated into the United States) At the time of the Declaration of Independence in 1776, Catholics made up less than two percent of all religious adherents in the English colonial population.[167] Most of the English American colonies discriminated against Catholics in their laws, and Catholic priests were arrested and exiled. (Anti-Catholicism was a powerful current for a surprisingly long time in American politics. For example, Catholics were legally prohibited from holding public office in the state of New Hampshire until late in the 19th century.)

Then things changed. In the early 19th century, the Louisiana Purchase and the Mexican-American War brought into the United States several regions where many Catholic families had lived, some for centuries. The real growth of Catholicism in the U.S. came with immigration from European Catholic populations such as Ireland, Germany, and Poland. By the late 19th century,[168] Catholics formed the largest single church in the country, a situation that remained in effect in 2012.

But there is nothing (you should pardon the expression) sacred about any of this. There is no sort of law of social development stating that religious groups with longer histories are insured of having more adherents in America.

No, the plurality status of Roman Catholics among American believers is not a given. That plurality status is to a very large extent an accident of history, and what history giveth, history sometimes doth take away.

---

[167] Finke & Stark (2005) Figure 3.1, p. 56.
[168] Finke & Stark (2005) pp. 117-120.

"The Mormons are falling away in droves."

A different kind of objection states that substantial numbers of Latter-day Saints are falling away from their church. Ultimately, or so this objection goes, such attrition will seriously undercut Mormon growth.

Little if anything in the way of actual statistical evidence is adduced by the Church's detractors to substantiate the claim of mass defections from Mormonism. What data does exist involves teenagers, and is highly favorable to the Saints. Researchers involved in a national survey reported this concerning youth aged 13-17:

> Conceived as a matter of retention of youth, conservative Protestant and Mormon parents are doing the best job, retaining 86 percent of their teens each, followed by Catholics at 83 percent, black Protestants at 81 percent, and Jewish parents at 75 percent. Only 68 percent of mainline Protestant parents' teens are mainline Protestant themselves.... Nonreligious parents at 63 percent are faring relatively poorly at retaining their youth as nonreligious.[169]

However, for the sake of discussion, let me ignore these data and take the objection here at face value. Let us consider the matter of attrition from the LDS faith.

All churches experience attrition. The rate of attrition from the LDS faith has accelerated somewhat over the last five to ten years.[170] However, this same acceleration of at-

---

[169] C. Smith & Denton (2005) p. 36.
[170] Marlin K. Jensen, quoted in Henderson & Cooke (2012).

trition, especially with regard to college-age youth, has been reported by other churches as well. As I note in Chapter 7, the American Millennial generation shows far lower rates of religious affiliation and practice than older age cohorts.[171] Attrition may indeed have become more pronounced in recent years; a nationwide Barna Group study conducted in 2009-2011 found that 59% of young adults (18-29 years old) with a Protestant or Catholic background "reported that they had or have 'dropped out of attending church, after going regularly.'"[172]

All of this is to say that recent accelerated attrition is not a uniquely Mormon problem. If attrition cuts into LDS growth, it will cut into everyone else's growth, as well.

Beyond that, the Church of Jesus Christ has a history of adapting to changing circumstances. For example, although at first the Church was very hesitant to explore the power of the Internet, it now has a plethora of websites, some with thousands of pages, to further its mission. Known as a church of families, the Latter-day Saints are constantly tweaking programs to better integrate single adults into the church. The immense humanitarian aid program of the Church is essentially a creation of the most recent generation or two of Mormon leadership. Even the missionary program has changed in recent years, such that missionaries in most locations donate a day of service weekly to the communities where they preach.

Given this history, it is no surprise that Church leadership is paying serious attention to the issue of increased attrition.[173] Stay tuned for updates as this story develops.

---

[171] Pew Research Center (2010) pp. 85, 90-93.
[172] Kinnaman (2011) pp. 23, 247-248.
[173] Marlin K. Jensen, quoted in Henderson & Cooke (2012).

Some claim that the roots of accelerated attrition from Mormonism lie in the way that the Internet has made available to readers a number of hitherto-obscure aspects of LDS history, such as supposedly compromising facts about its scriptures or church history.[174] Some bloggers have dubbed this phenomenon 'the Google Apostasy.'

However, by far most of the objections made to Mormonism on the basis of its history were made generations ago—and have long been successfully responded to by LDS scholars.[175] The real issue is that these responses have not been effectively communicated to the public; some scholars have noted that these issues are simply avoided in current LDS Sunday School manuals, for example.[176]

Here again, the Church of Jesus Christ has a history of changing teaching methods in response to a perceived need. I expect that the Church will take major steps to address positively the so-called Google Apostasy, for example, by teaching about historical issues that have long been neglected in its educational efforts.

---

[174] Stack (2012). An episode like this (supposedly lightly fictionalized) is depicted in Stephen Mansfield's *The Mormonizing of America* (2012), where a college student loses faith because of facts he discovered about the Mountain Meadows Massacre over the Internet. I address the 1857 massacre in *Mormon Controversies*, a forthcoming book in the same series as the present book; see also R.W. Walker, Turley, & Leonard (2008) and Turley & Walker (2009).

[175] For recent treatments of sensitive historical issues by LDS scholars, see Millet (2011), and my own forthcoming *Mormon Controversies*. Recent treatments of theological objections to Mormonism may be found there, and in Millet (2004, 2005, 2010). For other defenses of LDS theology, see D.C. Peterson & Ricks (1992) and Shuster & Sale (2010).

[176] Givens and R. L. Bushman, quoted in Stack (2012).

Chapter 5: Objections and Responses

In sum, I cannot respond definitively to this objection because that would require a response to statistical evidence—which is notably unsupplied by those who advance this objection. However, what data exist indicates that the LDS are at no special disadvantage relative to other faith communities in this respect. Beyond that, based on prior history, I feel confident that whatever LDS attrition is taking place, over and above historical norms, the Church's leadership will attempt to address it effectively.

"But Look at What the LDS Scriptures Say!"

I have reserved the concluding position in my parade of objections for one that might be made, not by the Latter-day Saints' detractors, but by the Saints themselves.

That quintessentially LDS scripture, the Book of Mormon, contains in its early pages an extensive vision of the future of the world—that is, the "future" from the point of view of the prophet receiving the vision in about 600 B.C. A portion of the vision considers a period that is so far in his future that it is in *our* future. In this portion, we read of an era that seems to involve the Church of Jesus Christ ("the church of the Lamb of God," the Lamb being Christ) pitted against a future church of Antichrist ("the whore of all the earth"). As the prophet wrote:

> And it came to pass that I looked and beheld the whore of all the earth, and she sat upon many waters; and she had dominion over all the earth, among all nations, kindreds, tongues, and people.
> And it came to pass that I beheld the church of the Lamb of God, and its numbers were few ...; I beheld that the church of the

Lamb, who were the saints of God, were also upon all the face of the earth; and their dominions upon the face of the earth were small, because of the wickedness of the great whore who I saw.[177]

If the numbers of the church of the Lamb of God will be "few," then how could that reflect the huge numbers of Saints in the projections that I have made?

I refer readers to Table 3-3 and Figure 3-5 (both regarding other global Christian churches), and also to Table 3-4 and Figure 3-8 (both regarding other global religions), focusing on the figures for 2120. Under my high-growth projection, the Saints certainly become a presence upon the world's religious landscape—2.6 billion people do count for something—but that number of Saints pales beside the 5.8 billion Muslims projected for that year. One would also do well to keep in mind at least the 2.2 billion Roman Catholics, 1.9 billion Hindus, 1.2 billion Protestants, 978 million independent Christians, 831 million Buddhists, and 737 million Chinese folk religionists, all of whom I project will share the Earth with the Mormons in 2120. In sum, even under my most liberal estimate for the growth of the Latter-day Saints, they will still be "few" in relation to all the other religious groups in the world in 2120.

*   *   *

My guess is that some readers will not receive the news of my projections very well at all. Here is the author (a Mormon himself, yet), predicting that the Latter-day

---

[177] Standard Works: Book of Mormon, 1 Nephi, chapt. 14, verses 11-12.

Saints will come to outnumber all but one other religious group in the world. This news is going to play badly in many quarters worldwide.

I ask only this: If critics wish to dispute these predictions, let them be specific about precisely where I have gone wrong. Let no one be satisfied with statements like "well, those kinds of numbers are just so ridiculously high," or "oh, you would *expect* to hear that from a *Mormon*, wouldn't you?" I have been very clear and specific in describing the assumptions that I have used in developing my projections; the reader and I have the right to expect responsible critics to be equally clear and specific in describing where those critics think I have gone wrong. Of course, because there is historical precedent behind even my most liberal estimates of Mormon growth, the burden is on the critic to demonstrate why we should ignore that historical precedent in criticizing a given model.

As it happens, I favor one model in particular for LDS growth: the high-growth model. In Chapters 6 through 9, I explain why I think that this is the model that will best reflect future LDS growth in reality.

Chapter 6
Why Religions Grow: A Model

In a discussion like ours it is very easy to get caught up in the statistics, the social trends, the political aspects of religious growth, and so forth, and forget that we are talking about a religion. Yet that is precisely what we are talking about: not just "religion" in the abstract, but a *specific*, living, breathing religion, a faith that believes some things and does not believe other things and outright denies yet other things altogether; a faith that supports some behaviors and eschews others and downright condemns still others. When we talk about "future Mormon growth," we are not just discussing changes in the size of a group; we are considering what might bring huge numbers of people into a body of believers. Given that over 90% of Mormon growth comes through conversion (see Chapter 1), we must ask: What forces will drive Mormon growth?

The projections that I have made regarding high rates of LDS growth are nothing but statistical exercises unless there is some reason to believe that these rates will actually occur. As it happens, there are several reasons why the best statistical bet on future Mormon growth is "high," rather than "small" or even "moderate." To put these reasons into context, we need a model of why religions grow. The very brief outline of a model that I present here has not been published before. Here is a formal statement of the principles involved:

In situations of free choice of religion, those religions will best prosper (that is, grow) that meet the following criteria (roughly in descending order of importance):

1. These religions are well-adapted to the social, geographic, cultural, and demographic situations of the people making religious choices (that is, their external reality). We may think of these demographic and other trends as forces outside the individuals themselves that exert a "pull" on these individuals, towards a given religion.
2. These religions respond explicitly and productively to the major hopes, aspirations, anxieties, and fears—one might say the obsessions—of the society of the people making religious choices (that is, their internal reality). We may think of these societal preoccupations as psychological forces inside the individuals themselves that exert a "push" on these individuals, towards a given religion.
3. These religions are effective in bringing their message to people making religious choices. These are 'knowledge forces,' which exert an attractive influence towards a given religion.
4. These religions best allow the preservation of the social and religious capital of people making religious choices.

As I see it, the LDS faith is particularly well-positioned for growth as predicted by these criteria. The growth of Mormonism will thus tend toward the high-growth scenarios that I have described earlier in this book.

In Chapter 7, I describe the "pulling" forces, the forces of demography and so forth, that will affect Mormon growth, considered separately for several areas of the world.

In Chapter 8, I consider the "pushing" forces, the societal themes—even obsessions—that are most relevant to Mormon growth, particularly in American society. (By extension, these are themes that have reached much of the rest of the industrialized world, at least, through the export of American media.)

In Chapter 9, I consider what we might call the "knowledge" forces, the way in which the Church of Jesus Christ is making its message available to the world.

The forces that incline people to preserve social and religious capital have already been well-described by Rodney Stark.[178] I touch on Stark's 'networks of faith' and 'religious capital' concepts in Chapter 7.

---

[178] See: Stark & Finke (2000) ch. 5; Stark (2005) ch. 3.

Chapter 7

Exterior Forces "Pulling" for Mormon Growth

In this chapter, I consider the demographic and other social forces that exert a "pull," positive or negative, on individuals, in a way that is relevant to Mormon growth. In particular, I consider the following areas, in this order:

- Central and South America and sub-Saharan Africa
- the United States
- Europe
- Mainland China
- India
- the lands of Islam

The reason for addressing these areas in this order is that Mormon growth is widely acknowledged to be booming in Central and South America, and in sub-Saharan Africa. On the other hand, the prospects for Mormon growth in the other areas have been called into question.

CENTRAL AND SOUTH AMERICA AND SUB-SAHARAN AFRICA

In Chapter 3, I noted that the per-decade growth rate required to sustain my LDS low-growth global model is 21.9%; that required for my moderate-growth global model is 48%; finally, the per-decade growth rate required for my high-growth global model is 70.8%. Now consider the data in the farthest-right column in Table 7-1.

	LDS Membership		Per-Decade Growth Rate
	1999[a]	2009[b]	
Central America			
El Salvador	84,683	105,501	24.6%
Guatemala	174,784	220,296	26.0%
Honduras	95,750	136,408	42.5%
Mexico	846,931	1,197,573	41.4%
South America			
Argentina	288,865	371,885	28.7%
Brazil	743,182	1,102,674	48.4%
Chile	502,153	561,920	11.9%
Ecuador	146,420	190,498	30.1%
Peru	333,828	480,816	44.0%
Sub-Saharan Africa			
DR Congo	8,197	23,615	188.1%
Ghana	17,278	40,872	136.6%
Nigeria	42,746	93,532	118.8%
South Africa	29,220	51,710	77.0%
Zimbabwe	8,287	17,632	112.8%

Table 7-1. **Per-decade LDS growth rates for selected countries in Central & South America and Africa, 1999-2009**

Notes to Table 7-1:

[a] Source: *Deseret News 2001-2002 Church Almanac* (2000).

[b] Source: *Deseret News 2011 Church Almanac* (2011).

Table 7-1 shows LDS membership and recent per-decade growth rates for the countries with the largest LDS populations in Central and South America, as well as sub-Saharan Africa. The low-growth per-decade growth rate is already exceeded in all but one of these countries. The per-decade growth rate required to maintain the moderate-growth projection is already exceeded in all the selected African countries and in Brazil, and is being approached in Honduras, Mexico, and Peru. Even the growth-rate required to maintain the high-growth projection is already exceeded in all the selected African countries.[179]

In Chapter 2, I described three factors that affect the number of LDS convert baptisms, and why I thought that each of these factors were likely to show major increases in strength in the very near future. That is, the LDS missionary force seems poised to increase by 20% to 30% over the

---

[179] Concerning those African countries: Some readers might object that the Church is too young and too small in most or all of those countries to yield stable figures for growth. Young the LDS faith certainly is in Africa, but in terms of size, the Church is already large enough in some parts thereof to yield stable growth figures. Working from Table 1-1, we can see that the Church's per-decade growth rate became stable enough to yield meaningful figures no later than 1870. **But in 1870, during the last decade of the Brigham Young era, total Church membership was only a touch over 90,000 members worldwide — or less than the LDS membership *in Nigeria alone* in 2009!** (See Table 7-1.) And the Church in Nigeria in 2009 had a per-decade growth rate that was 150% larger than the per-decade growth rate of the Church as a whole in 1870.

Thus, we see that the Church is already large enough in at least some parts of sub-Saharan Africa to yield stable per-decade growth rates. Those growth rates are already well into the high-growth-projection range. Even if the rest of my predictions were to fail to pan out, the Church of Jesus Christ is headed for a truly huge membership in sub-Saharan Africa.

next decade or so; the improved preparation of LDS missionaries seems to have raised the number of converts baptized per missionary by almost 14%; and, the LDS "networks of faith" on the frontier of the Church are substantially increasing in size, hence strength.

I think that these three factors will have at least an additive effect, increasing the number of convert baptisms in Central and South America and sub-Saharan Africa by *64% or more* over just the next decade or so. (This is the product of a 20% increase in the missionary corps, times a 14% increase in missionary effectiveness, times a 20% increase in the strength of LDS networks of faith.)

A 64% increase in LDS growth rate in heavily populated countries such as Mexico and Brazil would go a long way towards bringing all of Central and South America into the range of the LDS global high-growth projection. Sub-Saharan Africa is already there.

THE UNITED STATES

Who becomes a Mormon in the United States, anyway? The answer to this question has important implications for the future of the Church in America.

A recent survey showed that, of American Mormons in 2007, 74% had been raised LDS, and 26% had been raised in other faiths (that is, they were converts).[180] Figure 7-1 illustrates these data, showing converts' 'faiths of origin.'

Let us focus on the converts. Figures 7-2 and 7-3, and Table 7-2, show the distribution of American LDS converts by their former faiths, and, for comparison, the distributions of these faiths in the U.S. population. Table 7-1 also

---

[180] *U.S. Religious Landscape Survey: Religious Affiliation* (2008), p. 29.

Chapter 7: Exterior Forces "Pull" for Mormon Growth   143

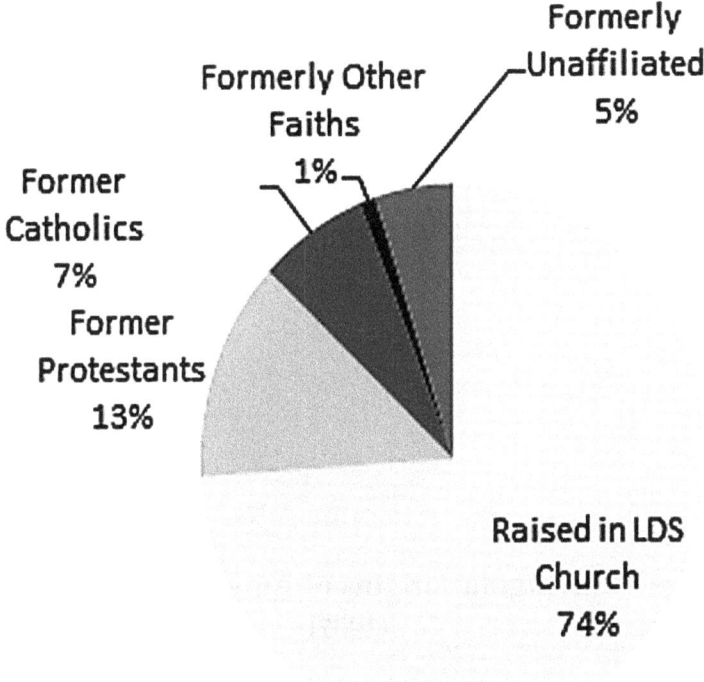

Figure 7-1. Religious origins of American Latter-day Saints (2007)

shows the extent to which each group is over- or underrepresented among American LDS converts, compared to the group's share of the U.S. population; see Fig. 7-4. These differences are statistically and practically significant.[181]

---

[181] Comparing the number of LDS converts we would *expect* from each group (based on the number of people raised in each group) with the number of LDS converts we actually *observe* from each group — all as shown in the *Landscape* report (pp. 24, 29, 72) — the differences are statistically significant: observed chi-squared = 31.31, df = 3, $p <$ .001. This shows a very large effect size: $w = 0.67$ (J. Cohen, 1992, p. 157); that is, in practical terms, the group differences are very large.

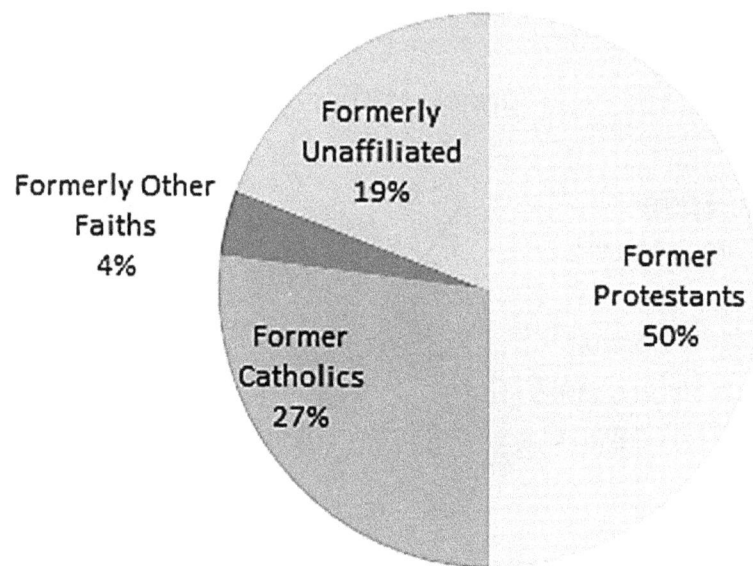

Figure 7-2. Religious origins of American LDS converts (2007)

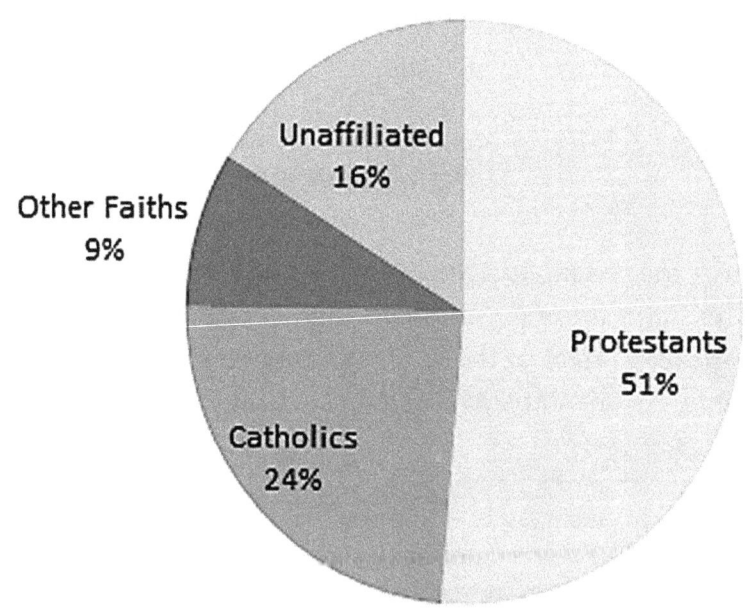

Figure 7-3. American population by faith group (2007)

Group	Proportion of American Population[a]	Proportion of LDS Converts from Group[b]	Amount Over- or Under-Represented Among LDS Converts[c]
Protestants	51.3%	50.0%	-2.5%
Catholics	23.9%	26.9%	+12.6%
Other Faiths[d]	8.7%	3.8%	-55.8%
Unaffiliated	16.1%	19.2%	+19.4%

Table 7-2. Religious origins of American LDS converts compared to American population (2007)

Notes to Table 7-1:

[a]Source: *U.S. Religious Landscape Survey: Religious Affiliation* (2008), p. 24.

[b]Source: Calculated from figures in *U.S. Religious Landscape Survey: Religious Affiliation* (2008), p. 29. (Formula: Divide percentage of the "Mormon" line that was raised in a given faith group by 26% [the proportion of all Mormons who were raised as something other than Mormon].

[c]Calculation: x = [(proportion of LDS converts from group) − (proportion of American population)] ÷ (proportion of American population). For $x > 0$, x is the degree to which this group is *over*-represented among LDS converts, rela-

tive to the group's size within the general American population. For $x < 0$, this is the degree to which this group is *under*-represented among LDS converts, relative to the group's size within the general American population.

[d]Includes individuals indicating affiliation with the Jews, Buddhists, Jehovah's Witnesses, Orthodox Christians, Muslims, Hindus, and other faiths. (Within only the column for "Proportion of American Population," this also includes Mormons, at 1.7% of the American population according to this survey.)

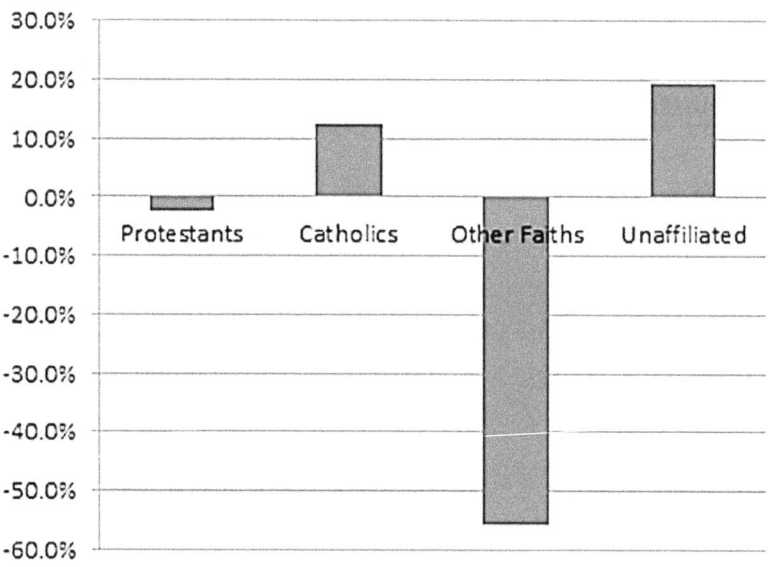

Figure 7-4. **Degree to which faiths are over- and underrepresented among American LDS converts (2007)**

Chapter 7: Exterior Forces "Pull" for Mormon Growth

The answer to "Who becomes a Mormon in the United States?" turns out to have different answers on different levels of depth. On a superficial level, the answer is, "anybody": Protestants, Catholics, Jews, and so forth, including the formerly unaffiliated (Figure 7-2, Table 7-2). However, on a deeper level, we see that not every group is equally likely to contribute converts to the LDS faith. As we see in Table 7-2 (far right column) and Figure 7-4, those raised in "other faiths" (Hindus, Jews, Muslims, and so forth), are under-represented among LDS converts; they are less than half as likely to convert to Mormonism as we might expect from the "other faith's" numbers in America.

This makes good sense from the point of view of Stark's ideas regarding "religious capital" as a factor in conversion. To review the concept:

> … any religion requires an adherent to master a lot of culture: to know the words and actions required by various rituals or worship activities, to be familiar with certain doctrines, stories, music, symbols, and history…. [O]ne's *religious capital* consists of the degree of [one's] mastery of and attachment to a particular religious culture.
>
> …, [o]ther things being equal, *people will attempt to conserve their religious capital*.[182]

Someone converting to Mormonism from Hinduism, Buddhism, or Islam is leaving behind a large body of religious capital: knowledge of many pages of sacred writings, mastery of religious rituals, and so forth. Such conversions do happen—I know people from the "other faiths" who have converted to Mormonism—but it is a steeper hill to

---

[182] Stark (2011) p. 74, italics in original, footnote omitted.

climb, and as such, fewer people climb it. It is thus no surprise that the "other faiths" group contributes a disproportionately smaller number of converts to Mormonism.

Now consider the groups that are *over*-represented among Mormon converts. The most noteworthy is clearly the "Unaffiliated," that is, people who were not affiliated with a religious group before they converted to Mormonism. The Unaffiliated contribute almost 20% more American converts to the LDS faith than the size alone of their group would predict. This also makes perfectly good sense in terms of Stark's religious capital approach to conversion; almost by definition, the Unaffiliated have less to lose in the way of religious capital than any other group when they convert—not just to Mormonism, but to *any* faith.

But who are the Unaffiliated? And what is their place in the American society of the future?

As the Pew organization's Religious Landscape Survey[183] reveals, and as Figure 7-5 shows, a small fraction of the Unaffiliated describe themselves as atheists, who take the position that a God or gods simply do not exist. This group amounts to only 10% of the Unaffiliated, or 1.6% of the American population as a whole. This sub-group of the Unaffiliated *does* have "religious capital" to lose by conversion to Mormonism: there is a large body of atheist teaching stretching back for centuries,[184] and there are organized atheist groups, all of which an atheist would be letting go of in a conversion to Mormonism (although, again, such conversions do occur).

---

[183] *U.S. Religious Landscape Survey: Religious Affiliation* (2008), p. 20.
[184] E.g., see Hitchens (2007b) and Joshi (2000).

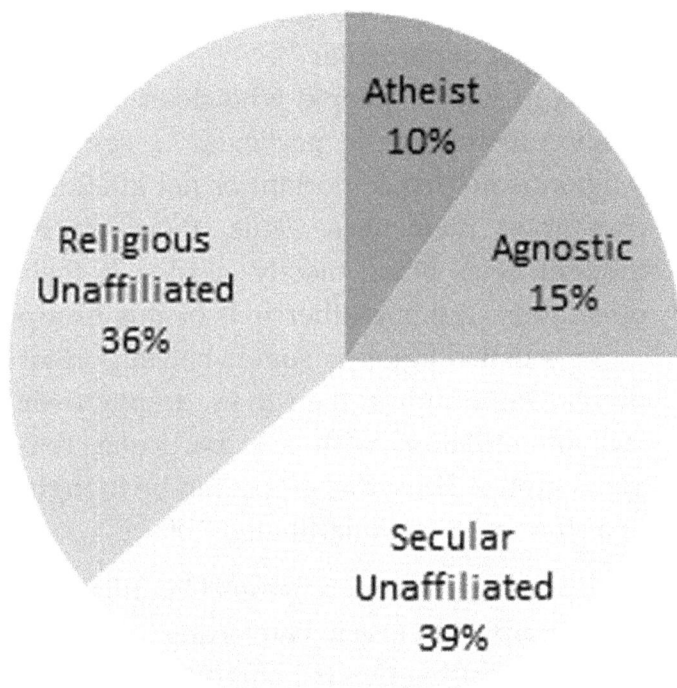

Figure 7-5. **Subgroups of Religiously "Unaffiliated" Americans (2007)**

Ninety percent of the Unaffiliated possess no such impediments to LDS conversion. Agnostics state that they do not know whether a God or gods exist. Although there is a "principled agnosticism"—the position that, *in principle*, knowledge of God is impossible or, at least, that evidence is lacking[185]—this seems a minority position even among agnostics. It seems that most agnostics simply claim that they *personally* do not know whether a God or gods exist.

Fully three-quarters of the Unaffiliated (amounting to 12.1% of the adult American population)

---

[185] See the papers by Huxley and Stephen in Joshi (2000).

> consists of people who describe their religion as "nothing in particular." ...
>
> About half of people who describe their religion as nothing in particular ... say that religion is not too important or not at all important in their lives. Thus, they can be thought of as being mostly secular in their orientation. But the other half of this group ... says that religion is somewhat important or very important in their lives, despite their lack of affiliation with any particular religious group. Thus, this group can be thought of as the "religious unaffiliated."[186]

Here again, both secular and religious Unaffiliated have little religious capital to lose in converting to Mormonism. Thus, it is not surprising that the Unaffiliated are disproportionately represented among American converts to the LDS faith.

There is every reason to believe that the Unaffiliated group will grow substantially. The fraction of the American population describing itself as Unaffiliated increases, the younger the age cohort (Fig. 7-6).[187] It is unclear whether this is truly a generational effect, where successively younger generations are more likely to be Unaffiliated. (It may be that, as people age, they are simply more likely to affiliate with a religious group.) But if this *is* a generational effect, then "growth in the size of the unaffiliated population may continue."[188]

---

[186] *U.S. Religious Landscape Survey: Religious Affiliation* (2008), p. 20.
[187] *U.S. Religious Landscape Survey: Religious Affiliation* (2008), p. 37.
[188] *U.S. Religious Landscape Survey: Religious Affiliation* (2008), p. 7.

Chapter 7: Exterior Forces "Pull" for Mormon Growth   151

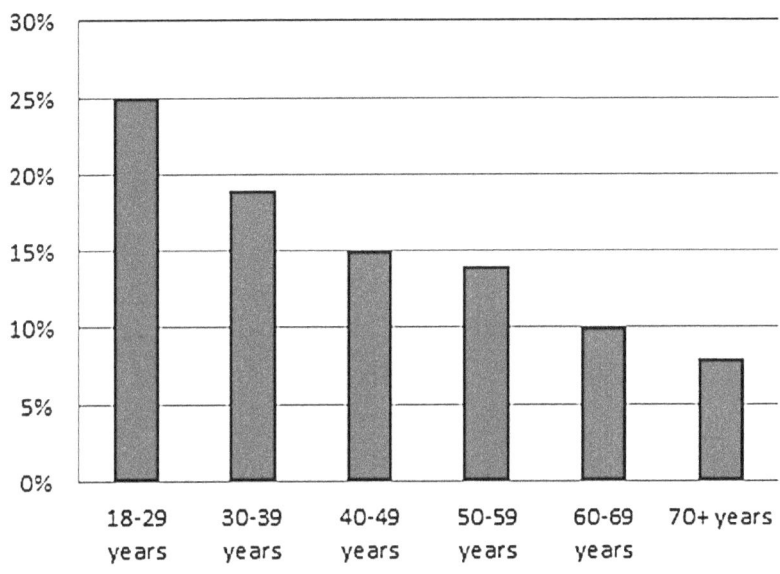

Figure 7-6. **Proportion of each American age cohort that is Unaffiliated (2007)**

The Unaffiliated have become a major 'religious group' in younger age cohorts. (Indeed, in the 18-to-29-year-old age cohort of the 2007 survey, there were more Unaffiliateds than either Catholics or evangelical Protestants.) If the effect shown in Figure 7-6 indeed shows inter-generational differences, then the number of adult Americans in the Unaffiliated group—the single 'religious group' *most receptive to converting to the LDS faith*—will become much, much larger over just the next few decades. If this LDS conversion-receptive group grows by, say, 50% over the next few decades (as the comparison of age cohorts in Figure 7-6 suggests it might), this could greatly increase the number of LDS converts.

Much the same could be said about the growth of the Catholic Church over the next century. In 2007, former Catholics were statistically over-represented by 12.6% among LDS converts (see Table 7-2 and Fig. 7-4). Using an annual growth rate of 0.75% for American Catholics (Table 4-1), I project the Roman Catholic Church will grow from 73 million in 2020 to 155 million in 2120 (Table 4-3). Again, the second-most "LDS-conversion-receptive" group cannot more than double in size over the course of the next century (as I project in Table 4-3) without substantially increasing the number of LDS converts.

In sum, the two religious groups whose members have proven to be the most receptive to conversion to the LDS faith may see a great deal of growth in the U.S. in the foreseeable future. This is an important reason to think that the LDS change rate in the United States will increase into the high-growth range of my American model.

EUROPE

It might seem laughable to think that the Saints will make substantial inroads in Europe. June 13, 2012 marked the 175th anniversary of the 1837 departure of Mormon elders from Ohio to open the British Mission of the Church. After all this time preaching in England and on continental Europe, the number of Saints in Europe is rather modest.

But there are important reasons to think that the Saints will see major growth in Europe over the next few generations. One reason involves the history of LDS missionary work in Europe; another concerns recent LDS growth rates in Europe; a third involves the type of people who convert to religions like the LDS faith.

LDS missionaries in Europe—only since *1946??*

It is rather silly to look at the current LDS population of Europe and count that as the fruit of 175 years of proselyting on that continent. If anything, one should look at the current LDS population of *Utah* for that fruit.

For much of the Church's first eight decades of existence, converts in America and Europe were strongly encouraged to migrate to the Church's center of gravity, in Ohio, Illinois, or Utah.[189] Over 100,000 converts came to join the Saints in the United States from Europe between 1840 and 1910 alone.[190] In this way, the central mass of the Saints grew stronger, fed by a stream of thousands of converts, especially from Europe—although this dynamic had a catastrophic effect on local European LDS congregations. As Rodney Stark has put it:

> We thus see that Brigham Young's immigration policies eventually all but destroyed the British mission, and indeed all other overseas missions, and set back Mormon missionary efforts in Europe by a century. ... But, I believe Brigham Young did the right thing. He preserved a Mormon homeland ....[191]

What a member of the Church hierarchy who held administrative responsibilities for northern Europe said about that area could apply just as well to all of Europe:

> The Church in northern Europe has almost a first-generation convert base. This is because

---

[189] For a brief overview of LDS immigration from Europe to the United States, see Hartley (1975) and R.L. Jensen & Hartley (n.d.).
[190] R.L. Jensen & Hartley (n.d.).
[191] Stark (1994) pp. 20-21.

during the Church's first century and a quarter, most converts in Europe immigrated to America, where they could enjoy the blessings of [an LDS] temple. In the early 1950s ... there were only about six thousand members left in the British Isles, despite more than a century of proselyting. The Church really began to be rooted there after the dedication of the London Temple in 1958.[192]

For all practical purposes, then, LDS proselytizing in Europe "began" (again) only with the return of American LDS missionaries to Europe after World War II.[193] In England, that occurred in January of 1946; in May of that year, the LDS mission in France was re-opened. So it went throughout Western and Northern Europe. In Southern Europe, the Church of Jesus Christ received permission for the first time in generations, or ever, to send missionaries, as they did in Italy (1965), Spain (1968), and Portugal (1974). As I have explained, it was not until the 1990s that LDS missionaries could be assigned to European countries that were formerly part of the Soviet Union.

The Church had begun advising converts to remain in their homelands rather than immigrate to the States beginning in the early years of the twentieth century. It renewed this advice strongly after World War II, and has periodically reminded the Saints of this advice, as it did in 1999.[194]

Consequently, there has not been a long time for the Latter-day Saints to build the kind of "networks of faith"

---

[192] Kenneth Johnson, quoted in "News of the Church: The Church in Northern Europe" (1994, p. 79).

[193] Stark (1994) pp. 20-21.

[194] *Deseret Morning News 2004 Church Almanac* (2004) p. 546.

that Rodney Stark has theorized are important to facilitate conversion. Over the course of the next generation or so, such networks should be sufficiently constructed that the LDS growth rate should improve throughout Europe.

LDS growth rates in some parts of Europe *are* impressive.

In the post-World-War-II period, the growth of the Church of Jesus Christ in Europe has varied greatly from country to country, as shown in Table 7-3. In some European countries, the Latter-day Saints languish in single-digit per-decade growth rates (Germany, Belgium, England). However, in other European countries, the LDS per-decade growth rate is quite respectable (Poland, Spain, the Czech Republic). Indeed, in Russia, the LDS per-decade growth rate strongly outpaced even the best Church-wide per-decade growth rates of the last 150 years. (Compare the Russian figures with those in Table 1-1. The Church in Ukraine also made a strong showing in this range.)

It is noteworthy that it is in Eastern Europe that so much of the LDS growth has occurred.[195] Of course, this is the very region that the LDS missionaries entered after 1990, at the cost of slowing global LDS growth for over two decades (see Chapter 1). The LDS investments of its missionary effort in the countries of the former Soviet Union were well made.

What implications does all this have regarding the overall growth of the Church of Jesus Christ in the future?

---

[195] This is so even omitting the statistics from countries like Latvia, where the Church is so young and tiny as to make it impossible to calculate a meaningful per-decade growth rate at present.

	LDS Membership		Per-Decade Growth Rate
	1999[a]	2009[b]	
Western Europe			
England	135,748	144,281	6.3%
France	30,541	35,427	16.0%
Belgium	5,771	5,980	3.6%
Central Europe			
Germany	36,303	37,796	4.1%
Austria	3,889	4,203	8.1%
Czech Repub.	1,654	2,198	32.9%
Southern Europe			
Spain	30,439	45,729	50.2%
Portugal	35,248	38,509	9.3%
Italy	18,599	24,430	31.4%
Eastern Europe			
Russia[c]	11,092	20,276	82.8%
Ukraine	6,369	10,722	68.3%
Poland	1,094	1,622	48.3%
Latvia	178	1,073	502.8%

Table 7-3. Per-decade LDS growth rates for selected European countries, 1999-2009

Notes to Table 7-3:
a Source: *Deseret News 2001-2002 Church Almanac* (2000).
b Source: *Deseret News 2011 Church Almanac* (2011).
c Many Saints included here live in Asian Russia.

The current LDS per-decade growth rate in Russia (82.8%) is far in excess of the sustained per-decade growth rate required by even my high-growth global model. Three other countries exceed the sustained per-decade growth rate required by my moderate-growth model: Poland (48.3%), Spain (50.2%), and Ukraine (68.3%). These four countries together have a combined estimated population of 264.8 million (a number equal to about 88% of the population of the United States). If growth in the moderate-to-high-growth-range were to occur in just these four countries, this would go a long way towards contributing to worldwide LDS growth in this range.

Today's Europe:
The ideal place to find potential LDS converts?

Certainly after reading the heading to this section (if not earlier), some readers will be tempted to doubt this author's sanity. Europe, the ideal place to find potential LDS converts? How could this be, when LDS growth rates are so low in places like England and Germany? The religious situation in Europe is a subject of vigorous debate and research,[196] even a summary of which would go beyond our purposes. However, a cursory examination will give us some hints about the Saints' possible futures in those parts of Europe where they are not yet growing quickly.

Americans sometimes seem to think that Europe, before the 20th century, was a land of great Christian piety. At least in North, West, and Central Europe, this is a fiction.[197] Huge figures for church membership reflect only the fact

---

[196] E.g., P. Berger, Davie, & Fokas (2008); Davie (1999); Micklethwait & Wooldridge (2001) chapter 1; Stark (2011) pp. 375-385.

[197] Here I follow Stark (2011), Chapters 15, 20, and 21.

that the state's established churches enrolled their members at birth. As Andrew Greeley has put it, "There could be no de-Christianization of Europe ... because there never was any Christianization in the first place. Christian Europe never existed."[198] Stark has summarized the process by which this state of affairs came about:

> ... the Christianity that triumphed over Rome was a dedicated, energetic social movement in a very competitive environment. Subsequent to the conversion of Constantine, Christianity left most of the rest of Europe only nominally converted, at best, being a lay monopoly church that sought to extend itself not by missionizing the masses, but by baptizing kings.... This left the task of missionizing the people to a "kept" clergy whose welfare was almost entirely independent of mass assent or support, with a predictable lack of results. This is the legacy that accounted for the remarkable lack of religious participation and Christian piety in medieval times—a lack that has continued to this day.[199]

This has left the masses of Europe in the position that they are in today, largely ignorant of even the basics of Christianity. A European Muslim who attends a public recitation of the entire Koran has heard more religious preaching about Jesus than most European Christians have—for the simple reasons that Jesus is mentioned with

---

[198] Quoted in Stark (2011) p. 375.
[199] Stark (2011) pp. 375-376, footnote omitted.

honor in the Koran, and the vast majority of Northern and Western European Christians do not attend church.

It is not that Europeans are alienated from Christianity, so much as that they are uninformed about it. For example, a recent report prepared for the Church of England revealed that, of those English young adults in so-called "Generation Y" (say, in their twenties and thirties), about one in eight was explicitly atheist in orientation. However, overall, when asked what they thought regarding Christianity, " 'I don't really know what to think' got 43% of the answers."[200] This may well be typical of Europe generally.

In a sense, then, much of Western, Northern, and Central Europe's young adults can be grouped into a category equivalent to the Unaffiliated group in the Pew organization's "U.S. Religious Landscape Survey"—despite the fact that, living in countries with state churches, many of these young adults technically have a church affiliation by default. And, as we have seen, the Unaffiliated category is the most LDS-conversion-acceptable religious group around.

So why, then, are young Mormon converts not already filling the pews of LDS chapels in Northern, Western, and Central Europe? LDS missionary work in Europe is impeded by several factors.[201] A popular perspective in Europe is philosophical relativism,[202] the principle that there is no such thing as any sort of absolute truth—an idea which undercuts the very premises of religious persuasion.

---

[200] "Is God Disappearing?" (2010).
[201] Here I follow Durham (1999/2008). See P. Berger, Davie, & Fokas (2008).
[202] For an exposition and critiques, see Krausz (2010) and Mosteller (2008).

A "scientistic" perspective,[203] in which *only* scientific knowledge is valid, is also popular in Europe; in such a context, "intense religiosity that becomes a central focus of life"—certainly a characteristic of the LDS faith and lifestyle—"tends to be thought of as something dated or fanatical."[204] State paternalism in religious matters leads to official investigations of smaller religious groups that often brand minority religions as suspicious. Majority churches with long histories make efforts to legally hinder minority religions' abilities to conduct missionary work.

Another inhibiting factor is inherent in LDS teaching itself. The lesson plans used throughout most of the last half century of LDS history have tacitly assumed a familiarity with the basics of Christian belief. That familiarity can no longer be assumed in Europe. As Grace Davie has noted, a situation where church affiliation is only nominal

> does lead to a dramatic generation-by-generation drop in religious knowledge. An ignorance of even the basic understandings of Christian teaching is the norm in modern Europe, especially among young people; it is not a reassuring attribute.[205]

Despite all this, there are reasons for the Saints to hope, cautiously, for major growth in Europe.

The first reason has to do with the longest English word that most Americans can even think of: "disestablishmentarianism," meaning a social movement to remove

---

[203] This is a variety of scientism, the position that science is more authoritative than other sources of knowledge (Sorell, 1991/1994 p. 1).
[204] Durham (1999/2008) p. 117.
[205] Davie (1999) p. 83.

Chapter 7: Exterior Forces "Pull" for Mormon Growth 161

official state sanction for a given religion. The three-centuries-old established position of the Church of Sweden ended in 2006.[206] One of the most powerful arguments advanced in support of the legislation to disestablish the Church of Sweden was the increasing multiculturality of that country; in 2012, this concept is easily and widely applicable throughout Europe. In addition, the economically disastrous circumstances afflicting Europe in general, and the euro zone in particular, as I write these words in 2012, are forcing many European countries to reconsider which programs and institutions they can afford to support. It is entirely possible, between the forces of multiculturalism on the one hand and fiscal austerity on the other, that disestablishmentarianism may spread to other European nations. Such a turn of events would make it easier for non-dominant religions generally to obtain converts.

Another reason for Mormons to hope is that some European college-age youth are becoming more interested in such topics as religious studies. Both at the upper levels of British high school and in college, "the number of candidates seeking to do theology or religious studies is growing, if at times unevenly…. Anecdotal evidence suggests that [the predilection for theology] is driven by an interest in ethics and the philosophy of religion …."[207] Such developments may herald the beginning of a more searching attitude towards religion among European youth.

There are plenty of "ifs" here. However, *if* the LDS missionary corps can find a way to effectively address a culturally sanctioned relativism and scientism; *if* disestablishmentarianism gains further hold in Europe; *if* the anecdotal evidence of a growing interest in religious studies

---

[206] Stegeby (1999).
[207] P. Berger, Davie, & Fokas (2008) p. 61.

points to something real; *if* LDS missionaries can find an effective way to connect with young European people who are ignorant even of Christian basics[208]—then the Saints may well find this field "ready to harvest." The better-prepared LDS missionaries of 2010 and on may be the generation to make this happen.

Mainland China

The government of mainland China has never permitted LDS missionaries to preach in any mainland province of the People's Republic of China (PRC).[209] Given the history of China, where foreign missionaries have been perceived as agents of unwelcome colonizing powers since the 19th century, the government may *never* permit American LDS missionaries to preach in country.

None of that matters in the slightest. The Church of Jesus Christ will grow in mainland China, and it will do so within whatever legal restrictions the Chinese authorities impose. The only question is how quickly the Church will grow. Of the LDS situation in China—past, present, and future—there are several important points to be made.

First, the Chinese government seems at least neutral towards the Saints, and may even show some positive inclination towards the Church of Jesus Christ. LDS apostle Elder Dallin H. Oaks, during the time he was president of

---

[208] Some assert that European youth learn the essentials of Christianity during their educations (Prothero, 2007/2008), for example, in history classes (Reed, 2010). My sense of the situation is that knowledge of Christian history does little in the way of conveying the essentials of Christian belief (see Davie's judgment, quoted earlier).

[209] The history of LDS activities regarding China through the mid-1990s is considered by Britsch (1998).

Chapter 7: Exterior Forces "Pull" for Mormon Growth 163

Brigham Young University in the mid-1970s, arranged for a series of performance tours by BYU musical and dance groups to mainland China; apparently, the Chinese authorities were impressed with the LDS groups' professionalism and wholesomeness, and their performance programs' lack of political content.[210] It is not unthinkable that the Communist government of mainland China might allow the LDS to formally organize local congregations, especially if there were no American missionaries involved.

Second, *there are already Latter-day Saints in mainland China*. The Saints have had missionaries continually in the former British colony of Hong Kong since 1955, and in the former Portuguese colony of Macau since 1976. These missionaries continue to work in these former colonies, even though these areas reverted to mainland rule in the late 1990s. Over 24,000 Saints—mostly mainland Chinese, by far—already live in Hong Kong alone.[211] The Saints feel so secure here that the LDS Hong Kong China Temple was dedicated in 1996, just a year before Hong Kong itself reverted to mainland Chinese rule.

The native Chinese Saints already resident in China can form a core of leadership for LDS congregations in mainland China, if the authorities of the PRC ever permit such congregations to be organized. Indeed, there are already signs that the organization of LDS congregations in mainland China is in the offing. In the summer of 2010, the LDS public affairs office in Hong Kong noted this:

> A series of high-level meetings between The Church of Jesus Christ of Latter-day Saints ... and an official from the People's Republic of

---

[210] Oaks (1991).
[211] *Deseret News 2012 Church Almanac* (2012) p. 457.

> China is expected to lead to "regularized" operations for the Church in China....
>
> "It is important to understand what the term regularizing means, and what it does not mean," Church spokesman Michael Otterson said. "It does not mean that we anticipate sending missionaries to China. That issue is not even under consideration.
>
> "The Church deeply appreciates the courtesy of the Chinese leadership in opening up a way to better define how the Church and its members can proceed with daily activities, all in harmony with Chinese law."[212]

The approach of 'growing the Church' through simply working through Saints already in China seems to be implicit within the reflections of LDS apostle, Dallin H. Oaks:

> People sometimes ask me about what can be done to "open China." In response, I state my belief that China is already "open"—it is we who are closed. We are closed because we expect the Orient to be the same as the West, China to be the same as Canada or Chile. We must open our minds and our hearts to the people of this ancient realm and this magnificent culture. We must understand their way of thinking, their aspirations, and their impressive accomplishments. We must observe their laws and follow their example of patience. We must deserve to be their friends.[213]

---

[212] "Church in talks to 'regularize' activities in China" (2010).
[213] Oaks (1991).

Third, there exists an immense Christian community in the PRC. As the editor-in-chief and a major columnist at *The Economist* noted in 2009:

> A conservative guess is that there are at least sixty-five million Protestants in China and twelve million Catholics .... Some local Christians think the flock is well over one hundred million.[214]

This is important because, following the American example, we would expect there to be a great number of LDS converts among those who are already Christian (see Figure 7-2 and Table 7-2).

Fourth, in 2007, 81% of surveyed mainland Chinese stated their religious affiliation as "None"—even though 31% of the mainland Chinese in a 2006 survey stated that they considered religion to be "very or somewhat important" in their lives.[215] As we have already noted, the single most productive category in terms of contributing converts to the Latter-day Saints, at least in the United States, are the Unaffiliated. In China, there may be somewhere around 1.05 *billion* Unaffiliated.

Fifth, many students from mainland China are now studying throughout the world—and that number is increasing. During the 2010-2011 academic year, China sent more students to the United States than any other foreign country; during that year, a total of 157,558 Chinese students came to the United States to study in undergraduate, graduate, and non-degree programs, an increase of 23.5% in a single year.[216] (Undergraduates alone increased 43% in

---

[214] Micklethwait & Wooldridge (2009/2010) pp. 4-5.
[215] *Pew Forum on Religion & Public Life* (2008).
[216] *OpenDoors 2011 "Fast Facts"* (2011), p. 1.

that year.[217]) This represents a large and growing opportunity for Mormons to 'preach their gospel abroad,' yet do it at *home*, an opportunity that the LDS leadership have noticed. As Elder Oaks put it:

> We cannot send missionaries to the People's Republic of China, but each year China sends thousands of its choicest sons and daughters to various foreign lands to study. In those places they quite naturally meet our missionaries, and many of these Chinese students are joining the Church. Some have already returned to China, and others will return when their studies are completed. We encourage our Chinese members to return to China. Their country needs them in China and the Lord needs them in China. The work of China will go forward with these young engineers, scientists, scholars, and artists. At the same time, the work of the Lord will go forward in a natural law-abiding way because of those who have received the message of the restored gospel. In every land, that message makes its recipients better citizens, better workers, and better friends.[218]

Indeed, this approach seems already to be working. When asked about indigenous members in mainland China, an LDS official noted:

> I will say that China is open [to the LDS faith], and it is open because Chinese citizens

---

[217] McMurtrie (2011).
[218] Oaks (1991).

are joining the Church throughout the world. Particularly in Sydney, Melbourne, England, Toronto, New York, Northern California, and Vancouver you see a growing number of Chinese students who are joining the Church and moving back to China. The government allows them to meet in groups, so we say China is open, but it is open in a different way.[219]

In sum, the government of the PRC seems to be neutral-to-positively disposed to the Mormons. Saints already living in Hong Kong and Macau can help to provide leadership to LDS congregations throughout the PRC if and when the government permits the formation of such congregations (which Elder Perkins, in the quote immediately preceding, implied may already be happening). The huge Christian community already in the PRC would prove to be a fertile ground for LDS missionaries, as would the almost unthinkably immense number of the Unaffiliated in mainland China. Many citizens of the PRC study abroad, where some of them convert to the LDS faith and bring their new religion back to the PRC. These factors may work to bring the Latter-day Saints in China well into the high-growth range in the 21st century.

INDIA

The LDS situation in India, a land of over 1.1 billion people, is complex.[220] On the one hand, the first branch of

---

[219] Perkins (2012) p. 11.
[220] *Deseret News 2001-2002 Church Almanac*, p. 341; *Deseret News 2011 Church Almanac*, p. 505; J. Walker (2012). The history of LDS activities in India through the mid-1990s is described by Britsch (1998).

the Church of Jesus Christ in India in living memory was established just in 1981, when government regulations permitted an LDS married couple called as missionaries to enter the country. The Church has been incorporated as a legal entity in India since 1982. There are already two LDS missions in India, one organized in the south at Bangalore in 1993, although a mission headquartered in India's capital, New Delhi in the north, was organized in 2007. In 2009, the Church counted 8,289 Indian Saints, an increase of 240% over the number of Saints (2,435) in 1999. As this book was being prepared for press, the first LDS stake in India was organized, in the southern city of Hyderabad, on May 27, 2012.[221]

On the other hand, the Church operates under serious restrictions in India. The Indian government permits only a very small number of non-Indian missionaries to operate in the country. In addition, the circumstances of Indian society present special challenges to LDS missionary work.

India has a long history of large-scale violence between religious groups (particularly between the 80.5% Hindu majority and the 13.4% Muslim minority, on the one hand, and between Hindus and the 1.9% Sikh minority, on the other); many thousands have died in this violence just since 1980. Political forces working to "purify" India of non-Hindu religions are on the rise.[222] Conversion of Hindus to other faiths has been a controversial issue for well over half a century.[223]

Violence against the Christian minority (about 2.3% of the Indian population) has increased tremendously since

---

[221] "Apostle creates first stake in India" (2012); J. Walker (2012).
[222] Nussbaum (2007).
[223] Kim (2003); Robinson & Clarke (2003).

Chapter 7: Exterior Forces "Pull" for Mormon Growth 169

the mid-1990s.[224] This violence has involved the burning of Christians themselves, the forcible reconversion of Christians to Hinduism, and the destructions of hundreds if not thousands of church buildings. The 1999 murder of Australian evangelical Christian missionary Graham Staines and his two sons—trapped in their car and burned to death by Hindu extremists—was publicized in the West, but other lesser-known incidents against native Indian Christians are numerous, including mutilations and fatal beatings; the Human Rights Watch organization has declared that the Indian government is complicit in many of these attacks.[225]

In this context, the Church must tread carefully in India. It is significant that the first Indian LDS mission in our times, organized in Bangalore, is in the south of India, where the majority of the Christian population live; the first LDS stake in India was organized in Hyderabad, also in the south of the country. The formation of the New Delhi Mission does not mean that the Saints have many converts there; the New Delhi Mission headquarters is responsible for the Saints in Bangladesh, Bhutan, Nepal, and Pakistan, a vast geographical area that it is sensible to direct from a centrally located large city with good air transportation. The Church of Jesus Christ in India is largely a church of Southern India, and primarily works among Christians.

What of the future of the Latter-day Saints in India? A few factors come to mind.

First, the per-decade LDS growth rate of 240% seen in India between 1999 and 2009 is impressive (albeit the absolute numbers involved are small). Clearly, something about LDS missionary efforts in India is working.

---

[224] Smita (1999).
[225] "Anti-Christian Violence on the Rise in India" (1999).

Second, the Indian LDS community has been fielding missionaries of its own since 1986.[226] In 2012, second-generation Indian missionaries—missionaries whose fathers or mothers had served LDS missions—may already be in the field. The Indian LDS community may soon be in a position to supply all of its own missionaries, if it is not already doing so. Of course, missionaries preaching in their own land function at a distinct advantage over foreign-born missionaries, in terms of their knowledge of language, culture, and folkways.

Third, the local Mormon membership in India is proactive in assisting the full-time LDS missionaries. Realizing that visa restrictions result in only very few foreign-born missionaries preaching in India, local Saints "provide plenty of referrals [to teach non-LDS friends and family], and [hence] ... missionaries do not have to do a lot of finding on their own."[227]

Fourth, as with the mainland Chinese, many Indian students come to the U.S. to study at colleges and universities. In the 2010-2011 academic year, India sent the second-largest number of students to study in the U.S. of any foreign country (just behind China); in that year, India sent 103,895 undergraduate, graduate, and non-degree students to study in America.[228] As with China, this presents an opportunity for the Saints to preach the gospel to Indians, without the difficulties and, indeed, dangers of doing so within India itself.

Fifth, the organization of the first LDS stake in India, the Hyderabad India Stake, in May 2012 is a watershed

---

[226] *Deseret News 2012 Church Almanac* (2012) p. 496.
[227] Perkins (2012) p. 11.
[228] *OpenDoors 2011 "Fast Facts"* (2011), p. 1.

Chapter 7: Exterior Forces "Pull" for Mormon Growth 171

event from the point of view of Stark's notion of networks of faith. The organization of a stake directly indicates that there is a breadth of membership and a depth of leadership sufficient to sustain the entire Church program independently; given that the Church program—worship services, religious education, local welfare and humanitarian assistance—is run and conducted by volunteers rather than professional clergy, the organization of a stake makes quite a statement about the maturity of the Church in the area covered by the new stake. Indirectly, the organization of a stake suggests that there is simply enough variety of members available in the area of the new stake to allow potential converts to make the kind of personal associations that facilitate conversion.

Indian LDS congregations have some of the highest convert retention rates, and members of the LDS priesthoods who are among the strongest in the faith, in all of Asia.[229] The LDS membership in India is maturing; this bodes well for future LDS growth in India. Taking all these factors into account, it is plausible that the growth of the Church of Jesus Christ in India will be in the high-growth range of my global projection.

I have noted that LDS missionaries in India seem primarily to work among Christians. Describing the LDS missionary effort in some cities of India, an LDS official stated:

> … in India our missionaries become quite adept, because it is so diverse there. The neighborhoods really vary: There is a Hindu neighborhood, a Christian neighborhood, a Muslim neighborhood, and our missionaries know where the neighborhoods are. They

---

[229] Perkins (2012) p. 10.

feel comfortable talking on the streets or maybe even knocking on a few doors in what is a Christian neighborhood but would not do that at all in a Muslim or Hindu neighborhood.[230]

In this connection, it is noteworthy that there are well over 20 million Christians in India; even if LDS missionaries were just to preach to them (which would arouse no resistance among India's Hindus, Muslims, or Sikhs), this would still be a very large field of potential converts. (Of course, Hindus and Muslims would still be free to seek out the LDS missionaries on their own.) Keeping Rodney Stark's notion of religious capital in mind, in preaching to the Christians of India, the Saints would be preaching to people who would preserve much of their religious capital in a conversion to the LDS faith (such as their use of the Christian Bible).

THE LANDS OF ISLAM

The lands of Islam—countries with a majority Muslim population—are virtually united in presenting barriers to the LDS missionary effort. Often-lethal violence directed against Christians in Muslim-majority countries (or even Muslim-majority regions within other countries) has become common, and is a growing phenomenon.[231] Given the many thousands of Muslims who participated in anti-American riots throughout the Middle East and Asia in late 2012 following the release of a single, 14-minute anti-

---

[230] Perkins (2012) p. 10.
[231] Ali (2012); Nossiter (2011).

Muslim video on YouTube,[232] this author does not see Latter-day Saint missionaries preaching in most of the lands of Islam anytime soon.

Aside from violence, there are often daunting legal and cultural problems regarding the establishment of Christian churches in the nations of Islam. The path to official, legal recognition for non-Islamic religious bodies either does not exist or does not function in many of these lands; without such recognition, meeting for religious worship is illegal.[233] The Church of Jesus Christ will not hold meetings for worship where it is illegal to do so.

What does all of this bode for LDS growth in the Muslim world? The Church takes a different approach with this region, as a Church official explained:

> It was in response to the reality of these political, social and legal constraints that the Church adopted a policy of not proselyting among Muslims. This policy, formulated during the early 1990s, prohibits teaching or baptizing Muslims who live in the United States or Europe but are planning to return to the Middle East. The premise for this policy is that Muslims who join the Church and go back to a Middle Eastern society find it almost impossible to honor their [LDS] covenants and practice their [LDS] religion.[234]

Describing the restrictions under which Mormon missionaries work in the lands of Islam, a Church official reported:

---

[232] Fassihi (2012), Gladstone (2012), Solomon & Lee (2012).
[233] Toronto (1999/2008).
[234] Toronto (1999/2008) p. 139.

> It varies by country. For example, the Church is growing very well in Pakistan, but we only work among Christian communities. Pakistani Muslims are not allowed to convert. In Malaysia, the Church is growing relatively rapidly [i.e., among Christians]. Ethnic Malays are Muslim by birth and, by law, not allowed to change their religion. We are not allowed to proselyte to them. In Indonesia, Muslims are allowed to change their religion, but our missionaries cannot actively tract, contact door-to-door, or talk on the streets. They can wear a badge, but the investigator has to raise a religious question before they can engage in a religious dialogue. They cannot say: "I have a message from the Church of Jesus Christ of Latter-day Saints." That gives you an idea of the restrictions in Muslim nations.[235]

The Church is engaged in a variety of humanitarian work and disaster relief projects in the lands of Islam. It also furthers Islamic academic research; the Church's Brigham Young University has a Middle Eastern Texts Initiative that includes a series in translations from Islamic literature that otherwise are unavailable in English.[236] What one LDS General Authority, Elder Dennis B. Neuenschwander, said about the Middle East is applicable to all the nations of Islam:

---

[235] Perkins (2012) p. 10.
[236] http://meti.byu.edu/islamic.php

> Our goal in the Middle East is not growth through traditional proselyting and conversion, but establishing a viable presence, building bridges of trust and friendship, and promoting goodwill.[237]

To recap, there is reason to believe that the higher-growth projection is within reach for the Latter-day Saints, certainly in the United States, and, I suspect, likely also in Europe. In China and India as well, there is reason to expect Mormon growth in this range. Even if there is little or no Mormon growth within the nations of Islam, that still leaves a lot of world in which to preach the Mormon message. As we shall see in Chapter 9, that message is readily available on the Internet, in more and more of the languages of the world. All these factors combine to make the case that Mormon growth, both in the world in general, and in the United States in particular, will be in the "high-growth" range.

---

[237] Quoted in Toronto (1999/2008) pp. 138-139.

Chapter 8

Interior Forces "Pushing" for Mormon Growth

The way in which different religious teachings are received by an individual is often related to the reigning concerns of that individual's society. This is so, entirely apart from any considerations about the origins of these teachings, their ultimate truth, or even the centrality of these teachings to the followers of the religion in question.[238]

For example, it has been noted that Mormon teachings about a universal apostasy from the ancient Christian church—teachings found in the Book of Mormon and in other revelations reported by Joseph Smith[239]—were especially appealing to many people in 19th century America who already were seeking the restoration of primitive Christianity.[240] It has been claimed that the appeal of Mormonism for many early 19th century converts was related to the LDS faith's distinctive teachings about life after death, when premature death was much more commonplace than it is in the early 21st century (given massive in-

---

[238] For a recent statement of central LDS beliefs, see Oaks (2011).
[239] LDS Standard Works: The Book of Mormon, 1 Nephi chapter 13; the Pearl of Great Price, Joseph Smith—History 1:5-20. The classic LDS treatment of this subject is Talmage (1909/1994). See also Nibley (1961/1987) and Reynolds (2005).
[240] Harper (2000); Vogel (1988). See also Shipps (1985) chapt. 4.

fant mortality, and widespread infectious diseases untreatable before the development of antibiotics).[241]

Below, I address ways in which LDS teachings respond productively to some of our cultural preoccupations—our societal obsessions, if you will—as these can be discerned in the United States in the early 21st century. Even working within these limitations, I think that it is possible to discern some cultural themes that will be valid over the course of the next century or so.[242] These themes are "pushing" forces from within an individual's mind, forces that will serve to attract people to the LDS faith—in ways that these forces will *not* attract people to any or most other Christian churches, at the least.

It is important to understand that I am *not* claiming that people will *become* Mormons because of these social themes. People become Latter-day Saints primarily because of spiritual confirmations of the truth of the Gospel as the Latter-day Saints teach it (see Appendix C). What I *am* saying here is that certain LDS beliefs and practices address certain themes found in the culture at large—and address these themes quite directly, at that, and in ways that other Christian churches' beliefs and practices do not. As this state of affairs becomes more widely known, it will attract the attention of the many people in the general population who are concerned about this or that cultural theme. Of these people, it is quite likely that a number will

---

[241] S.M. Brown (2012).

[242] One might easily fault this approach because I lean so heavily on themes from contemporary American culture. I would point out that American culture—as expressed in motion pictures, television shows, and books—is a dominant force in world culture, at least in the industrialized world. This dominance shows no signs of abating in the foreseeable future.

proceed to investigate LDS beliefs more generally, and go on to become Mormons themselves.

I am keenly aware that this chapter is the most speculative of any in this book. This is necessarily the case: I am leaving the realms of religious demographics, where concrete numbers rule, and entering deeply into the realm of the depth psychology of culture and religion, a rather 'squishier' area of discourse even among the social sciences. Consequently, I have taken the approach of documenting heavily what I consider to be social themes, giving plentiful references to the academic and general nonfiction literature, and to items of popular culture. If it seems that I am being somewhat obsessive myself in the level of detail I use in my examples, at least the reader will understand why I have taken this tack.

Specifically, I describe the following cultural themes,[243] and how LDS beliefs respond to them:

- the power of science and technology;
- the struggle to survive the end of civilization;
- the ambition to transform beyond the human;
- the discovery of extraterrestrial (intelligent) life.

THE POWER OF SCIENCE AND TECHNOLOGY

Humanity has long had legends of what we would today call applied scientists, or technologists: skilled or even divine craftspersons, such as Daedalus and Hephaestos of ancient Greek legend, or Wayland the Smith in Norse legend. But science has come a long way since Plato and Aristotle discoursed on physics and biology. Over the course of

---

[243] Technically, these are four cultural *metathemes*, 'over-themes,' the half-obscured Themes *behind* the more obvious themes that directly appear in, for example, scientific writing, or popular entertainment.

time from the invention of modern science during the European Enlightenment until today, science and technology have become a part of everyday life in a way unthinkable before, say, the mid-18th century and the beginning of the Industrial Revolution.

Examples of the perception of the superiority of science as a path to health, prosperity, and knowledge is so widespread that actually listing it seems superfluous. Popular works on science, many by scientists themselves, are bestsellers.[244] The news is full of articles involving the development of new technology.[245] Our medicine depends upon high technology to diagnose our disorders, and more high technology to treat them. In Chapter 7, I described *scientism*, the idea that scientific knowledge is inherently more authoritative than other sources of knowledge.[246] It would be fair to say that a substantial fraction of the American public are adherents of scientism.

Such attitudes have an impact on religion. The Barna Group, a research organization that focuses especially on evangelical Christianity, reported that 59% of young (evangelical) Christians "disconnect" (i.e., drop out) from their churches after age 15. One of the major reasons for this disconnection is that these individuals feel that there is a conflict between science and Christianity, with 29% of the under-30-aged survey respondents stating that "churches are out of step with the scientific world we live in," 23% saying that they have "been turned off by the creation-versus-evolution debate," and 25% endorsing the

---

[244] E.g., Baggott (2012), Close (2011), Kahneman (2011), Penrose (2011).
[245] Consider the volume of news coverage when a leading company releases a new smart phone.
[246] Sorell (1991/1994) p. 1.

statement that "Christianity is anti-science."[247] (Of course, many of the so-called New Atheists would agree that Christianity—as they understand it—is anti-science, and as such should be discarded from the mental furniture of every thinking person.[248])

As it happens, **Mormonism has usually been on very good relations with science.** This is apparent in many ways, including traditional Mormon teachings about miracles (the supposedly unscientific nature of which is a favorite target of the New Atheists[249]). As Brigham Young (1801-1877), second President and Prophet of the Church, taught:

> The providences of God are all a miracle to the human family until they understand them. There are no miracles, only to those who are ignorant. A miracle is supposed to be a result without a cause, but there is no such thing. There is a cause for every result we see; and if we see a result without understanding the cause we call it a miracle.[250]

Essentially, miracles are simply the result of superior knowledge, applied to the natural elements of the reality; so-called miracles, to Mormons, are essentially products of a superior knowledge of scientific principle.[251] Speaking of various New Testament miracles, Brigham Young taught:

---

[247] Barna Group (2011). See also Kinnaman (2011) p. 23 and chapter 7.
[248] E.g., Dawkins (2006) pp. 282-286, Stenger (2009) chapters 2-4.
[249] E.g., Dawkins (2006) pp. 58-61, Hitchens (2007a) chapter 10.
[250] Widtsoe (1954) p. 339.
[251] One is reminded of the saying of noted scientist and science fiction author Arthur C. Clarke: "Any sufficiently advanced technology is indistinguishable from magic"—or a miracle.

> At the wedding in Cana of Galilee, ... [t]he Savior converted the water into wine.[252] He knew how to call the necessary elements together in order to fill the water with the properties of wine. The elements are all around us ... and Jesus, understanding the process of calling them together, performed no miracle except to those who were ignorant of that process. It was the same with the woman who was healed by touching the hem of his garment[253]; she was healed by faith, but it was no miracle to Jesus. He understood the process .... The case of the Centurion's servant[254] is a striking instance of this.... Jesus counteracted the disease preying upon the system of this man but to himself, knowing the principle by which the disease was rebuked, it was no miracle.[255]

Concerning organic evolution and the origin of species, there has long been a range of opinion among the Saints. Some LDS leaders over the years have favored the idea that some form of evolution resulted in the present state of life on Earth, while others have opposed that idea.[256] David O. McKay (1873-1970), who long served (1951-1970) as the ninth President and Prophet of the Lat-

---

[252] LDS Standard Works: Bible, New Testament, John, ch. 2, vv. 1-11.
[253] LDS Standard Works: Bible, New Test., Matthew, ch. 9, vv. 20-22.
[254] LDS Standard Works: Bible, New Testament, Matt., ch. 8, vv. 5-13.
[255] Brigham Young, quoted in Widtsoe (1954) pp. 340-341. See also *Teachings of Presidents ... Brigham Young* (1997) pp. 255-256.
[256] E.g., B.H. Roberts (1928/1996) being pro-evolution, and Joseph Fielding Smith (1954) being anti-evolution. See also Sherlock (1980).

ter-day Saints, is reported to have stated privately, while he was LDS President, that he personally believed in organic evolution.[257] Yet his biographers note:

> He kept his views private ... for a ... reason that he raised in another private conversation: "The thing you need to remember about evolution is that the Lord has never revealed anything about the matter. People have their opinions but the Lord has not revealed the details of how He created the earth."[258]

Subsequent LDS prophets have not reported revelation that would settle the matter. LDS teachings emphasize that God created the world and humanity. The mechanisms involved, concerning which nothing has been revealed to the Saints, are not discussed in Church teaching. As the highest level of Church leadership, the LDS First Presidency, put it in 1910, after quoting from the LDS scriptures about the creation of humankind 'from the dust of the ground':

> These are the authentic statements of the scriptures, ancient and modern, and it is best to rest with these, until the Lord shall see fit to give more light on the subject. Whether the mortal bodies of man evolved in natural processes to present perfection, through the direction and power of God ... [and other related issues] ... are questions not fully answered in the revealed word of God.[259]

---

[257] Prince & Wright (2005) pp. 46, 417n20.
[258] Prince & Wright (2005) pp. 46 (footnote omitted), 417n21.
[259] The LDS First Presidency in 1910, quoted in Evenson & Jeffery (2005) pp. 43-44.

In 1931, the then-First Presidency noted the following (in a statement that has long been distributed, as part of "the evolution packet," to students at the Church's Brigham Young University, or BYU):

> Upon the fundamental doctrines of the Church we are all agreed. Our mission is to bear the message of the restored gospel to the world. **Leave geology, biology, archaeology, and anthropology, no one of which has to do with the salvation of the souls of mankind, to scientific research**, while we magnify our callings in the realm of the Church.[260]

And so the matter has remained. LDS Church teachings today are remarkably free of the rancor one sometimes encounters in the writings of people from different religious organizations, concerning science and various scientific theories. Perhaps because of this, there are many faithful Saints in the basic and applied sciences, as well as other areas of scholarship.[261] Church leaders have emphasized the compatibility of scholarship and faithful involvement in the Church.[262] BYU's Museum of Paleontology's website proclaims that it "houses one of the top five collections from the Jurassic Period in the world," and explains that the Jurassic Period extended from about 210 to 140 million years ago.[263] No distortion of science here.

---

[260] LDS First Presidency in 1931, quoted in Evenson & Jeffery (2005) p. 38, emphasis added. The full "evolution packet" is available on the internet, e.g., Evenson (1992a). The quotation in Evenson & Jeffery is specifically from Evenson (1992b), which is available online.
[261] See Henry Eyring (1967), and papers in Black (1996).
[262] E.g., Henry B. Eyring (1999).
[263] "BYU Museum of Paleontology" (2006).

My point is clear. I earlier quoted research showing that a substantial proportion of the youth leaving evangelical Christian churches are doing so, at least in part, because of a perceived anti-science attitude in their churches. People who reject a church because of its stance on science will continue to have questions about religion and spirituality. When such individuals—and many others who wonder about this issue—encounter the LDS faith, **they will find that the Church of Jesus Christ is uniquely well-suited among Christian churches to address the relationship between science and religion in a positive, productive way.** This fact will pave the way for some of these people to investigate the Church in more detail; some of those who do so will become Saints themselves. So it is that our modern societal preoccupation with science and technology may actually lead to Mormon growth.

THE STRUGGLE TO SURVIVE THE END OF CIVILIZATION

American culture has become obsessed with the end of civilization. This theme developed to obsessional proportions after the dawn of the nuclear age, and it has notably blossomed just since the turn of the 21st century.

Apocalypticism is nothing new to human society. The biblical book called Apocalypse by Catholics and Revelation by Protestants is a foundational text of Western civilization, influencing religion, politics, art, and popular culture for almost two thousand years.[264] (Every would-be social rebel wearing "666" on a tee-shirt or a tattoo borrows the number of the Beast directly from the Book of Revelation.[265])

---

[264] Kirsch (2006).
[265] LDS Standard Works: Bible, New Test., Revelation, ch. 13, v. 18.

In our generation, Christian apocalypticism has been the subject of a great deal of interest, especially from the evangelical Christian community, an interest that grew particularly after the publication of Hal Lindsey's *The Late Great Planet Earth* in 1970.[266] Christian apocalypticism is still a lively topic of concern in the new millennium, again, especially within the evangelical Christian community[267]; it has been the subject of some of the best-selling books of all time, the *Left Behind* series and its spin-offs.

However, America's cultural obsession with the end of civilization has grown far beyond the boundaries of Christian apocalypticism. This is reflected in several ways.

Natural Catastrophe

Claims that human civilization would be destroyed by natural catastrophic disasters—polar magnetic reversals, displacements of the Earth's crust—were once the domain of obscure authors and very small groups on the fringe of public discourse.[268] Such claims have now come into the mainstream, with some authors stating that the end of most or all human life could come about through long-term variations in global climate patterns,[269] and others finding our end in variations in solar flare activity.[270] This theme is also found in popular entertainment.[271]

---

[266] Lindsey (1970); this book was in its 50th printing in 2011, after reportedly selling over 15 million copies. See also Lindsey (1984).

[267] E.g., Horn et al. (2011); LaHaye (1999); Robertson (1994).

[268] E.g., Kueshana (1963); Noone (1982).

[269] McGuire (2002) chapters 2-4.

[270] A search at amazon.com of media related to "2012 Mayan calendar" or "solar flare" will yield many listings.

[271] E.g., the blockbuster motion picture *2012* [released 2009].

Human-Caused Environmental Catastrophe

Conversely, the notion that the world will be destroyed through environmental catastrophe caused by human activity has steadily picked up steam, at least since the publication of *The Limits to Growth*[272] in 1972. This book (the famous Club of Rome report) publicized the notion that unchecked population growth and industrialization could bring about the collapse of civilization.

A large and plausible literature has grown up around these ideas,[273] as well as around ways to avert these catastrophes,[274] to resist the socioeconomic forces that ultimately create such catastrophes,[275] and to prepare to survive these disasters and preserve civilization.[276] These ideas, too, have found their way into popular entertainment.[277]

Societal Collapse Through Energy Crisis

The case for this scenario has been made by several authors, with greater frequency in recent years.[278] The idea

---

[272] Updated: Meadows, Randers, & Meadows (2004); Bardi (2011).

[273] E.g., Eldredge (1995/1997, 1998); D. Jensen (2006a); Lopez (2011); Martenson (2011); E.O. Wilson (2002).

[274] E.g., in addition to the references in the preceding footnote, see Brand (2009); L.R. Brown (2003, 2011); Jackson (2009/2011); Lomborg (2010); J. Martin (2006).

[275] E.g., D. Jensen (2006b); Lopez (2011); McBay, Keith, & Jensen (2011).

[276] E.g., Greer (2008, 2009).

[277] E.g., the blockbuster motion picture *The Day After Tomorrow* [2004].

[278] Kunstler (2005) is a good place to start in this literature; see also Casti (2012) ch. 7. Authors differ somewhat in their approaches to these issues (e.g., some are more inclined to predict societal collapse, others transformation), and in their recommendations for action. A variety of viewpoints are represented among Brand (2009),

here is that modern civilization is built around energy and materials (such as plastics and fertilizers) obtained from irreplaceable fossil fuels (coal, natural gas, and especially oil). However, we have reached "peak oil," when half the oil ever in the ground has been pumped out; much the same can be said of gas and coal. With demand for fossil fuels rising, but supply decreasing, industrialized civilization will inevitably collapse, according to this literature.

This and similar themes now appear in popular entertainment. James Kunstler's *World Made by Hand* novels[279] depict an oil-depleted-era America where technological society has collapsed. Other novelists describe a post-apocalyptic America where technology has been incapacitated by a massive electromagnetic pulse (EMP); at least one of these has been recommended from the floor of the assembled U.S. Congress.[280]

Global High-Lethality Pandemic

Recent years have seen a great deal of attention paid in the nonfiction literature to the idea that some emerging microbe could bring on a global pandemic with massive fatalities worldwide.[281] For example:

- Studies of the Black Death of medieval Europe, and the bubonic plague thought to have been the infectious agent in that pandemic, have multiplied.[282]

L.R. Brown (2011), Doring (2008), Goodstein (2004), Heinberg (2011), Martenson (2011), P. Roberts (2004), and Ruppert (2009).

[279] Kunstler (2008, 2010).

[280] Forstchen (2009). In television, see NBC's *Revolution* [2012].

[281] E.g., Casti (2012) ch. 8; L. Garrett (1994); Levy & Fischetti (2003); Zimmerman & Zimmerman (2003).

[282] E.g., Cantor (2001); Marriott (2002); Orent (2004); Scott et al. (2004).

- Much has been written about the so-called Spanish Flu, the global influenza pandemic of 1918-1919.[283]
- Following the 2005 avian flu outbreak, the notion that pandemic influenza is a threat to today's world was the subject of an extensive workshop sponsored by multiple U.S. government agencies,[284] and was the topic of cover stories in major magazines.[285]
- As this book goes to press, news reports quoted a spokesperson for the World Health Organization, stating that an outbreak of Ebola virus in the Democratic Republic of the Congo was "not in control."[286]

Potentially high-lethality pandemics, leaping from non-human species to humans, are a disturbingly real possibility in today's world.[287] This theme also has been featured in popular entertainment.[288]

Nuclear War

Since the deployment of the first nuclear weapons in 1945 ended the Second World War, the possibility has been raised that civilization might be destroyed in a global nuclear war. This theme appeared frequently in the 1950s and

---

[283] E.g., Barry (2004); Crosby (1976/1989, 2003); Pete Davies (1999/2000); Duncan (2003); Kolata (1999).

[284] Knobler, Mack, Mahmoud, & Lemon (2005).

[285] E.g., Appenzeller (2005). The July/August 2005 issue of *Foreign Affairs* had a special section titled "The Next Pandemic?", including articles by L. Garrett (2005) and Osterholm (2005), among others.

[286] "Ebola Outbreak in DRC" (2012).

[287] Quammen (2012).

[288] E.g., novels: Stewart (1949); King (1990 extension of 1978 novel), adapted for a 1994 TV miniseries. Major motion pictures: *Outbreak* [released 1995], *Contagion* [2011], *The Stand* [forthcoming, 2013].

early 1960s in nonfiction books,[289] novels,[290] and television and motion pictures.[291] Nuclear war as a theme showed a spike in the 1980s, during the decade, immediately before the collapse of the Soviet Union, when that superstate built to the peak of its nuclear arsenal. So it is that the theme of nuclear war and its aftermath appeared in popular nonfiction,[292] novels,[293] and video entertainment.[294]

It is noteworthy that the public has shown more interest in the theme of nuclear war and post-nuclear apocalypse in recent years, perhaps as the result of the perceived increased threat in nuclear terrorism. This theme has been prominent in both nonfiction[295] and entertainment.[296]

Asteroid Strikes

One type of disaster from which there would be no hope of human survival would be the impact of a massive asteroid, such as the one that ended the reign of the dinosaurs 65 million years ago.[297] This theme has been behind some hugely popular motion pictures in recent years, including the aptly named *Armageddon* and *Deep Impact*, both released in 1998, and the 2009 ABC television miniseries

---

[289] E.g., Kahn (1960).
[290] E.g., Frank (1959), Miller (1960), Shute (1957).
[291] E.g., the 1959 film adaptation of *On the Beach*, the 1960 television adaptation of *Alas, Babylon*, and the 1964 film *Dr. Strangelove*.
[292] E.g., Ehrlich et al. (1984); Sagan et al. (1986); Schell (1982, 1986).
[293] E.g., Strieber & Kunetka (1984).
[294] E.g., the 1983 television movie *The Day After* and the film *Testament*.
[295] E.g., Allison (2007), Langewiesche (2007), Schell (2007).
[296] E.g., the CBS 2006-2008 television series *Jericho*. The ABC television show, *Last Resort*, premiering in the Fall 2012 season, revolves around the theme of averting nuclear war.
[297] McGuire (2002) ch. 5.

Impact. Two recent films examine the human side of this type of end to the world, including 2011's *Melancholia* and the 2012 release, *Seeking a Friend for the End of the World*; it may be especially noteworthy that, in the latter two films, the world and all life on it do indeed come to a violent end.

We could go on to consider the realm of unadulterated fantasy—Americans, at the least, being obsessed in their popular entertainment with such civilization-ending occurrences as the zombie apocalypse,[298] the vampire plague,[299] and attacks by malevolent robots equipped with artificial intelligence,[300] H.P. Lovecraft's alien gods,[301] or other malicious extraterrestrial beings.[302] But there is no

---

[298] E.g., novels: Brooks (2003, 2006), Cronin (2010), King (2006); motion pictures: *Night of the Living Dead* [released 1968], *28 Days Later* [2002], *Resident Evil* [2002], *Zombieland* [2009], and sequels; TV series: *The Walking Dead* [2010—current], The theme has found its way into scientific papers (Munz, Hudea, et al., 2009; Smith? [*sic*], 2009, a parody) and public health messages (Khan, 2011).

[299] E.g., Matheson (1954)—adapted for major movies three times.

[300] E.g., D.H. Wilson (2011), and the 1984 motion picture *The Terminator*, along with its many movie and television sequels. See Casti (2012), ch. 10, for a nonfiction treatment of this theme.

[301] E.g., Joshi (1997, 1999/2011); Joshi & Cannon (1999); Lovecraft (1982). See also Lovecraftin stories by such well-known literary authors as Michael Chabon and Joyce Carol Oates in Datlow (2009). In film, potential invasions by Lovecraftian aliens drive the plots of several films by notable directors John Carpenter (his "Apocalypse Trilogy": *The Thing* [released 1982], *Prince of Darkness* [1987], and *In the Mouth of Madness* [1995]), Sam Raimi (*The Evil Dead* [1981] and sequels), and Guillermo del Toro (*Hellboy* [2004] and sequel), as well as the popular film *The Cabin in the Woods* [2012].

[302] E.g., the motion pictures *Invaders from Mars* and *War of the Worlds* [both released 1953], *Invasion of the Body Snatchers* [1956, remade 1978, 1993, and 2007], *Village of the Damned* [1960, remade 1995], *The Puppet Masters* [1994], *Independence Day* [1996], *Signs* [2002], *Battle:*

need: we have ample evidence of a cultural obsession with the end of civilization from the voluminous literature and popular entertainment cited above regarding natural disasters, environmental catastrophe, pandemics, energy crises, nuclear war, and planet-killing asteroid strikes.

The Mormon Response to Catastrophe and Hardship

The question now becomes, how might the LDS faith address our societal obsession with end-of-civilization catastrophes? As it happens, among the religious people of the world, the Latter-day Saints are uniquely organized to deal with catastrophe and hardship.

From their earliest days, the Mormons as a people were oriented to communal action to provide, not only for prosperity, but for their very survival. Even before the Latter-day Saints were driven out of their city of Nauvoo, Illinois, in the late 1840s, and forced to migrate to what is now Utah (see Introduction), the Saints had developed an ethic of small- and large-scale cooperation. During and after that Mormon Exodus, the Saints nourished that ethic into what is now a deeply rooted approach to dealing with challenges as a community, rather than as just a group of individuals forced to make do on their own. Examples abound.

The first Mormon prophet, Joseph Smith, reported receiving revelations[303] in which the Saints were to live according to something called the United Order, which prac-

---

Los Angeles [2011], and *Battleship* [2012], and the TV series *The Invaders* [broadcast 1967-1968], *V* [miniseries 1983 and 1984, series 1984-1985, rebooted 2009-2011], *The X-Files* [1993-2002], *Dark Skies* [1996-1997], *Invasion* and *Threshold* [both 2005-2006], and *Falling Skies* [2011-current]. This theme is addressed in numerous novels.

[303] E.g., LDS Standard Works: Doctrine & Covenants, Sections 51 & 70.

ticed what was called the law of consecration.[304] This involved the deeding of personal property to the community, which then deeded property back to the individual, sufficient for his or her needs. Excess property was then used to care for the poor and needy. This early form of communal property ultimately was revised into the teaching of tithing, but the United Order is still held as an ideal by the Saints, and the attitudes behind the Order—caring for the good of the community above oneself, treating property and wealth as a stewardship to be used to further the purposes of God, considering all people as social equals—are recommended by many Saints today.[305]

When it came time for the persecuted Saints to leave their city of Nauvoo for what is today Utah, the Mormon Exodus was carefully organized. Brigham Young reported receiving a revelation in which the Saints were set in order for the trip west. The revelation is now part of the LDS scriptures,[306] and represents a marvel of social organization. Although there were mishaps and fatalities in the trek west, these were far fewer than circumstances would otherwise have predicted.

Once ensconced in Utah, the Saints created settlements throughout the Intermountain West in such a way as to benefit the overall community. For example, colonists were "called" from the pulpit of the Saints' semi-annual general conferences to colonize specific areas to raise particular crops or develop specific industries.[307]

---

[304] The definitive work on the United Order as practiced under Joseph Smith and Brigham Young is by Arrington, Fox, & May (1976).

[305] For how Saints in modern times have interpreted the United Order ethic, see Lucas & Woodworth (1999) and Nibley (1989).

[306] LDS Standard Works: Doctrine & Covenants, Section 136.

[307] Arrington, Fox, & May (1976).

Beginning in the early 20th century, the LDS leadership developed the Church Welfare Program to help empower and meet the needs of the poor.[308] This program helps the unemployed to find work, sometimes providing employment through its chain of Deseret Industries thrift stores; "bishop's storehouses" throughout the world directly provide food for the poor, in exchange, whenever possible, for service (such as tutoring, or custodial work).

From pioneer times forward, the Church of Jesus Christ has maintained a structure that serves to strengthen group cohesion and mitigate the effects of community crises. In today's LDS congregation—which typically only numbers about 400-500 individuals—the ward bishop is connected to every ward member through a network of what are called "home teachers" (male priesthood holders) and, in the case of female adults, additionally through a network of "visiting teachers" (adult female members of the Relief Society). It is simply harder for people to 'slip through the cracks' in an LDS congregation than in other comparable religious congregations. In addition, LDS wards are used to engaging in communal projects. In pioneer times, this would have included barn raisings; today, ward members help with bringing meals to new parents, community service projects, cleaning their own ward buildings, and assisting in the rehabilitation of the residences of needy ward members and others.

---

[308] Arrington, Fox, & May (1976) ch. 15; "How the Lord Provides for His Own" (2004); Rudd (1995, 2011); Wrigley (2012). The current President and Prophet of the Church, Thomas S. Monson, is only the most recent to state that the program has a divine origin; as he put it, "I declare that the welfare program of The Church of Jesus Christ of Latter-day Saints is inspired of Almighty God" (Monson, 2011a, p. 90).

At a higher level of organization, LDS stakes (similar to Catholic or Protestant dioceses) are organized to facilitate community-wide action. For example, LDS stakes and local wards coordinated their own disaster-relief efforts after Hurricane Katrina in 2005, aided by relief supplies from Church headquarters in Salt Lake City.[309] For instance, some members of my then-congregation in central Florida, the Winter Park Ward, volunteered to work in Louisiana in the relief effort. During the hurricane season of 2004, when four major hurricanes made landfall upon Florida, Saints from all over the state—including several from my congregation at the time, the small Goldenrod Ward—travelled to hard-hit areas to clear away fallen trees (yes, for Mormons and non-Mormons alike). The yellow "Mormon Helping Hands" shirts worn by many local LDS relief volunteers are a welcome sight after a disaster.

Another aspect of the LDS faith that equips its members for disaster is the Church's long-held focus on emergency preparedness. For example, as part of its policies regarding the encouragement of self-reliance among its members, the Church teaches the following:

> To help care for themselves and their families, members should build a three-month supply of food that is part of their normal diet. Where local laws and circumstances permit, they should gradually build a longer-term supply of basic foods that will sustain life. They should also store drinking water in case the water supply becomes polluted or disrupted.[310]

---

[309] "Church providing relief" (2005); Hart (2005).
[310] *Handbook 2* (2010) p. 34.

The upshot of all this is that the Church of Jesus Christ is uniquely well-equipped to deal with catastrophic events, because of (1) its structure, (2) the ethic of cooperation and communal action that have been instilled into its membership over the course of nearly two centuries, and (3) its focus on emergency preparedness. In the event of some catastrophic natural disaster, local, regional, and international Church authorities will coordinate relief and even rescue activities involving the activities of many Saints. In the event of some societally disruptive event—a massive EMP, for example—the micro-society of the local LDS congregation will endure, and will care for its members, and as many other people as it can. In the event of a pandemic, the Saints who have stored food will be able to avoid crowds at the market, and hence avoid infection. In situations that call for evacuation, the Saints will organize and evacuate in an efficient and orderly way.

As I have documented earlier, a variety of societally disruptive scenarios have been predicted by responsible researchers (the least speculative ranging from extreme weather resulting from global warming, to social disruptions resulting from the post-peak-oil situation). This will make the LDS propensity to weather storms—both real and figurative—a matter of greater awareness and interest to the general public. **This awareness itself will attract people to look farther into the LDS faith.** Some of these people will become Latter-day Saints themselves. So it is that our societal anxiety concerning the struggle to survive the end of civilization may wind up bringing more people into contact with LDS beliefs and practices, and thereby leading to more Mormon growth.

THE AMBITION TO TRANSFORM BEYOND THE HUMAN

Human society has been preoccupied, to the point of obsession, with the idea of somehow transforming beyond the traditional limitations of being human. As it happens, this theme dovetails with a controversial but central doctrine of the LDS faith.

The psychologist Abraham Maslow (1908-1970) posited that human motivations were arranged in a hierarchical fashion. According to Maslow's scheme, after basic survival needs and social needs are met, the need to actualize one's unique potentials becomes dominant in one's life. However, in the relatively little-known final version of his theory,[311] as these self-actualization needs are addressed, the overarching need that emerges is *self-transcendence*: the need to connect with something greater than the self, be that the search for Beauty and Truth, a social cause, or a divine Power. One way to think of self-transcendence is that it ultimately represents a motive to *become* that Something greater than the self, to join with Beauty, with Truth, with Justice—or with that divine Power.

As I show below, the motive to transcend the limitations of humanity has revealed itself in cultural productions throughout history, including those of modern American popular and scientific sub-cultures. Although I must apologize for being highly selective for reasons of space, what I do present will do to make my point.

---

[311] Koltko-Rivera (2006).

From ancient Egypt into the 20th century West

At least as early as Egypt's Dynasty VI (24th to 22nd centuries BC), deceased people were envisioned as having the potential to transform into deities. The so-called Book of the Dead depicts the deceased's soul reciting how the very members of his or her body took on the gods' qualities:

> My hair is the hair of Nu....
> My eyes are the eyes of Hathor.
> My ears are the ears of Ap-uat.
> My nose is the nose of Khenti-Khas.
> My lips are the lips of Anpu....
> My hands are the hands of Ba-neb-Tattu....
> My backbone is the backbone of Suti....
> My feet are the feet of Ptah.
> My fingers and leg-bones are the fingers and leg-bones of the Living Gods....
> There is no member of my body which is not the member of a god. The god Thoth shieldeth my body altogether, and I am Rā day by day.[312]

In late antiquity (circa 2nd century AD), the practitioners of esoteric Hermeticism and the followers of Gnosticism sought *gnosis*, which is commonly translated as "knowledge." However, this was a knowledge that would thoroughly transform the very nature of the knower, a knowledge of the divine that would lead to union with (and perhaps transformation into) divinity.[313] As the schol-

---

[312] Wallis Budge (1899/1979) pp. 197-198, punctuation modernized. The quotation is from Chapter 42 of the Book of the Dead.

[313] van den Broek (1998); see also Faivre (1994) p. 13, and Goodrick-Clarke (2008) p. 19.

Chapter 8: Interior Forces "Push" for Mormon Growth 199

ar Hans Jonas put it, the Gnostics thought that their special knowledge "transforms the knower himself by making him a partaker in the divine existence."[314] This dovetails with the gnostic notion that each human being carries a divine spark, and it is the purpose and mission of each human life to reunite that spark with its divine source.[315]

Many centuries later, during the European Renaissance, we find evidence that the notion of alchemical "transmutation" was applied to human nature itself in esoteric circles.[316] The 20th century analytical psychologist, C. G. Jung, wrote of medieval alchemy as a symbolic representation of the stages of individual psychological development to its most advanced stages.[317] Although Jung considered the medieval alchemists as having largely *unconsciously* symbolized the work of psychological development,[318] other scholarly opinion differs, with some claiming that at least some of the medieval alchemists explicitly framed the alchemical "work" as a program of psychological transformation, intended to bring about the development of the most advanced human capacities.[319]

In modern esoteric groups, the idea of human transmutation, transformation, and metamorphosis has remained prominent. The Golden Dawn, a 19th century magical order founded in England (and revived in the late 20th century), had their most advanced students make a pledge that included the following statement:

---

[314] Jonas (2001) p. 35.
[315] Rudolph (1987) p. 57.
[316] Faivre (1998) p. 120.
[317] Jung (1953), e.g., p. 231 [par. 342].
[318] Jung (1953) p. 258 [par. 380].
[319] E.g., Faivre (1994) p. 55, Godwin (2007) p. 118, Goodrick-Clarke (2008) ch. 4.

I further promise and swear that with the Divine Permission I will, from this day forward, apply myself to the Great Work—which is, to purify and exalt my Spiritual Nature so that with the Divine Aid I may at length *attain to be more than human*, and thus gradually raise and unite myself to my higher and Divine Genius, and that in this event I will not abuse the great power entrusted to me.[320]

Modern American popular culture

We live in an age in which even the occasional motion picture or television drama addresses the issue of how human beings would handle godlike powers.[321] However, the theme of human transformation into the godlike has a great deal more, and more subtle, evidence than this.

Be it the change that allows the dead to identify with the Egyptian gods, transformational Gnostic knowledge, the personal transmutation of the alchemists, or the union with one's Divine Genius in the Golden Dawn, it is clear that Western civilization for many centuries has featured an undercurrent focused on transformation to something beyond the 'everyday' human. Since the mid-20th century, an obsession with this topic has been evident, not just among secret societies and esoteric study groups, but at many newsstands, bookstores, and convenience stores—wherever comic books are sold.

---

[320] Regardie (1989) p. 230, emphasis added.
[321] E.g., *Chronicle* [2012], of which the DVD release asks as a tagline on the front cover: "What are you capable of?" On television: the "It's a *Good* Life" episode [1961] of the original series, *The Twilight Zone*; the "Rush" episode [1999] of *The X-Files*.

Chapter 8: Interior Forces "Push" for Mormon Growth 201

For what are most comic book superheroes but an expression of the human desire to transform into something beyond the human? Into something indistinguishable from what earlier generations would have called 'gods'?

Yes, some superheroes—Batman, for example[322]—are normal humans with special training and perhaps technology. However, most of the most prominent superheroes are just that: *super*, which is to say, beyond human; thus, they are *transhumans* in the proper sense of the word.[323] The most obvious example is Superman, an extraterrestrial transformed by the effect of the yellow sun on his alien body.[324] Other examples of "transhuman" superheroes include natural mutants[325]; "normal" humans empowered by highly advanced technology[326] or outright magic[327]; members of other species diverted from *homo sapiens*[328]; artificial intelligences[329]; and straightforward demi-gods.[330]

However, what seems to be the most well-populated category of transhuman superheroes includes people whose bodies have been altered artificially by the effects of radiation, chemicals, or technology, including genetic engineering.[331] Some of America's best-loved comic book su-

---

[322] Also: Black Panther, Black Widow, Green Arrow, Hawkeye.
[323] Munkittrick (2010). I say more about transhumanism below.
[324] Other examples of extraterrestrial superheroes include Captain Mar-Vell and the Martian Manhunter.
[325] E.g., each of the X-Men.
[326] E.g., Adam Strange, Green Lantern, Iron Man.
[327] E.g., Scarlet Witch, Dr. Strange.
[328] E.g., Aquaman, Sub-Mariner.
[329] E.g., Brainiac 5, the Vision.
[330] E.g., Thor, Wonder Woman.
[331] E.g., Ant-Man, Captain America, the Atom, Doctor Manhattan, the Flash, the High Evolutionary, Metamorpho, Spider-Man, the Fantastic Four, the Hulk, the Inhumans, the Wasp.

perheroes thus had their origins in what would be, in the real world, branches of the transhumanism movement.

Comic book superheroes are the most widespread expression of a societal obsession with the concept of transformation beyond the human. Of course, these superheroes have influenced popular culture since the 1930s, through comic books, novels, magazines, television shows, and motion pictures too numerous to mention.

The connection between comic book superheroes and human ambitions, including spiritual aspirations, has been addressed by several authors in recent years. As one comic book writer and artist, Christopher Knowles, puts it in the title to his book: *Our Gods Wear Spandex*[332]; that is, "superheroes have come to fill the role in our modern society that the gods and demigods provided to the ancients."[333] Knowles goes on to describe the roots of modern superhero myths in spiritual teachings throughout the ages.

However, Knowles has also emphasized that superhero stories create *demand* for improved human capacities:

> How much longer will young audiences [of superhero films] be satisfied with the ordinary? How long before they demand increased or supernatural powers for themselves? And will that lead to an expectation of greater human abilities that can only take the form of a totally new human reality?[334]

Another comic book writer, Grant Morrison, asks,

---

[332] If superheroes really existed, in many cases their colorful, tight-fitting costumes presumably would be made of spandex.
[333] Knowles (2007) p. xv.
[334] Knowles (2007) p. 219.

Chapter 8: Interior Forces "Push" for Mormon Growth

> Could the superhero ... be the best current representation of something we all might become, if we allow ourselves to feel worthy of a tomorrow where our best qualities are strong enough to overcome the destructive impulses that seek to undo the human project?
>
> We live in the stories we tell ourselves. In a secular, scientific rational culture lacking in any convincing spiritual leadership, superhero stories speak loudly and boldly to our greatest fears, deepest longings, and highest aspirations.[335]

To go a step farther, for religious studies scholar Jeffrey J. Kripal, comic book superhero stories are a cultural expression of actual paranormal capacities existing within humanity. For Kripal, these cultural expressions can guide humanity in developing those very capacities.[336]

One also discerns the quest for transformation in the appearance in popular culture of two distinct mythological characters. These are the magician and the vampire.

The superhumanly powerful magician has been the theme of the best-selling book series of all time: J. K. Rowling's *Harry Potter* series.[337] In turn, this series has spawned many imitators, as well as a critically acclaimed postmodern literary take on the whole notion of the magician.[338]

---

[335] Morrison (2011/2012) p. xvii.
[336] Kripal (2011) pp. 2, 5.
[337] Rowling (1997) and its 6 sequels. These books have also been made into a series of 8 blockbuster movies, 3 of which were the highest-grossing films in the world during their respective years of release.
[338] Grossman (2009).

The vampire is inherently transformative, a literal transmutation from mortal to immortal. One is "made" a vampire, and vampires possess powers far beyond human capacity. Vampires are almost unimaginably popular in American culture. The four installments of Stephenie Meyer's *Twilight* series of books are the third-best-selling book series among those begun since 1995.[339] Anne Rice's 12-installment *The Vampire Chronicles* has sold about 80 million copies. The premium-cable television series *True Blood* (broadcast 2008-present) has received high Nielsen ratings and sold millions of units of DVDs of each season released. Vampire-themed novels, graphic novels, television shows, and motion pictures are far too numerous to list.

The academic Victoria Nelson, in her analysis of the genre fiction, comics, and other popular entertainment of our times, ultimately arrives at a puzzling question about the divine images that are encased within the popular super/natural heroes of this entertainment:

> Why human gods and not a set of new invented deities? What is there in this heterodox idea ... that makes it so pervasive in the popular culture sub-Zeitgeist at this moment in time?
> I do not have the answer to this question....

---

[339] Meyer (2005) and its sequels have sold about 116 million copies to date. Among best-selling book series begun since 1995, it ranks only behind the aforementioned *Harry Potter* and the *Chicken Soup for the Soul* series. (In an odd coincidence, both the *Twilight* and *Chicken Soup* series are authored by Mormons.) The *Twilight* books have also been adapted for several blockbuster motion pictures.

I do know that *Twilight* fans do not want to worship the vampire goddess Bella Swan. They want to *be* her. They want to have Bella's superpowers and her perfect, immortal love. That does not necessarily mean they will get fitted out with prosthetic incisors and join the Temple of the Vampire. It does mean that the notion of self-deification is somehow in the metaphysical air surrounding all these various narratives.[340]

The answer to Victoria Nelson's perceptive question—why human gods?—is that the search for divinization has long been an element of human psychology, often submerged due to cultural constraints, but now emergent. As we have seen, human society has long been engaged in a very active search to transcend (and thus perfect) their humanness, the same way that caterpillars transcend and thus perfect their caterpillarness by becoming butterflies.

High technology and self-transcendence

The mapping of the human genome, completed in 2000, has opened the possibility of *improving* that genome, for the purposes of creating individuals who have genetic advantages in terms of intellect, health, or physical attributes (such as strength and beauty). A burgeoning nonfiction literature discusses the pros, cons, and ethics of engineering superior individuals (either from scratch, or by improving already living people) through genetic manipulation and/or pharmacology: in a word, through bioen-

---

[340] Nelson (2012) pp. 262-263, emphasis in original.

hancement.³⁴¹ The title of one of *Time* magazine's early articles on genomic medicine is revealing in this respect: for *Time*, the development of genomic medicine was "Seeking a Godlike Power."³⁴²

The theme of artificial enhancement of human capacities through biological means has found its way into popular culture, not only through sports doping scandals, but also through novels,³⁴³ television shows,³⁴⁴ and movies.³⁴⁵

Parallel to attempts to enhance human ability through biological means, a great deal of research is currently being conducted to enhance human cognitive capacities through the use of computer technology.³⁴⁶ This is the focus, for example, of *augmented cognition* (AugCog) projects, which seek to adapt software function to the human user's cognitive state, in real time.³⁴⁷ It is also the focus of projects to provide ever *more* information to humans by computerized systems, while yet making *less* demand on human cognitive systems.³⁴⁸

---

[341] E.g., Agar (2010), Boylan & Brown (2001), Bowring (2003), Buchanan (2011), Carlson & Stimeling (2002), Chapman & Frankel (2003), Fukuyama (2002), Garreau (2005), Harris (2007/2010), Hughes (2004), Mehlman (2003), Naam (2005), President's Council on Bioethics (2003), Rothman & Rothman (2003), Stock (2002).

[342] Jaroff (1992).

[343] E.g., Glynn (2001), Herbert (1965), Keyes (1966), Kress (1993).

[344] E.g., *Space: Above and Beyond* [1995-1996], *Andromeda* [2000-2005], *Dark Angel* [2000-2002].

[345] E.g., *Gattaca* [1997], *Splice* [2009], and, in 2011, *Captain America: The First Avenger* and the adaptation of Glynn (2001), titled *Limitless*.

[346] Much of this research is funded by the U.S. Department of Defense's Defense Advanced Research Projects Agency (DARPA). This is the case with both AugCog and ELADIS, cited here.

[347] E.g., Schmorrow, Stanney, et al. (2012).

[348] "Extremely Low Attention Demand ... (ELADIS)" (2006).

Chapter 8: Interior Forces "Push" for Mormon Growth

One can consider virtual reality (VR) as a technological effort to enhance human cognition and experience. The capacity for virtual reality to change one's sense of self has been addressed explicitly by some VR researchers:

> ... in virtual reality, the rules of grounded reality are suspended.... In virtual reality, people have abilities that just don't exist in the physical world. Avatars can age, grow, shrink, teleport, and fly at will. They can use ... superpowers—for example, large-scale mimicry and gaze. They can even wear other people's faces and bodies.
> In sum, ... avatars can be "more human than human."[349]

That last phrase is significant. Implicit in the idea that virtual avatars can be "more human than human" is the notion that the true range of human capacities goes beyond the limits of what we consider everyday normality. Certainly it is the case that the 'seamless' VR of the future will allow humans to virtually experience superhuman, even divine capabilities. As I have noted elsewhere, VR can allow one "to react in [a] virtual space with the gods themselves .... [or] to become the embodiment of a god or goddess (the original meaning of 'avatar')."[350] Given the large number of video games that permit identification with at least semi-divine characters,[351] it seems a safe bet that we will see the same when 'seamless' VR becomes reality.

---

[349] Blascovich & Bailenson (2011) p. 262.
[350] Koltko-Rivera (2005) p. 6.
[351] E.g., *Populous* [1989], *ActRaiser* [1990], *Gods* [1991], *Afterlife* [1996], *Dungeon Keeper* [1997], *Doshin the Giant* [1999], *Black & White* [2001] (the box of which features the slogan, "Find out who you really

Virtual reality is the subject of large technical,[352] academic,[353] and popular nonfiction[354] literatures. It is also an element of productions in popular culture too numerous to list comprehensively.[355]

Yet another path for enhancement, not just described but advocated by some, is the actual *incorporation* of computer technology and other equipment into the human body. This is the cyborg movement, which also has amassed a large nonfiction literature.[356] This theme has also found its way into popular culture, through novels too numerous to mention, as well as through television shows[357] and motion pictures.[358]

The cyborg movement has recently been overshadowed by the transhumanism movement (often designated by the symbols "H+" or "h+"), which seeks to apply the

---

are"), *Ghost Master* [2003], *Pocket God* [2009], *Dungeons* [2011], *From Dust* [2011]. Most of these belong to the "God game" genre.

[352] E.g., Sherman & Craig (2003), Stanney (2002), Stanney & Cohn (2012).

[353] E.g., Heim (1993).

[354] E.g., Blascovich & Bailenson (2011), Rheingold (1991).

[355] Some landmarks would include, on TV, the holodeck on *Star Trek: The Next Generation* [broadcast 1987-1994], and in motion pictures, *eXistenZ* [1999], *The Matrix* [1999] and its sequels, and *Avatar* [2009].

[356] E.g., Gray (1995, 2001), Warwick (2002). Some contend (explicitly or implicitly) that humanity are already cyborgs, and should embrace that identity, e.g., Clark (2003), Mazlish (1993), Prensky (2012).

[357] E.g., the Cybermen in *Doctor Who* [broadcast 1963-1989, revived 2005-present], Steve Austin in *The Six Million Dollar Man* [1974-1978], the Borg in *Star Trek: The Next Generation* [1987-1994], the Cylons in the reimagined *Battlestar Gallactica* series [2003-2009].

[358] E.g., the Terminators in *The Terminator* [released 1984] and sequels on film and TV. The high-technology exoskeleton worn by the Tony Stark character in *Iron Man* [2008] makes him a part-time cyborg.

idea of enhancement on a wider scale. Transhumanism advocates transforming the human species through multiple technologies (including nanotechnology, biotechnology, artificial intelligence, cybernetics, and network science) into "transhuman beings" with superior longevity, health, intellect, beauty, and physical performance capabilities. The ultimate hypothetical outcome of technological development in this manner has been called the *transcendent posthuman*, which one author described as follows:

> **Transcendent Posthumans:** This is what we (most of us [i.e., transhumanism theorists]) wish we were. Flawless, immortal, godlike. Abilities so above and beyond humans that they are almost unimaginable.[359]

Transhumanism has amassed a large nonfiction literature debating its means, implications, pros, and cons.[360] In popular culture, transhumanism is the explicit focus of the webseries *H+* (originally released 2012).[361] However, as we have seen in relation to comic book superheroes, transhumanism has appeared pervasively throughout popular culture for decades, albeit somewhat disguised.

One branch of the transhumanism movement deals with what is called the technological Singularity, "the Singularity" for short. The notion here is that technological progress is accelerating to the point where it inevitably and

---

[359] Munkittrick (2010).
[360] E.g., Bostrom (2005), Cole-Turner (2011), Elliott (2003), Hansell & Grassie (2011), Hughes (2004), Young (2006). Much of the literature on transhumanism is online; e.g., see *h+ Magazine* (http://hplusmagazine.com/) and the *Journal of Evolution and Technology* (http://www.jetpress.org/).
[361] http://www.youtube.com/HplusDigitalSeries

irrevocably will change human nature itself, by doing two things: (1) creating self-aware machines—essentially, "hard" artificial intelligence—and (2) creating technology by which human consciousness and artificial intelligence can merge, a future event (the eponymous Singularity) beyond which predictions are impossible. Singularity activists hope that human beings will join with these self-aware machines, uploading their individual consciousnesses to a kind of electronic immortality, having transcended the very need for a biological foundation to human life. The Singularity is a movement as well as a concept, and it has generated much press[362] and nonfiction literature.[363]

Different aspects of the Singularity concept (the "hard," self-aware form of artificial intelligence, or AI; human consciousness merging with AIs; the transformation of humanity through advanced science) have been the subject of numerous novels and stories since at least the 1950s; AI-enabled robots have been a staple of motion pictures and television shows for equally as long. (Examples are far too plentiful to mention in any number.[364])

---

[362] E.g., Grossman (2011).

[363] E.g., Broderick (2001), Kurzweil (2005), Prensky (2012) ch. 8, Watson (2012) chs. 13 and 14. Here, too, much Singularity literature is online; e.g., see *h+ Magazine* and *Journal of Evolution and Technology* (URLs noted above), as well as Singularity Hub (singularityhub.com/), Singularity Institute (singularity.org/), and Singularity University (singularityu.org/). I have made the case elsewhere that humanity should prevent the technological Singularity from occurring (Koltko-Rivera, 2011b).

[364] Milestones of the appearance of these elements would include: in novels, Asimov (1950), Clarke (1953), and Gibson (1984); in motion pictures, *The Creation of the Humanoids* [released 1962], the conclusion of *2001: A Space Odyssey* [1968], and *Colossus: The Forbin Project* [1970]; in television, the "Kill Switch" episode of *The X-Files* [1998].

Whether we consider a post-Singularity being who merges human and AI consciousness, or the "transcendent posthuman," earlier generations would simply have called them gods of a sort. The transhumanism and Singularity movements are both expressions of an impulse for transformation beyond the limitations of 'ordinary humanity,' an expression of Maslow's drive to self-transcendence.

As we have seen, the search for self-transcendence through transformation—even transmutation—has taken several paths through history, and has a number of manifestations today. What these modern paths have in common, to put it bluntly, is the desire for humans to become godlike. Among modern religions, especially in the West, the LDS faith is uniquely suited to address this desire.

Self-transcendence and the LDS doctrine of exaltation

One of the most distinctive central doctrines of the LDS faith involves the Mormon doctrine of *exaltation*.[365] Joseph Smith recorded a revelation in 1843 that stated the following, concerning those who (1) marry in LDS temples under the proper authority to have those marriages last eternally, and (2) then go on to actually keep the covenants for righteous living they have made in the temple:

> .... when they are out of the world [i.e., at some point in the afterlife] ...they shall pass by the angels, and the gods, which are set there, to their exaltation and glory in all things ... which glory shall be a fulness and a continuation of the seeds forever and ever [i.e., eternal family life].

---

[365] See *Gospel Principles* (2009) chapter 47; Pope (1992).

> Then shall they be gods, because they have no end; therefore shall they be from everlasting to everlasting, because they continue; then shall they be above all, because all things are subject unto them. Then shall they be gods, because they have all power, and the angels are subject unto them.[366]

In other words, the LDS faith teaches that human beings *can* literally become gods (albeit in the afterlife). This journey to godlike capacities is far different for the Saints than the journey depicted in most of the other literature and artifacts of popular culture that we have considered thus far. For the Saints, becoming godlike is not a matter of accidental encounters with extraterrestrial or magical artifacts, or the implantation of technology. Rather, it is a divine gift that requires moral worthiness and personal holiness of the recipient, an orientation of selfless service to others, self-sacrifice, and obedience to the Lord.

The doctrine of exaltation opens the possibility for families to last for all eternity (as in the Mormon catchphrase, "forever families"). The doctrine of exaltation is the basis of Mormon temple-building, which provides opportunities for people to make the covenants for faithful, clean living that one must make and keep to bring about exaltation and forever families.[367] The doctrine of exaltation is behind LDS genealogical activity, which makes it possible to extend temple blessings to earlier generations.[368] In brief, the doctrine of exaltation is central to the LDS faith.

---

[366] LDS Standard Works, Doctrine & Covenants, Section 132, vv. 19-20.
[367] *Gospel Principles* (2009) chapters 36 and 38.
[368] *Gospel Principles* (2009) chapter 40.

The Latter-day Saints have been stigmatized as un-christian, especially by evangelical Christians, for the doctrine of exaltation. However, it is slowly becoming more common knowledge throughout at least the academic religious studies community that the ancient Christian Church taught something very much like exaltation: the doctrine of *theosis*,[369] a form of which is taught to this day in the Orthodox Christian Churches[370] (such as the Greek and Russian Orthodox). According to the doctrine of theosis, the faithful shall "partake of the divine nature"; this is divinization, deification, 'becoming God.' Scholars are rediscovering theosis in the writings of Paul the apostle of ancient Christianity,[371] and in the writings of Christian teachers in later ages, including the late Middle Ages.[372] The Christian heritage of the doctrine of theosis and its implications are being explored in other churches today.[373] (It is noteworthy that Victoria Nelson explicitly connects modern super/natural heroes to the ancient doctrine of theosis.[374])

There are those who claim that the Latter-day Saint doctrine of exaltation is somehow something different from, or a distortion of, the ancient Christian doctrine of theosis.[375] This kind of criticism is likely to fade—

---

[369] Christensen & Wittung (2007), Finlan & Kharlamov (2006), Kharlamov (2011), Russell (2005).

[370] Russell (2009).

[371] Gorman (2009). See Russell (2005), and papers in Christensen & Wittung (2007), Final & Kharlamov (2006), Kharlamov (2011).

[372] N.J. Hudson (2007).

[373] In the Roman Catholic tradition, see Keating (2007). In the Lutheran tradition, see Kärkkäinen (2004).

[374] Nelson (2012) p. 265; see also pages indexed s.v. "divine human."

[375] In a refreshing contrast to those making such claims, the Roman Catholic priest Fr. Jordan Vajda, O.P., in a close analysis of theosis and exaltation, determined that the two doctrines were "functional-

especially once it becomes known that Jesus himself taught what seems like a direct—even blunt—statement of the LDS doctrine of exaltation.[376]

The ancient Christian leader and teacher, Clement of Alexandria (ca. 150-215 A.D.), is remembered today especially for his *Exhortation to the Greeks*.[377] In it, he quotes various sayings of Jesus. In the same style of language, Clement states what I believe is just another quotation from Jesus (albeit undetected as such for nearly twenty centuries):

> Verily I say, the word of God became a man, truly in order that you too might learn from a man how at length then a man may become a god.[378]

Could there be any more clear and concise a statement of the LDS doctrine of exaltation, including the role of the Atonement of Jesus Christ in bringing about that exaltation for humankind? As the top leadership of the Church of Jesus Christ stated in 1909:

> Man is the child of God, formed in the divine image and endowed with divine attributes, and even as the infant son of an earthly father and mother is capable in due time of becoming a man, so the undeveloped offspring of celestial parentage is capable, by experi-

---

ly equivalent" (Vajda, 2002, p. 50). Of course, he found important differences between the Catholic and Mormon doctrines of God.

[376] For a full discussion of this matter, see the forthcoming book in this series, *What Mormons Believe*.

[377] Titled in some English translations *Exhortation to the Heathen*.

[378] This author's very literal translation of the Greek of *Exhortation to the Greeks*, chapter 1. See Butterworth (1919) pp. 22-23 for the original Greek and an alternative translation.

ence through ages and aeons, of evolving into a God.[379]

For many centuries, humankind has aspired to transcend the limitations of humanity, and to become, in some fashion or another, godlike. In our own day, one can see this aspiration expressed in the transhumanism and cyborg movements, in the fascination with the Singularity, and in the super/natural hero narratives that comprise a huge fraction of our popular entertainment.

At some point, this age-old yet oh-so-modern preoccupation with transcendence will collide with information about the LDS doctrine of exaltation. When this occurs, **people who are consciously concerned with transcendence of human limits—by whatever means—will find that the LDS faith is a religion for which the concept of transcendence and human transformation is central.** Some of these people will go on to investigate the LDS faith, and then to become Latter-day Saints themselves. So it is that our society's preoccupation with transcending the limits of humanness may well lead to greater LDS growth.

THE DISCOVERY OF EXTRATERRESTRIAL (INTELLIGENT) LIFE

The discovery of life—particularly intelligent life—beyond the confines of the Earth has been an increasingly prominent theme at least in American society, especially since the 1970s, as serious scientific inquiry in this area has picked up momentum.[380] A substantial nonfiction literature has grown up around issues like the philosophical issues raised by the possibility of extraterrestrial intelli-

---

[379] "The Origin of Man" (1909/2002).
[380] Boss (2009), Dick (1996), Koerner & LeVay (2000), Lemonick (2012).

gence,[381] why Earth scientists have not yet discovered intelligent extraterrestrial life,[382] and what the societal and even religious implications of 'first contact' might be.[383] The 1996 discovery in Antarctica of a Martian rock that contained evidence of microscopic life (evidence ultimately determined to be ambiguous at best) caused a national sensation.[384] The 2012 mission on Mars of the NASA rover Curiosity had the explicit purpose of searching for chemical signs that life on Mars, past or present, might exist.[385]

Of the potential discovery of extraterrestrial intelligent life, I can say three things. First, the theme has shown up in all avenues of popular entertainment, in instances too numerous to mention comprehensively, thus demonstrating the strength of this idea in the popular consciousness.[386]

Second, it has been predicted that even the discovery of nonintelligent alien life might have profound social consequences on Earth. As one physicist put it:

> ... the discovery of just a single bacterium somewhere beyond Earth would force us to revise our understanding of who we are and where we fit into the cosmic scheme of things, throwing us into a deep spiritual identity crisis that would be every bit as

---

[381] E.g., Regis (1985).

[382] E.g., Burger (2003), Webb (2002).

[383] E.g., Dick (2000), Harrison (1997), Maruyama & Hawkins (1975), Michaud (2007).

[384] Goldsmith (1997).

[385] "Closer to Encounter" (2012).

[386] Landmarks in motion pictures alone would include *Forbidden Planet* [released 1956], *Alien* [1979], *E.T.: The ExtraTerrestrial* [1982], and *Prometheus* [2012] — each one a commercial blockbuster.

dramatic as the one Copernicus brought about in the early 1500s, when he asserted that Earth was not at the center of the universe.[387]

Third, **the Latter-day Saint faith is uniquely well-suited to cope with the discovery of intelligent extraterrestrial life.** This is because LDS scriptures already contain what seem to be direct and unambiguous references to the existence of intelligent extraterrestrial beings.

At one point in the LDS narrative regarding the ancient prophet Moses (recorded as a revelation by Joseph Smith in 1830), the prophet and the Lord are in conversation, when the Lord opens up a vision to Moses' sight:

> … Moses cast his eyes and beheld the earth, yea, even all of it; and there was not a particle of it which he did not behold, discerning it by the spirit of God.
>
> And he beheld also the inhabitants thereof, and there was not a soul which he beheld not; and he discerned them by the Spirit of God; and their numbers were great, even numberless as the sand upon the sea shore.
>
> **And he beheld many lands; and each land was called earth, and there were inhabitants on the face thereof.**
>
> And it came to pass that Moses called upon God, saying: Tell me, I pray thee, why these things are so, and by what thou madest them?

---

[387] Paul Davies (2003). The callout to Paul Davies' article provocatively asks, "Could earthly religions survive the discovery of life elsewhere in the universe?"

… And the Lord God said unto Moses: For mine own purpose have I made these things. Here is wisdom and it remaineth in me.

And by the word of my power, have I created them, which is mine Only Begotten Son, who is full of grace and truth.

And worlds without number have I created; and I also created them for mine own purpose; and by the Son I created them, which is mine Only Begotten.

…

But only an account of this earth, and the inhabitants thereof, give I unto you. For behold, there are many worlds that have passed away by the word of my power. And there are many that now stand, and innumerable are they unto man; but all things are numbered unto me, for they are mine and I know them.

And it came to pass that Moses spake unto the Lord, saying: Be merciful unto thy servant, O God, and **tell me concerning this earth**, and the inhabitants thereof, and also the heavens, and then thy servant will be content.

And the Lord God spake unto Moses, saying: ….

And now, Moses, my son, I will speak unto thee **concerning this earth upon which**

thou standest; and thou shalt write the things which I shall speak.[388]

The Lord revealed a vision to Moses in which Moses saw all the Earth and its inhabitants, and then saw a variety of *other* worlds, each called 'earth,' with *their* inhabitants. Moses asks to learn about these alien worlds; the Lord declines to reveal any more about these other inhabited worlds; Moses then asks just to learn about our Earth, and the Lord accedes to this much more limited request.

In a vision that Joseph Smith recorded in 1832 (received, he said, with his associate Sidney Rigdon), Smith reported the following about Jesus Christ:

> And now, after the many testimonies which have been given of him, this is the testimony last of all, which we give of him: That he lives!
>
> For we saw him, even on the right hand of God; and we heard the voice bearing record that he is the Only Begotten of the Father—
>
> That by him, and through him, and of him, the worlds are and were created, and the inhabitants thereof are begotten sons and daughters unto God.[389]

This is the sum total of what the LDS Standard Works have to say explicitly about the existence of intelligent extraterrestrial life. We may conclude that the "inhabitants" Moses saw possessed language—they "called" their respective planets "earth"—but that is all that one might

---

[388] LDS Standard Works: Pearl of Great Price, Moses, chapter 1, verses 27-33, 35-37, 40, emphases added.

[389] LDS Standard Works, Doctrine & Covenants, Section 76, vv. 22-24.

conclude from the scriptural narrative. We may also conclude that these aliens have something like our two sexes: they may, through Christ, become "sons and daughters unto God." But there is nothing said here about the relative abundance of inhabited worlds among the planetary systems in the universe, let alone our own galaxy, or galactic neighborhood. There is nothing even stated about whether the "inhabitants" of those alien worlds are humanoid.

Despite the brevity of these passages, they have powerfully shaped LDS expectations about intelligent life on other worlds. The Mormon consensus about the subject was well expressed by the late LDS Apostle, Elder Neal A. Maxwell: "We cannot comprehend it all, of course. We do not know how many inhabited worlds there are, or where they are. But certainly we are not alone."[390]

These teachings do not take up much space in a Saint's mental landscape; LDS teaching is far more concerned with how the inhabitants of *this* Earth live, not how the inhabitants of other worlds do. However, **if and when evidence of life on other worlds is discovered, the Saints will be the only Christian community of faith to have declared in advance, clearly and as a matter of scripture, that extraterrestrial life exists.**[391] If and when evidence of extraterrestrial *intelligent* life is found, the Saints will not be fazed in their faith, for their scriptures have declared for nigh on two centuries that they are not alone in the uni-

---

[390] Maxwell (1990/2001), p. 25.

[391] The widely reported 2009 conference at the Vatican's Pontifical Academy of Sciences merely resulted in a statement by Catholic officials (not even including the Pope) that intelligent life *might* exist on other worlds (Kaufmann, 2009). This declaration is just an opinion, and does not constitute Catholic doctrine.

verse as sentient creatures. And if and when either of these discoveries occurs, **the LDS position on extraterrestrial life will attract the attention of a great many people**, some of whom will be attracted to the faith itself. In this way, our society's long-standing interest in the possibility of extraterrestrial life may lead to greater Mormon growth.

Conclusion

I have shown in detail the existence of several overarching themes that exist within the mindset of modern American society: the power of science and technology; the struggle to survive the feared future end of civilization; the ambition to transform somehow beyond the limitations of everyday humanity; and, the discovery of extraterrestrial life. I make no claims that these are all of our society's super-memes, or even the most powerful. (Our society's powerful obsessions with wealth and hedonism, for example, do not work into this chapter.)

However, Mormonism does have specific beliefs and practices to offer as productive responses to these social themes—beliefs and practices that other religions, by and large, simply do not possess. As these LDS beliefs and practices become more widely known, they will attract the attention of large numbers of people. (That is, after all, one central aspect of an obsession: anything that relates to it receives one's attention.) Some of these people will go on to study the LDS faith more seriously, and of those, some will go on to become Latter-day Saints themselves.

In this way, the interior, psychological "pushing" forces will promote Mormon growth. Given the prominence of these societal themes, it is entirely possible that these forces will promote Mormon growth into the high-growth range of my projections.

Chapter 9

Knowledge Forces and Mormon Growth

In Chapter 6, I take the position that religions will grow, in part, to the extent that they are effective in putting their message in front of people who are making religious choices, using "knowledge forces" to bring potential converts to them. The LDS leadership has taken steps to put their message in front of potentially billions of people.

The Church has embraced online technology to bring its message to the world. One way it is doing this is through making its signature scripture, the Book of Mormon, available online in Asian languages—something the Saints see as crucial to their missionary effort. (It has been available in European languages for generations.) As explained by a member of the LDS General Authorities, Elder Anthony D. Perkins:

> Looking forward, technology may be the key for populous Asian nations to access the Book of Mormon. Today, because of various legal restrictions, only 5 percent of the people in Asia can possibly find a full-time missionary in their city who can give them a [copy of the] Book of Mormon …. Yet almost everyone [sic] in Asia owns a mobile device, if not a computer or tablet. Book of Mormon text is now available on the Internet in most Asian languages with mobile versions now availa-

ble in Cambodian, Chinese, Indonesian, and Mongolian, with additional languages forthcoming. Efforts are underway for text and audio scriptures on mobile devices.

The first and most crucial step to bring the Church out of obscurity in Asia remains publication and distribution of the Book of Mormon in any format. We cannot invite all to come unto Jesus Christ without this sacred volume of scripture.[392]

However, bringing the Book of Mormon to the world is only one part of the Church's approach to technology.

The Church has an asset that will prove extremely valuable as it spreads its message to the world: its Internet presence. It appears that the Church of Jesus Christ has the most sophisticated Internet presence of any Christian church. The Church takes online communication very seriously, the Church Internet Committee being composed of four members of the Quorum of the Twelve Apostles and other high officials.[393] The Church uses its online presence vigorously, to bring its message to its own membership and to the world at large. I describe some of the websites that are part of this online presence below.

www.lds.org

The website at "www.lds.org" is one of the Church's major official websites. It is a cornucopia of resources related to the Latter-day Saints and their message. There are pages with the full text of the LDS scriptures, the Church's

---

[392] Perkins (2012) p. 4.
[393] Colemere (2012) p. 24.

many manuals for teaching their membership, and over forty years' worth of the Church's magazines. Special pages are dedicated to descriptions of LDS beliefs and history, and the LDS temples; a sophisticated online newsroom is also featured.[394] A media library features videos and music. In late 2011, the Church began to release online video vignettes produced about the life of Jesus Christ; as of September 2012, the growing set contains over 30 vignettes, all available for free download online.[395]

All or most of the lds.org website is available in ten languages: Chinese, English, French, German, Italian, Japanese, Korean, Portuguese, Russian, and Spanish—thus covering the first languages of about 2.6 billion people.[396] Selected portions of the website are available in over 85 additional languages as of late September 2012, including Amharic, Arabic, Bengali, Fanti, Hindi, Igbo, Indonesian, Kazakh, Latvian, Malay, Mongolian, Polish, Tamil, Thai, Turkish, Twi, Ukrainian, Urdu, Vietnamese, Xhosa, Yoruba, and Zulu.[397] Other languages, no doubt, will be added.

The lds.org website contains everything needed for the basic instructional needs of an LDS congregation, family,

---

[394] The newsroom is actually another website that the Church makes available to the public, specifically one for the news media (MormonNewsroom.org). Other public websites include one focused on video and audio with "inspirational and uplifting content for members and those with similar values" (MormonChannel.org), family history and genealogy (FamilySearch.org), and one for people interested in learning more about the LDS faith 'from scratch': mormon.org, which I describe presently. A portion of the main LDS website is devoted to youth: https://www.lds.org/youth

[395] http://www.lds.org/bible-videos/videos/

[396] Author's calculations from data in Lewis (2009).

[397] See http://www.lds.org/languages . Or, on www.lds.org, click on the globe icon (🌐) at the top of the page to see a list of languages.

or individual member. It contains a great deal of interest to the member of the general public who is curious about the LDS faith. However, the Saints have a different website for that purpose: www.mormon.org (see below).

The Church website, "lds.org"

Official LDS Country Websites

The Church has begun to develop "lds.org"-like websites specifically for individual countries outside the United States.[398] Thirty-seven countries and regions are listed as having their own individual sites on the LDS "Country Sites" webpage as of late September 2012, although more countries actually have LDS sites that have yet to migrate

---

[398] For a partial list of LDS country sites, see http://www.lds.org/countries

to a listing on the official page; I estimate that, in all, at least 70 LDS country websites exist.

LDS country pages provide a mix of "headquarters" material and local content. The Mexican country site[399] (all in Spanish) has lots of local LDS news, and online articles about Mormon history in Mexico; even the Latvia country site,[400] which has much less content than Mexico's, recently carried notices about an then-upcoming conference in Riga. Some countries share sites at present; for example, Argentina, Paraguay, and Uruguay share a common Spanish-language country site, which recently featured a call for volunteers to help at the public open house preceding the rededication of the LDS Buenos Aires Temple.[401] On the India country site,[402] the majority of the site is in English, one of the official languages of India, although the site provides a monthly message from the LDS First Presidency translated into Hindi, Tamil, and Telugu. In Hong Kong, there are two separate websites with identical content, including lots of local news—one site being in Chinese,[403] the other in English.[404] All of these websites feature pages about the basics of the LDS faith; some feature videos on the subject, carefully dubbed in the local language.

In the near future, the Saints will have sophisticated websites making it possible for a very large proportion of the human race to learn a great deal about the LDS faith in their own languages, online, in both text and audiovisual form. This can only help to spread the LDS message.

---

[399] http://www.lds.org/?lang=spa&country=mx
[400] http://www.jezuskristusbaznica.lv/
[401] http://www.countrywebsites.lds.org/ar/
[402] http://www.lds.org.in/
[403] http://www.lds.org.hk/
[404] http://www.lds.org.hk/en/

www.mormon.org

The website www.mormon.org is all about the beliefs and practices of the Latter-day Saints, written specifically for the benefit of those who are not members of the LDS faith. There are pages devoted to LDS beliefs about Jesus Christ, the Book of Mormon, and so forth. Other pages are devoted to explaining LDS values, such as the importance of strengthening families, and the importance of service.

However, the most extensive section of the website is headed "Our People," and it is devoted to personal narratives contributed by individual Latter-day Saints, presented in both video and text form.

A few of these narratives involve Saints who are prominent in the public eye, such as Kevin Fedderson, professional skateboarder (whose profile is highlighted on the site, in the screenshot below). For the most part, though, these narratives have been submitted by members with no special standing in the eye of the public.

These "I'm a Mormon" narratives put a human face on the Church, and allow people to learn how a "regular person" became a Latter-day Saint, why they remain a Mormon, and how they live their LDS faith in their everyday lives. (This author has contributed his own personal narrative to this collection: http://mormon.org/me/1777/ ; see below.)

Chapter 9: Knowledge Forces and Mormon Growth 229

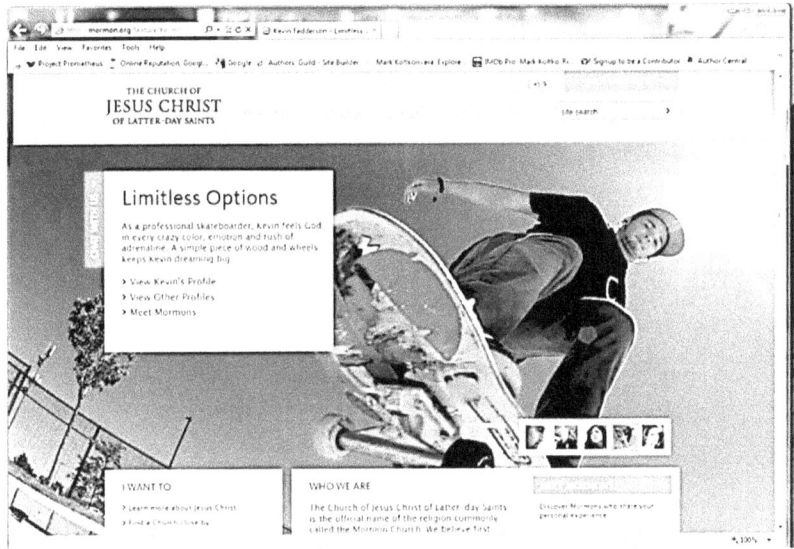

The Church website, "mormon.org"

The author's "I'm a Mormon" web page on
www.mormon.org

Individual Mormon Blogs

The Mormon presence on the Internet is not confined to official Church productions. If anything, the 'unsponsored' sector of the Mormon online universe is even larger.

The last decade or so has seen the rise of the LDS blogger and videographer.[405] Thousands of blogs and video channels have been created by Saints to convey some aspect of their LDS experience. Group weblogs,[406] and other websites focus on tracking the many Mormon blogs and video channels.[407] Even this author has two such blogs.

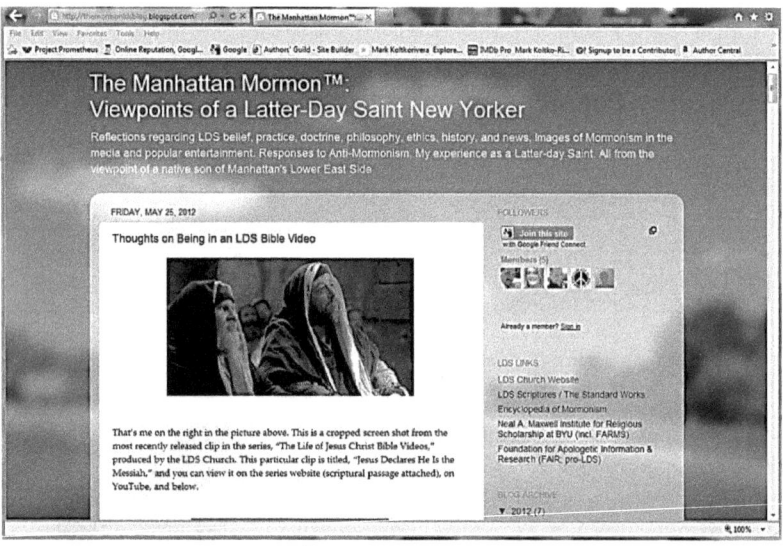

The author's blog, "The Manhattan Mormon™"[408]

---

[405] The LDS "bloggernacle" is described broadly in Otterson (2012).
[406] Such as "By Common Consent," http://bycommonconsent.com/
[407] Such as "Mormon Blogs," http://mormonblogs.org/ ; "Mormon Archipelago," http://www.ldsblogs.org/ ; "Bloggernacle Times," http:// www.bloggernacle.org/
[408] http://themormonldsblog.blogspot.com/

Chapter 9: Knowledge Forces and Mormon Growth   231

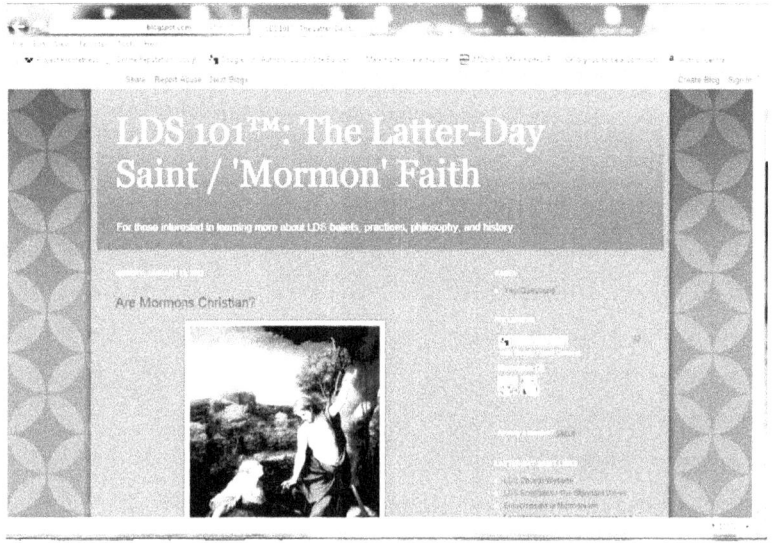

The author's blog, "LDS 101™"[409]

Impact of the LDS Online Presence

What will be the impact of this sort of online presence? It is now the most common of truisms to state that people find their information online; indeed, a teacher like myself sometimes hears students say, "if it's not online, it doesn't exist for me." Even for such, the Church of Jesus Christ exists, in a very vigorous way. Through its thousands of official and unsponsored websites, the LDS faith can reach billions of people in seconds, every day.[410]

This will have a particular effect on the American Millennial generation, roughly composed of those individuals born in the United States between 1980 and 2000. Understanding how that is so is important to understanding why

---

[409] http://lds101mormonism.blogspot.com/
[410] At year-end 2011, world internet usage was estimated to reach over 30% of the global population, or about 2.3 billion people, including over one-third the population of Asia (*Internet World Stats*, 2012).

the Internet is likely to lead to high growth rates for the Church, and not just in the United States, but worldwide.

The American Millennial generation has the reputation, in some quarters, of being less religious than others. We have seen that this cohort has the largest proportion of Americans unaffiliated with a religious organization; in a 2010 survey, this amounted to 26% of Millennials, compared with 13% of Baby Boomers.[411] The Millennials also show less frequent religious practice on several measures (such as worship attendance, daily prayer, and so forth),[412] although "among those who *are* affiliated, generational differences in worship attendance are fairly small"[413]; much the same can be said about other religious practices.

However, in terms of *convictions*, Millennials are really not so different from their elders, especially when we consider the 75% or so of Millennials who have a religious affiliation. Among the affiliated, a smaller proportion of Millennials than older people have an absolutely certain belief in the existence of God, but not *that* much smaller (74% vs. 80%). About the same proportion of all Millennials as older people believe that their holy book is the word of God, whether religiously affiliated (71% of both Millennials and their elders) or not (26% of Millennials, 25% of their elders).[414] Among the affiliated, a slightly *greater* proportion of Millennials (82%) versus their elders (79%) believes in a life after death; among the unaffiliated, a *greater* proportion of Millennials than elders believes this (54% vs. 45%).[415]

---

[411] Pew Research Center (2010), p. 85.
[412] Pew Research Center (2010), pp. 90-93.
[413] Pew Research Center (2010), p. 90.
[414] Pew Research Center (2010), p. 98.
[415] Pew Research Center (2010) p. 100.

Thus, with the Millennial generation in America at least, we are confronted with a distinctive demographic group that shows somewhat less religious *behavior* than those older than they are, but a very similar degree of religious *conviction*. As one commentator has put it:

> Suggestions that the Millennial generation are signaling the secularization of American culture are premature and ignore the rather nuanced religious identity of this age cohort. Belonging to a religious organization is a behavior. Belief is a conviction. As regards belief, Millennials have much in common with other Americans.[416]

At some point, Millennials, like those of any generation, have questions about religion and spirituality. Very much *un*like the generations before them, however, the Millennials will find answers to those questions online.

The Millennials are aggressively connected to online technology. Of those Millennials who said that their generation had a unique, distinctive identity—and 61% of them thought they do—24% of them said that what makes their generation unique was their use of technology (the single most popular response).[417] In a 2010 survey, 75% of Millennials said that they had a profile on a social networking site (compared with 41% of the general population).[418] Eighty-three percent of Millennials use the Internet or email at least occasionally (compared with 68% of the general public).[419] A full 20% of Millennials have posted a vid-

---

[416] Lindner (2012) p. 17.
[417] Pew Research Center (2010) p. 5.
[418] Pew Research Center (2010) p. 1.
[419] Pew Research Center (2010) p. 27.

eo of themselves online, compared with only 6% of the next older age cohort, the members of Generation X.[420] In the 24 hours just before completing the survey, 32% of Millennials reported that they had watched a video online, compared with 9% of individuals from the Baby Boomer generation.[421] And, perhaps most revealingly, fully 59% of Millennials said that the Internet was a main source for their news, compared with 30% of Baby Boomers.[422]

Thus, every indication suggests that when the Millennials have religious questions, they will look online, perhaps using social networking sites to further their quest for answers. As that day arrives, Millennials will find thousands upon thousands of webpages—video, audio, and text—by individual Latter-day Saints and the Church itself, setting forth the Mormon message.

We may already be seeing the beginning of this. Kevin Fedderson's video, posted not only to the www.mormon.org website but also to YouTube, has been viewed over 121,000 times as of early June 2012; former NFL player Gabe Reid's video has received over 712,000 views; Sheryl Garner, a school teacher in Washington, DC, posted a video that has had over 133,000 views.[423] As an LDS-owned newspaper put it:

> The videos are ultimately changing missionary work for the better. Jeremy Kidd, an elementary school teacher in Pasco, Wash., said the videos are incredibly easy to share and show that members of The Church of Jesus

---

[420] Pew Research Center (2010) p. 25.
[421] Pew Research Center (2010) p. 36.
[422] Pew Research Center (2010) p. 35.
[423] Winchel (2012).

Christ of Latter-day Saints are normal people with a variety of jobs and family situations.... "It breaks down some barriers," he said. "You don't have to go across the street and knock on their door and invite them [i.e., non-LDS friends and neighbors] to a discussion [i.e., a missionary lesson]."[424]

Of course, the Internet is global, and although hard data is scarce to support this proposition, it appears that the technology-savvy American Millennials have similarly tech-savvy same-generation companions around the world.[425] What holds for the American Millennials probably holds for their international counterparts—including the likelihood that they will seek to answer their religious and spiritual questions online.

In sum, the Church and its members have created a large online infrastructure to bring their message to the world through the Internet—an infrastructure that seems much more developed than that of any other single faith or religious organization that I know of. The Millennial generation of the United States, and their tech-savvy counterparts throughout the world, will go to the Internet to obtain answers to their spiritual and religious questions—and when they do, they will find Mormon faces, voices, and points of view in abundance. These factors will help to put Mormon growth rates in the high-growth range that I have predicted, over the course of the next century.

---

[424] Winchel (2012).

[425] Anecdotal evidence abounds. The Egyptian uprising, part of the Arab Spring of 2011, was facilitated by the use of social networking sites such as Facebook and Twitter, and the use of cell phones to send Short Message Service (SMS) text messages.

Chapter 10

The Potential Impact of High Mormon Growth: A 'More Mormon' World

I have demonstrated that there is good reason to believe that the Latter-day Saints will grow to be an extremely numerous people over the course of the next century, with a major presence, not only in the United States, but in the world as a whole. Now it is time for me to ask that quintessentially New York question, for the third, the last, and the most important time in this book:
So what?
As it happens, a major Mormon presence in the U.S. and the world could have various important consequences. One does not introduce a distinctive worldview to over two billion people *without* introducing major consequences. In this chapter, I consider the potential impact of the high rate of Mormon growth that I have projected over the next century. That is, I sketch out what a 'more Mormon' world would look like.

Of course, even in my high-growth projection, this is by no means the 'Mormonizing' of either the world or America.[426] I project that Mormons become an important,

---

[426] The title of Stephen Mansfield's (2012) book—*The Mormonizing of America: How the Mormon Religion Became a Dominant Force in Politics, Entertainment, and Pop Culture*—at best is silly, and at worst

yet still minority, presence on each of the global and U.S. religious landscapes. Thus, what I have to present is not 'the Mormon world,' but rather, 'a *more* Mormon world.' But first, I have some preliminary issues to consider.

First of all, I do *not* believe that the large-scale spread of the LDS faith would mean the global replication of Utah Mormon culture. Although the State of Utah does have the highest concentration of Latter-day Saints in the United States at present, Utah Mormon culture is a product, not only of the numerically dominant religion, but of the history of the *region*—or, strictly speaking, the *peoples* of the Intermountain region, who carry the baggage of their own backgrounds, including their racial, ethnic, and social histories, as moderated by the geographic realities of the Intermountain West. Different regions of the world, of course, come with very different such histories and background factors, and so as members of the LDS faith become more numerous around the U.S. and around the world, of course the Utah component of their identity must of necessity become less prominent; in fact, even the American component of Mormon identity must become less prominent. This process is already far advanced, as we can see from the data in Table 10-1, which compares the Mormon people as it existed in 1980 with that people as it existed thirty years later, in 2010.

---

panders to a lowest-common-denominator type of taste for the sensational.

Chapter 10: A 'More Mormon' World

	1980[a]	2010[b]	% Change
LDS in world	4,638,000	14,131,467	+204.7%
LDS in USA	2,810,541	6,144,582	+118.6%
% of LDS in world	60.6%	43.5%	-28.2%
LDS Intermountain[c]	1,634,092	3,207,286	+96.3%
% of LDS in USA	58.1%	52.2%	-10.2%
% of LDS in world	35.2%	22.7%	-35.5%
LDS in Utah	1,025,990	1,910,343	+86.2%
% of LDS in USA	36.5%	31.1%	-14.8%
% of LDS in world	22.1%	13.5%	-38.9%

Table 10-1. **LDS Membership in the world, the U.S., the Intermountain West, and Utah: 1980 and 2010**

[a]Sources: Raw year-end figures from *Deseret News 1982 Church Almanac*, pp. 218-220. Proportions calculated by author.

[b]Sources: Raw figures from *Deseret News 2012 Church Almanac*, pp. 4, 324-415. Proportions calculated by author.

[c]Includes Arizona, Colorado, Idaho, Montana, Nevada, New Mexico, Utah, and Wyoming. These states comprise the Mountain division within the West region of the U.S.A., as defined by the U.S. Census (United States Department of Commerce, n.d.), and are considered the "Intermountain West" by some news organizations (e.g., Harrop, 2008).

Several facts become clear from Table 10-1:

- During this 30-year period, the number of Mormons more than tripled in the world as a whole (205% growth), more than doubled in the U.S. (119% growth), and showed substantial growth in both Utah (86% growth) and throughout the Intermountain West (96% growth).

- Despite this, the *proportion* of the Mormons worldwide that was comprised by the American Saints dropped significantly (from 61% to 44%). Most Mormons in the world today reside outside the United States—a milestone reached early in 1996.[427]

- Similarly, most American Mormons reside outside Utah, and the proportion residing in Utah is dropping (from 36% to 31%). A bare majority of American Mormons reside in the Intermountain West, but this proportion too is dropping (from 58% to 52%).

- Utahns have come to comprise a far smaller proportion of the world's Saints (from 22% to 14%). Similarly, Mormons in the Intermountain West have come to comprise a far smaller proportion of the Saints in the world (from 35% to 23%).

This process is irreversible. Mormonism has internationalized itself. It will only become 'more international' (i.e., less American/Intermountain/Utahn) with each passing year.

---

[427] *Deseret News 1999-2000 Church Almanac* (1998) p. 519.

Having said that, the American Mormon experience offers *some* guidance for what the world will be like when there are more Mormons in it. Hence, with great caution, I shall generalize from how the Saints in America are different from their neighbors today to how Saints worldwide might make the world a bit different in the future.

Places where cultures make contact are interesting. In midtown Manhattan, I sometimes eat *kosher*, sometimes *halal*, simply because many Jews and Muslims work in Midtown, and so these foods are available. Similarly, having a lot more Saints in the world will make certain attitudes and behaviors more common, and others less common. So, what might a 'more Mormon' world look like?

Religion is multidimensional. Therefore I have organized my responses to this question in terms of a venerable model (that of Charles Glock) which posits five dimensions to religion: (1) the consequential dimension, which refers to the consequences of religion in one's life, (2) religious belief, (3) religious practice, (4) religious knowledge, and (5) religious or spiritual experience.[428]

THE CONSEQUENTIAL DIMENSION

Some behaviors have an obviously religious context to anyone (such as attendance at worship, or prayer). Other behaviors only have religious meaning to some people, and not others. Mormonism features many 'not-obviously-religious' behaviors, which have a religious meaning for the Saints but not in general society; in turn, some of these behaviors have important consequences for individuals and communities. A more Mormon world would see these behaviors, and their consequences, become more common.

---

[428] Glock (1962). See also Koltko-Rivera (2006-2007).

A more Mormon world would be physically healthier.

One distinctive aspect of the LDS lifestyle is its health code, whereby Latter-day Saints abstain from tobacco, alcohol, and illicit drugs (as well as tea and coffee).[429] That this practice has substantial health benefits for the Saints has long been known, and often demonstrated.[430]

The world health toll from tobacco, alcohol, and illicit drug use is immense. In a more Mormon world, this toll would be greatly reduced. In addition, as many people in the West today embrace the health benefits of yoga without converting to Hinduism, it may well be that the Mormon example will encourage others to embrace this aspect of the LDS lifestyle independently of the LDS faith itself. This alone would have a major effect on world health.

A more Mormon world would be more mentally healthy.

One researcher summarized a review of 72 years' worth of professional literature as follows:

> Analysis of the data indicates that Latter-day Saints who live their lives consistent with their religious beliefs experience greater general well-being and marital and family stability, and less delinquency, depression, anxiety, and substance abuse than those who do not.[431]

---

[429] LDS Standard Works: Doctrine & Covenants, Section 89. See *Gospel Principles* (2009) chapter 29.

[430] E.g., Bahr (1994); Enstrom (1998a, 1998b); Tumulty (2012).

[431] Judd (1998) p. 473.

A separate review of the literature yielded similar conclusions.[432] The claim, oft-repeated on the Internet, that LDS women are more depressed than others, has no basis in fact; among more educated women who are more active in the Church, the opposite seems to be the case.[433]

A more Mormon world, then, at least has the potential to be a more psychologically healthy one.

A more Mormon world would be better educated.

In the distinctively LDS scriptures, God is quoted as saying that "the glory of God is intelligence."[434] This is reflected in a strong emphasis on education within the LDS community. A recent President of the Church gave advice to LDS youth regarding education; because this advice speaks to the sense of mission that the LDS faith engenders in its adherents, I quote it here at some length:

> You must get all of the education that you possibly can. Life has become so complex and competitive. You cannot assume that you have entitlements due you. You will be expected to put forth great effort and to use your best talents to make your way to the most wonderful future of which you are capable. Sacrifice a car; sacrifice anything that is needed to be sacrificed to qualify yourselves to do the work of the world. That world will in large measure pay you what it thinks you are worth, and your worth will

---

[432] Bergin, Payne, Jenkins, & Cornwall (1994).
[433] Bergin et al. (1994) pp. 142-146.
[434] LDS Standard Works: Doctrine and Covenants, Section 93, verse 36.

increase as you gain education and proficiency in your chosen field.

The Lord Wants You to Be Educated

You have a mandate from the Lord to educate your minds and your hearts and your hands. The Lord has said, "Teach ye diligently ... of things both in heaven and in the earth, and under the earth; things which have been, things which are, things which must shortly come to pass; things which are at home, things which are abroad; the wars and the perplexities of the nations, and the judgments which are on the land; and a knowledge also of countries and of kingdoms—that ye may be prepared in all things" (Doctrine & Covenants 88:78–80).

The Lord wants you to train your minds and hands to become an influence for good as you go forward with your lives. And as you do so and as you perform honorably and with excellence, you will bring honor to the Church, for you will be regarded as a man or woman of integrity and ability and conscientious workmanship. In addition, your education will strengthen your service in the Church. A study was made some years ago that indicated the higher the education, the greater the faith and participation in religious activity.

The Lord wants you to educate your minds and hands, whatever your chosen field. Whether it be repairing refrigerators, or the work of a skilled surgeon, you must train yourselves. Seek for the best schooling available. Become a workman of integrity in the world that lies ahead of you.[435]

As I have mentioned, the Church sponsors a Perpetual Education Fund to help Saints outside the U.S. obtain postsecondary education. Within the U.S., fully 60% of surveyed Mormons stated that they had at least some college education, compared with 50% of the general population, 48% of Protestants (44% of evangelicals), 47% of Catholics, 68% of Orthodox Christians, and 78% of Jews.[436]

Interestingly, although in the general population there is a negative relationship between degree of education and religious belief and observance, this relationship does not hold for Saints. Rather, among U.S. Mormons at least, there is a strong positive relationship between degree of education and religiosity.[437] As one researcher summarized it:

> Whether we are talking about personal value placed on religious beliefs, attendance at church, financial contributions, frequency of personal prayer, or frequency of gospel study, the impact of increased education among Latter-day Saints is positive. These relationships also hold when we control for such other variables as attendance at church-sponsored schools, geographic area of the country, and so on. The secularizing influ-

---

[435] Hinckley (2007a). This address was printed in a magazine published for LDS youth of high school and early college age.
[436] *U.S. Religious Landscape Survey: Religious Affiliation* (2008) p. 56.
[437] Albrecht (1998); Albrecht & Heaton (1998).

ence of higher education simply doesn't seem to hold for Latter-day Saints.[438]

The ongoing emphasis that the Church of Jesus Christ puts on education strongly suggests that a more Mormon world will be a more educated one. In a world that seeks technological ways out of its many problems, a more educated population would be highly desirable.

A more Mormon world would have more stable families.

Analyzing data from the late 1980s,[439] researchers found that the divorce rate in the 3-to-10-years-after-marriage range was 24% less for Mormon women than for other women in the U.S.[440] To some extent, this is the effect of Church programs that favor building strong families, such as Family Home Evening[441] (where families reserve one night weekly for activities at home as a family).

As of 2008, the divorce rate in the United States was 49% of the marriage rate.[442] In the United Kingdom in 2000, the divorce rate was 50% of the marriage rate, while in Germany in 2008, the divorce rate was 51% of the marriage rate.[443] In a more Mormon world, divorce would be substantially less common—with beneficial effects for the welfare of children, both in their youth and later on in their

---

[438] Albrecht (1998) p. 286.
[439] *A National Survey of Families and Households* (2008).
[440] The Mormon rate was .026, and the non-Mormon rate .034; Heaton, Goodman, & Holman (1994) p. 95.
[441] See, e.g., *Family Home Evening* (2012) and *Family Home Evening Resource Book* (1997).
[442] The divorce rate was 5.2/1,000 population, while the marriage rate was 10.6/1,000; United States Census Bureau (2012a).
[443] Author's calculations from United States Census Bureau (2012a).

lives, considering what research has revealed about the long-term consequences of divorce for children.[444]

A more Mormon world would have more young children.

LDS families tend to have more children than non-LDS families, by and large. The LDS faith favors marrying and starting a family relatively earlier in life than is typical in American society.[445] Researchers have found that, as of the late 1980s, American LDS mothers had an average of 2.96 children, while American non-LDS mothers had an average of 2.04 children.[446] If that pattern—Mormon families having one more child than non-Mormon families, within a given country—were to hold up, at least in industrialized countries throughout a more Mormon world, this would have a major effect on the world economy and polity.

For all the talk over the last few decades about overpopulation, the fact is that vast swaths of the industrialized world are shrinking in population. Europeans have been reproducing well below replacement level for generations. China, with its one-child policy, has a graying population with a relatively smaller younger generation to support it. Japan, with what amounts in practice to its own one-child "policy," is in much the same situation or worse.

This has created a situation in which some researchers have predicted a variety of negative consequences for many countries in the industrialized world: potentially disruptive transformations of national identity,[447] econom-

---

[444] E.g., Wallerstein, Lewis, & Blakeslee (2000).
[445] See, e.g., Deakyne (1997); "Strengthening the Family" (2005).
[446] Heaton, Goodman, & Holman (1994) p. 98.
[447] Teitelbaum & Winter (1998).

ic and political disruption both globally[448] and in the U.S.[449] As a variation of this theme, the practice of "disposing" of female embryos or even born female infants, practiced particularly in China and India, has been hypothesized to lead to so great a surplus of males as to predispose these nations to international war.[450]

In a more Mormon world the imbalance between generations would be at least somewhat corrected, with more younger people being available to contribute to society, advance the economy, and support the elderly within a given country. As a matter of policy, "The Church opposes elective abortion for personal or social convenience."[451] The Church does not tolerate the murder of infants under any circumstances. Following these policies would help to alleviate the gender imbalance, or male surplus, in China and India. Overall, the presence of more children in a more Mormon world would have a beneficial effect on the safety, peace, and prosperity of society.

A more Mormon world would have greater multicultural expertise.

A substantial fraction of the LDS missionary corps consists of Americans serving outside the U.S. Usually, this involves learning a foreign language. The experience always involves becoming familiar with the culture of the country to which the missionary is assigned. In a world

---

[448] Longman (2004).

[449] Kotlikoff & Burns (2004).

[450] V.M. Hudson & Boer (2004).

[451] *Handbook 2* (2010), section 21.4.1, page 195. The Church maintains an anti-abortion policy, with exceptions for rape, incest, serious threats to maternal health, or severe, life-threatening fetal defects.

that is becoming increasingly interconnected in its economy and the communication of its ideas, greater multicultural expertise is a very valuable skill—one that will make a more Mormon world a more multiculturally knowledgeable place. One may conjecture that this may in turn increase intercultural understanding, and the opportunities to create a more peaceful world.

For many years, the LDS faith has explicitly held the belief that God has guided the various peoples of the world, Christian or not. This does not seem to be a common belief among the Christian churches of the world. But on February 15, 1978 the Church's highest leaders issued a "Statement of the First Presidency Regarding God's Love for All Mankind," which states in part:

> The great religious leaders of the world such as Mohammed, Confucius, and the Reformers, as well as philosophers including Socrates, Plato, and others, received a portion of God's light. Moral truths were given to them by God to enlighten whole nations and to bring a higher level of understanding to individuals....
>
> Consistent with these truths, we believe that God has given and will give to all people sufficient knowledge to help them on their way to eternal salvation, either in this life or in the life to come.
>
> We also declare that the gospel of Jesus Christ, restored to his Church in our day, provides the only way to a mortal life of happiness and a fullness of joy forever. For those who have not received this gospel, the

opportunity will come to them in the life hereafter if not in this life.[452]

At the risk of mentioning the obvious, this is not the sort of statement that Christian churches seem to have made all that frequently. For our purposes, the point of interest is that there is great respect given here to non-Christian religious leaders and philosophers; the Mormon leadership all but names them vehicles of God's grace.

In a world that becomes more multiculturally diverse by the minute, this kind of respect for different traditions will only lessen inter-religious and inter-ethnic tensions. The more widespread this ethic is, the better—and in a more Mormon world, it would be quite widely spread.

A more Mormon world would be more productive.

The modern LDS scriptures are full of injunctions admonishing the Saints simply to *work*. Some of this involves religious tasks—missionary work, temple building—but some of this counsel is given concerning temporal work, work to support oneself and one's family. Idleness is strictly condemned, and personal industry is praised. For example, the Lord is quoted as stating, in a series of 19th century revelations:

> Thou shalt not be idle; for he that is idle shall not eat the bread nor wear the garments of the laborer.[453]
>
> Wo unto you poor men, whose hearts are not broken, whose spirits are not contrite, ...

---

[452] The entire Statement is quoted in "I Have a Question" (1988).
[453] LDS Standard Works: Doctrine & Covenants, Section 42, verse 42.

and whose hands are not stayed from laying hold upon other men's goods, whose eyes are full of greediness, and who will not labor with your own hands![454]

Let every man be diligent in all things. And the idler shall not have place in the church, except he repent and mend his ways.[455]

Cease to be idle; ... cease to sleep longer than is needful; retire to thy bed early, that ye may not be weary; arise early, that your bodies and your minds may be invigorated.[456]

The early leadership of the Church also taught that the division between the temporal and the spiritual was artificial; all that we do, with the right attitude, is an act of worship. As Brigham Young put it:

> With God, ... there is no difference in spiritual and temporal labors—all are one. If I am in the line of my duty, I am doing the will of God, whether I am preaching; praying, laboring with my hands for an honorable support; whether I am in the field, mechanic's shop, or following mercantile business, or wherever duty calls, I am serving God as much in one place as another; and so it is with all, each in his place, turn and time.[457]

---

[454] LDS Standard Works: Doctrine & Covenants, Section 56, verse 17.
[455] LDS Standard Works: Doctrine & Covenants, Section 75, verse 29.
[456] Standard Works: Doctrine & Covenants, Section 88, verse 124.
[457] Brigham Young, quoted in Widtsoe (1954) p. 8. See also *Teachings ... Brigham Young* (1997) p. 22.

We came upon LDS President Spencer W. Kimball in Chapter 1, in regard to presentations he made in the 1970s that changed the face of LDS missionary efforts. He also had much to say to the Saints about the principle of work:

> With regard to all phases of our lives, I believe that men should help themselves. They should plow and plant and cultivate and harvest and not expect their faith to bring them bread.
>
> Work is a spiritual necessity as well as an economic necessity.
>
> Work brings happiness, self-esteem, and prosperity. It is the means of all accomplishment; it is the opposite of idleness. ...
>
> ... For work is important to human happiness as well as productivity. The world's way, however, places greater and greater emphasis on leisure and upon the avoidance of work.[458]

The Church has a section of its website devoted to "Happiness in Family Life." One of the values underlying this goal, to which a separate webpage is devoted: Work.[459]

Given all this emphasis upon work, it is not surprising that Mormons have earned a reputation as hard workers. As *The Economist*'s columnist "Schumpeter" put it:

> Less than 2% of Americans are Mormons, yet their commercial prominence belies their numbers.... Had Max Weber lived a century

---

[458] *Teachings of ... Spencer W. Kimball* (2006) pp. 118-120.
[459] http://www.lds.org/family/work

later, he might have made sweeping generalisations about the "Mormon work ethic"....

What explains the Mormons' success? Clean living probably helps: alcohol clouds judgment and lubricates bad deals. A history of persecution may breed self-reliance: 19th-century Mormons trekked westwards across plains and mountains to escape the kind of bigots who murdered their founder, Joseph Smith, in 1844.... But some of the answer may lie in the faith itself. Mormonism—the only global religion to have been invented in the past 200 years—is in some ways more business-friendly than its more ancient rivals.

Mormons revere organisation. They believe that God created the world out of chaos, rather than out of nothing. They also believe that men and women are capable of "eternal progression" towards "Godhood", so long as they conduct themselves like busy little bees. The church is probably the best-organised in the world .... Church members begin to perform in public at the age of three. They become "deacons" at 12 and are given more demanding jobs as they grow older....

The fiercest crucible for young Mormons is the mission.... They are expected to proselytise for ten hours a day, six days a week. Few other groups experience anything as demanding at a similar age....

Missionary work also teaches young Mormons to persevere despite harsh odds....

After that, selling airline seats or life insurance must be a doddle.[460]

The injunction to work—to fulfill one's duty—applies as well to community service. The Church periodically invites Saints worldwide to give a special day of service to their communities. A recent report of a 2012 Church-wide day of service recounted projects held on five continents, and included projects like cleaning homeless shelters, tutoring low-income youth, painting schools, and many more.[461] Members throughout the United Kingdom conducted a day of service in 2012 to celebrate the Queen's diamond jubilee; projects included cleaning of public property, serving at a jubilee fair for the elderly and underprivileged, providing cushions and quilts for a women's shelter, and so forth.[462] The New York New York Stake holds its own annual day of service; we often clean up public parks.

The upshot of all this is that a more Mormon world would have more of this sort of work ethic. In a world with a host of problems to address, a Mormon work ethic and an LDS orientation to community service would be welcome. The effect on global productivity could be marked.

A more Mormon world would have less economic inequality.

The distinctively LDS scriptures include a narrative describing how the ancient prophet Enoch founded a city of righteousness, known as Zion:

---

[460] "The Mormon way of doing business" (2012). The term "doddle" is informal British English, indicating something that is easy to do.
[461] Olson (2012).
[462] Oliver (2012).

Chapter 10: A 'More Mormon' World

> And the Lord called his people ZION, because they were of one heart and one mind, and dwelt in righteousness; and there was no poor among them.[463]

The LDS scriptures teach that a similar society formed when the resurrected Christ visited the New World:

> And they had all things common among them; therefore there were not rich and poor, bond and free, but they were all made free, and partakers of the heavenly gift.[464]

Many revelations reported by the first LDS prophet, Joseph Smith, concern divine commandments to provide for the poor. For example, he recorded that the Lord said:

> If thou lovest me thou shalt serve me and keep all my commandments.
>
> And behold, thou wilt remember the poor, and consecrate of thy properties for their support that which thou hast to impart unto them, with a covenant and a deed which cannot be broken.
>
> And inasmuch as ye impart of your substance unto the poor, ye will do it unto me ....[465]

---

[463] Standard Works: Pearl of Great Price, Moses, chapter 7, verse 18.

[464] Standard Works: Book of Mormon, Fourth Nephi, chapter 1, verse 3.

[465] Standard Works: Doctrine & Covenants 42:29-31. See also, e.g., Doctrine & Covenants 38:35; 42:30-31; 78:3; 83:6. See Index to the "Triple Combination" (the Book of Mormon, the Doctrine & Covenants, and the Pearl of Great Price) s.v. "Poor" for many such references, including several, in the Doctrine & Covenants, with highly specific

The ideal of a Zion society has powerfully affected the LDS people. This concern for lifting people up temporally shows itself in many concrete ways in the modern Church.

The Church, as I mentioned earlier, places a strong emphasis on education, and backs this emphasis in the developing world with the Perpetual Education Fund, which provides direct financial assistance for technical and professional training. The Church devotes substantial resources to its Church Welfare Program, which provides a variety of assistance to the poor and needy, such as financial assistance, foodstuffs, and job training. In addition:

- LDS converts come into the Church from a wide variety of social, cultural, and educational backgrounds. The Church recognizes that some converts lack even basic skills in nutrition and sanitation. Consequently, it provides materials to be used at the congregation level for teaching basics of disease prevention, cleanliness and sanitation, nutrition, first aid, and so forth[466]—all as local circumstances warrant. (The Church also sends non-proselyting missionaries focused on improving people's skills in health and nutrition, primarily to the Third World.)

- The Church emphasizes training in basic life skills as part of the faith. This training is conducted in a number of ways, including in classes taught on Sundays to the youth and adult men and women of the Church, as local needs dictate. The sorts of topics addressed can be seen from the class manual

---

instructions regarding how the Church should provide for the poor.

[466] E.g., *Basic Physical Health with Limited Resources* (2010).

used to teach a religion class taught at the Church's Brigham Young University, *The Gospel and the Productive Life* (2004). This class, which can be taught anywhere in the Church Educational System (which spans the Church worldwide), covers such topics as goal-setting, time management, financial management, and the development of talents, in addition to a variety of more obviously spiritual topics (such as "The Guidance of the [Holy] Spirit").

- The Church has produced materials to help individuals build stronger families for themselves, one weekly Family Home Evening at a time.[467]

- The Church provides extensive materials to train help families in how to manage their finances.[468] Similarly, the Church provides materials for career guidance.[469] These materials are used, not only in local congregations, but in many locations where one of the Church's social services arms, LDS Employment Resource Services, has offices to help local Saints in need of training.

- The Church continually focuses on teaching principles of leadership. Many of these teaching materials are online and available to anyone.[470]

A more Mormon world would have more people in it who would have, not only the basic skills needed to handle life in any economy, not only leadership training, but also

---

[467] *Family First* (1992); Family *Home Evening Resource Book* (1997). A variety of materials (manuals, kits, and other resources) are available at the Church's "Family Home" (2010) online homepage.

[468] E.g., *The Family Finance Workshop* package (2010).

[469] E.g., *The Career Workshop* package (2004).

[470] E.g., *Leadership Training Library* (2011).

a marketable education (perhaps paid for with Church funds through PEF). Whether by education, or the Church Welfare Program, including job training, the poor would be assisted out of poverty. A world in which more people are so equipped—in the U.S. as well as anywhere else—would be one in which more people achieve economic security. This explicitly addresses a Church ideal, to help all people ultimately become self-reliant.[471]

The inevitable result of these activities is that there would simply be less economic inequality worldwide. In a world where gross income inequality has been blamed as a cause of the global financial crisis of 2007 and thereafter,[472] greater economic opportunity and income equality, such as the LDS program promotes, would be most welcome.

A more Mormon world would give more widespread service to the poor and needy.

We have spoken of the Mormon notion of work. There is another side to this: providing for the poor and needy.

The Latter-day Saints have long had an ethic of service to others, especially to the less fortunate. As it is stated by a king-prophet in the Book of Mormon itself:

> And behold, I tell you these things that ye may learn wisdom; that ye may learn that when ye are in the service of your fellow beings ye are only in the service of your God.[473]

---

[471] E.g., see this LDS website: http://www.providentliving.org/self-reliance

[472] Reich (2011).

[473] Standard Works: Book of Mormon, Mosiah, ch. 2, v. 17. This is one of the 100 scriptures (25 from the Book of Mormon) that observant

Chapter 10: A 'More Mormon' World

Direct assistance to the poor is something commanded in the modern LDS scriptures to the faithful. For example:

> Wo unto you rich men, that will not give your substance to the poor, for your riches will canker your souls; and this shall be your lamentation in the day of ... judgment, and of indignation: The harvest is past, the summer is ended, and my soul is not saved![474]

Seventy-three percent of surveyed U.S. Saints stated that working to help the poor is *essential* (not just "important") for being a good Mormon.[475] Perhaps reflecting this, 54% of surveyed U.S. Saints stated that they participate at least monthly in community or volunteer work through their place of worship, compared with 19% of the general public, 24% of Protestants (27% of evangelicals), 16% of Catholics, and 19% of Orthodox Christians.[476]

In LDS congregations, such service might involve the production of sanitation kits for people in disaster areas, or work at a Church-owned cannery to can food for the poor.[477] One year recently, the women's Relief Society in my own congregation sponsored a project to produce personal care kits for victims of Hansen's disease (more commonly known as leprosy). The congregations in the LDS

Mormon high schoolers memorize while attending LDS "Seminary" (religion classes, held before or after the school day).

[474] LDS Standard Works, Doctrine & Covenants, Section 56, verse 16.

[475] *Mormons in America* (2012) pp. 13, 112. This is much higher than the proportion (49%) who believe that not drinking coffee or tea is essential for being a good Mormon, even though that practice plays a more significant part in the Church's public image. For LDS teachings on service, see *Gospel Principles* (2009), Ch. 28, pp. 161-166.

[476] *U.S. Religious Landscape Survey: ... Beliefs and Practices* (2008) p. 42.

[477] Rudd (1995, 2011).

New York New York Stake—14 wards and branches in Manhattan—take turns making sure that the local Bishop's Storehouse (our food bank for the poor and needy) is staffed by our membership every Saturday.

The Church leadership encourages their membership to take the initiative in serving the poor and needy. The official current counsel states:

> Through His Church, the Lord has provided a way to care for the poor and needy. He has asked Church members to give generously according to what they have received from Him. He has also asked His people to "visit the poor and the needy and administer to their relief" (D&C 44:6). Church members are encouraged to give personal compassionate service to those in need. They should be "anxiously engaged in a good cause," serving without being asked or assigned (see D&C 58:26-27).[478]

That last scriptural reference is worth giving in full, as it provides a rationale for Mormons to take the initiative to do good in the world. In 1831, Joseph Smith reported receiving a revelation in which the Lord said, in part:

> ... it is not meet that I should command in all things; for he that is compelled in all things, the same is a slothful and not a wise servant; wherefore he receiveth no reward.
>
> Verily I say, men should be anxiously engaged in a good cause, and do many things

---

[478] *Handbook 2* (2010) p. 35.

of their own free will, and bring to pass much righteousness;

For the power is in them, wherein they are agents unto themselves. And inasmuch as men do good they shall in nowise lose their reward.

But he that doeth not anything until he is commanded, ... the same is damned.[479]

One will see more people take the initiative to serve the poor and needy in a more Mormon world. Under the best of circumstances, service to the poor and needy would be a welcome thing in the world. Given the possibility of looming economic crises worldwide,[480] such pro-social behaviors would be especially welcome—and needed.

A more Mormon world would be better prepared to deal with disasters and crises.

I have alluded throughout this book to the predictions of researchers, to the effect that the 21st century will be a time of multiple serious challenges to global society, including a crisis in energy, generational imbalance, environmental catastrophe, and the risk of multiple international wars.[481] Any one of these would threaten the stability of society; several of them concurrently would stress global society, perhaps beyond the ability of the world's polities and economies to sustain themselves peacefully.

---

[479] LDS Standard Works: Doctrine & Covenants, Section 58, vv. 26-29.
[480] Kunstler (2005).
[481] E.g., Friedman (2009/2010); Hudson & Boer (2004); Kunstler (2005); Longman (2004); Meadows, Randers, & Meadows (2004); Teitelbaum & Winter (1998).

How would the Church of Jesus Christ face these challenges? With prayer, surely—but also with preparation before any disaster had occurred, organized effort during a disaster, and a great abundance of work after the disaster. Understanding each of these facets of the Church's approach to adversity is important to understanding what a more Mormon world *in crisis* might look like.[482]

Let us begin with after-disaster actions. The Church of Jesus Christ is slowly becoming better known for its massive humanitarian aid and disaster relief projects. These projects encompass local Church members responding to local or distant needs, as well as headquarters projects that involve assistance for large-scale disasters. Local projects might include college women assembling 44,555 hygiene kits, 14,942 school kits, and 4,952 kits for newborns, for use overseas,[483] or Saints cooperating with local American Muslims to prepare 10,000 family hygiene kits to send to Iraq.[484] Headquarters projects might involve sending $650K of medical supplies and blankets to accompany those hygiene kits to Iraq,[485] or sending six semi-trailers of disaster relief materials and food to Mexico after Hurricane Isidore,[486] or sending 515 wheelchairs to Samoa and another 450 to Central America and thousands to Mexico,[487] or sending 12 ship containers of educational books to Gha-

---

[482] The Church recommends this three-part approach to its own members as they contemplate facing natural disasters; Ellis (2012).
[483] *Deseret Morning News 2004 Church Almanac* (2004) p. 564.
[484] *Deseret Morning News 2004 Church Almanac* (2004) p. 564.
[485] *Deseret Morning News 2004 Church Almanac* (2004) pp. 564-565.
[486] *Deseret Morning News 2004 Church Almanac* (2004) pp. 549-550.
[487] *Deseret Morning News 2004 Church Almanac* (2004) pp. 552-553, 567, 572.

na,[488] or pledging $3 million to eradicate measles in Africa,[489] or sending 160 tons of porridge mix aboard a Church-sponsored cargo plane and ocean containers to Ethiopia to ease a hunger crisis, bringing the total of food the Church sent to Ethiopia one year to 4,000 tons.[490]

This was some of what the Church did in humanitarian service—in one year (late 2002—early 2003). Similar activities have been a part of the Church's life every year for at least a generation, long before Latter-day Saint Charities was formed in 1996 "to help the Church deliver humanitarian aid to the poor and needy people of the world."[491]

So the Church knows how to act in a rehabilitation mode, after a crisis has emerged. How about *during* one?

Every LDS congregation is structured so as to become a local emergency or disaster control center. There is a clear line of responsibility from the head of the congregation—the ward bishop, or the branch president—through the priesthood home teachers and the Relief Society visiting teachers, to each individual member of the congregation. This allows for quick communication in emergencies.

Now let us consider preparation and prevention. The Church of Jesus Christ, while not promoting any specific scenario for disaster or challenge, has long counseled its members to prepare for challenging circumstances, as part of its well-established focus on what it calls "provident living."[492] As aspects of provident living, the LDS leadership has counseled the Saints to prepare for emergencies and difficult times, in a variety of ways: storing food and wa-

---

[488] *Deseret Morning News 2004 Church Almanac* (2004) pp. 550-551.

[489] *Deseret Morning News 2004 Church Almanac* (2004) p. 571.

[490] *Deseret Morning News 2004 Church Almanac* (2004) pp. 558-559, 566.

[491] *Deseret News 1999-2000 Church Almanac* (1998) p. 7.

[492] http://www.providentliving.org/

ter, saving financial assets, upgrading job and professional skills, and improving physical, spiritual, and emotional health and strength. For all the Church's assistance to people in crisis near and far, the Church teaches its members to be self-reliant, a crucial value among the Latter-day Saints. As one of the guiding documents for Church procedure puts it (in a document on the Church's website, for all members to study):

> Church members are responsible for their own spiritual and temporal well-being. Blessed with the gift of [moral] agency, they have the privilege and duty to set their own course, solve their own problems, and strive to become self-reliant. Members do this under the inspiration of the Lord and with the labor of their own hands.
>
> When Church members are doing all they can to provide for themselves, but cannot meet their basic needs, generally they should first turn to their families for help. When this is not sufficient or feasible, the Church stands ready to help.[493]

Self-reliance includes advance preparation for crisis. This is the current Church counsel on home food storage:

> To help care for themselves and their families, members should build a three-month supply of food that is part of their normal diet. Where local laws and circumstances permit, they should gradually build a longer-

---

[493] *Handbook 2* (2010) p. 34.

term supply of basic foods that will sustain life. They should also store drinking water in case the water supply becomes polluted or disrupted.[494]

Imagine what life would be like for the eight million inhabitants of New York City if there were a disruption of the food supply chain. (It has been estimated that there are only two or three days of food on the city's grocery shelves, at any given time. The city depends on constant deliveries.) This disruption extends for three weeks. Consider the human suffering, the civil unrest, and the violence that would likely occur, as a city containing over 2% of the population of the entire United States struggled for food— all crowded into merely a 15-mile radius.

Now imagine the same scenario—except that, say, a quarter of the population had stored at least a three-month supply of food, and a lifetime supply of an ethic of sharing. It would be uncomfortable, but it would be *survivable*. That is what a more Mormon world would be like in a crisis.

The LDS approach to crisis is well-expressed by one of their scriptures: "if ye are prepared ye shall not fear."[495] In a more Mormon world, large numbers of people would be better prepared in advance, not only to weather crises themselves, but to help others to do so. During a crisis— even the 'long emergency' scenario that some have predicted[496]—local Church congregations would be capable of coordinating relief and care. After a crisis, the social organization and physical machinery is already in place for the allocation of relief resources.

---

[494] *Handbook 2* (2010) p. 34.
[495] Standard Works: Doctrine & Covenants, Section 38, verse 30.
[496] Kunstler (2005).

At year-end 2011, there were 28,784 LDS wards and branches worldwide,[497] each one capable of functioning as an emergency or disaster control center. In a world with hundreds of millions or even billions of Saints, the number of such congregations would be greater by orders of magnitude. In aggregate, the local and headquarters organization of the Saints would be able to offer assistance to hundreds of millions and even billions of people, including both the Saints and their non-Mormon neighbors.

All of this—LDS efforts at preparation, crisis intervention, and crisis relief—would raise substantially what we might call the 'resilience quotient' of global society. A world where hundreds of millions or even billions of Saints were prepared to handle disruptions and emergencies is simply a hardier, more resilient, and safer world in which to live, for everyone.

A more Mormon world would have less demand for potentially addictive materials.

As mentioned earlier, the LDS Word of Wisdom prohibits Saints from using tobacco, alcohol, or, by extension, illicit drugs. For that matter, the Church of Jesus Christ is strictly opposed to pornography,[498] and the potential for sexual addiction that comes with the viewing of pornography. The Church's Addiction Recovery Program is free, and open to those with issues involving either substance or pornography use.[499]

---

[497] "Statistical Report, 2011" (2012) p. 30.
[498] http://www.lds.org/topics/pornography
[499] http://addictionrecovery.lds.org/ ; *Addiction Recovery Program* (2005).

A more Mormon world would have that much less demand for tobacco, alcohol, or illicit drugs, the latter of which is the basis of so much criminal activity and violence throughout the world. It would have less demand for pornography, and the deleterious consequences that can result from the use of pornography.

A more Mormon world would lay the foundation for a new Renaissance in arts and letters.

One of the more readily noticeable developments of a more Mormon world would be a blossoming of culture built around LDS themes. This would be the Mormon version of a new Renaissance.

It has been widely noted that there is a malaise overshadowing our era's arts and letters. In literature, as one controversial critic put it, certain celebrated literary authors write as if they "believe that an incoherent world dictates incoherent writing."[500] In the visual arts, some have proclaimed "the end of art," as the postmodern elevates the banal and the narrowly ideological, effectively ending the aesthetic import of art itself, in favor of its commercial import.[501] The critic Donald Kuspit puts it in direct terms:

> In short, art these postmodern days seems to have become another depressing way of passing time rather than of reaching beyond time, which is what it was for van Gogh. Art is no longer the path to salvation it was for him, but rather confirms that life is damned because it is meaningless, which is ultimately why art is meaningless, since it can do noth-

---

[500] Myers (2002) p. 35.
[501] E.g., Kuspit (2000; 2004, esp. pp. 147, 155).

> ing to rescue life from itself. Today's postart seduces us to death not life.... The void left by the absence of faith in art is filled by the presence of money.[502]

Is this an overstatement? What Kuspit says is not true of all artists, but Kuspit is certainly accurate in seeing existential bleakness in much of today's art. Kuspit's statement seems like the logical consequence of a trend apparent in art for quite some time. Consider the opening of a 1951 talk delivered by the French painter and sculptor Jean Dubuffet (1901-1985) at the Arts Club in Chicago:

> I think, not only in the arts, but also in many other fields, an important change is taking place, now, in our time, in the frame of mind of many persons....
>
> I have the impression that a complete liquidation of all the ways of thinking, whose sum constituted what had been called humanism and has been fundamental for our culture since the Renaissance, is now taking place, or at least, going to take place soon.[503]

Let us consider Renaissance humanism. The great artists and writers of the era—Dante, Da Vinci, Michelangelo, Dürer, and many others—created their lasting masterpieces on a dual foundation: the version of Christianity they had inherited from the Late Middle Ages, and the humanism that they had rediscovered from the classical era of Greece and Rome. Inspired by these cross-currents, they created a body of cultural capital that is still inspiring to

---

[502] Kuspit (2004) p. 160.
[503] Dubuffet (1960/1996) p. 192.

humanity centuries later, both in its art and its science. Even the great scientific advances of the last few centuries are built on a religiously informed science rooted in the Renaissance era and its successor, the Enlightenment; perhaps the greatest scientific mind in human history, Isaac Newton, was guided by a religious mindset in which a rational God created a universe whose workings could be discovered and understood by the rational human mind.[504]

Well did the philosopher and theologian Paul Tillich (1886-1965) state this about art:

> Each period has its peculiar image of man. It appears in its poems and novels, music, philosophy, plays and dances; and it appears in its painting and sculpture. Whenever a new period is conceived in the womb of the preceding period, a new image of man pushes towards the surface and finally breaks through to find its artists and philosophers.[505]

Perhaps it is only to be expected, after a century that has seen two world wars, multiple episodes of large-scale genocidal murder, the first uses of nuclear weapons, massive environmental degradation, and other horrors, art should reflect more the "negative side in the fight for humanity," as Tillich put it.[506] But do our arts and letters have to be trapped in that aspect of human existence?

Now consider that more Mormon world. In light of what Tillich had to say—"Each period has its peculiar image of man"—consider the literary, artistic, and scientific possibilities inherent in a faith where all humans have al-

---

[504] White (1997).
[505] Tillich (1959/1996) p. 183.
[506] Tillich (1959/1996) p. 184.

ways been sister and brother since before the world was made; where magnifying one's talents and intelligence is a divine command;, where humanity may look forward to fully developing its potential for divinity; and where some of the greatest divine service is service to humanity.

Now imagine the vigorous cultural and scientific creations that could arise from that sort of inspiring vision, as a huge band of self-reliant, healthy, well-educated and well-trained people goes forth to put their words to paper, apply their colors to canvas, their hands to clay and stone, their feet to the wooden floors of the dance studio, and their minds to the blackboard and the instruments of the laboratory. One can glimpse in the mind's eye the millions upon millions of bright minds, young and old, engaged in bringing their gospel's tale of suffering and trial and redemption and triumph to the world, and exploring the many and varied implications of that tale for the people of this complicated planet.

This is no hollow speculation; there are almost two centuries of precedent for the idea that the Saints are especially inspired aesthetically by their faith. LDS writers and artists have shown an enthusiasm for artistic creation completely out of proportion to their numbers. This is evident in the massive literary output of the Saints, dating back to the earliest days of the Church[507] and continuing to the present day,[508] as well as in the art created for their temples and elsewhere.[509] Today, this aesthetic impulse is evident in the fiction, poetry, and art published in such in-

---

[507] E.g., Cracroft & Lambert (1974).
[508] E.g., England (1992), Hallstrom (2010).
[509] E.g., Dant (1999), M.B. Brown & Smith (1997), Welch & Dant (1997).

Chapter 10: A 'More Mormon' World 271

dependent Mormon periodicals as *Dialogue*,[510] *Irreantum*,[511] *Sunstone*,[512] and elsewhere. It is evident in the artwork submitted to the Church's triennial International Art Competition,[513] and its International Youth Art Competition.[514] If this is true for a church of just over 14.4 million members in 2012, it will be much more true for a church ten times that size in 2066, a hundred times that size in 2109, and beyond.

What a 19th century Mormon apostle said of the literary arts applies just as well to the plastic arts and the performing arts, and to the sciences and mathematics. Addressing himself to an LDS audience in 1888, Elder Orson F. Whitney—three-time missionary, once presiding over the entire Mormon mission in Europe—wrote this on the subject of Mormon writers:

> Above all things, we must be original. The Holy Ghost is the genius of "Mormon" literature…. No patterning after the dead forms of antiquity. Our literature must live and breathe for itself. Our mission is diverse from all others; our literature must also be….
>
> We will yet have Miltons and Shakespeares of our own. God's ammunition is not exhausted. His brightest spirits are held in reserve for the latter times. In God's name

---

[510] https://www.dialoguejournal.com/archive/
[511] http://irreantum.mormonletters.org/
[512] https://www.sunstonemagazine.com/
[513] Reproductions of examples of art in this competition were published in "Testifying of Christ" (2012).
[514] Information about both competitions is available online at http://www.lds.org/churchhistory/museum/competition/1,16118,4091-1,00.html

and by his help we will build up a literature whose top shall touch heaven, though its foundations may now be low in earth....

Let us onward, then, and upward, ... living not in the dead past, nor for the dying present. The future is our field. Eternity is before us.[515]

And with their Miltons and Shakespeares, the Saints shall have their Da Vincis, Michelangelos, Dürers, and their Austens and Henry Jameses, their Borges and Kafkas, their Chekovs, Baldwins, Bellows, Bradburys, and Clarkes, as well as their Arthur Millers, their Moores, Noguchis, and Braques, their Picassos and Rothkos, their DeMilles, their Grahams, Aileys, and Balanchines, their Nijinskys, their Robesons. I daresay they shall have their Platos and Aristotles, their Newtons and Einsteins, their Cantors and Gödels, their Jennings' and Pasteurs and Carvers—although their Nietzsches will declare that God lives, their Freuds that religion is anything but an illusion, and their Darwins will note that the tale of biology serves to elucidate the power and utter strangeness of His ways.

The Saints shall have their prodigies on every inhabited continent, in most every language. The resulting efflorescence of culture and science ultimately may be the most obvious aspect of that more Mormon world, in the consequential dimension of religion.

Religious Belief

A substantial increase in the Mormon population would greatly increase the number of people who believe

---

[515] Whitney (1888/1974) p. 206.

in the central and essential doctrines of Christianity. This is suggested by findings of recent U.S. national surveys conducted by the Pew Research Center. For example:

- 98% of surveyed Mormons stated belief that Jesus rose from the dead, compared with 83% of the general public.[516]
- 92% of surveyed Mormons stated belief that the Bible is the word of God, compared with 63% of the general population, 77% of Protestants (89% of Protestant evangelicals), 62% of Catholics, and 59% of Orthodox Christians.[517]
- 88% of surveyed Mormons were *absolutely certain* of a life after death, compared with 50% of the general population, 62% of Protestants (71% of Protestant evangelicals), 45% of Catholics, and 47% of Orthodox Christians.[518]
- 95% of surveyed Mormons stated belief in a heaven where people who have led good lives are eternally rewarded, compared with 74% of the general population, 84% of Protestants (86% of evangelicals), 82% of Catholics, and 74% of Orthodox Christians.[519]

In sum, a more Mormon world would be one in which certain basic Christian beliefs would be more common,

---

[516] *Mormons in America* (2012) pp. 35, 108. Relevant LDS teachings: *Gospel Principles* (2009) ch. 11, p. 57.

[517] *U.S. Religious Landscape Survey: Religious Beliefs* (2008) pp. 31, 235. Relevant LDS teachings: *Gospel Principles* (2009), Ch. 10, pp. 45-49.

[518] *U.S. Religious Landscape Survey: Religious Beliefs* (2008) pp. 32, 230-231. Relevant LDS teachings: *Gospel Principles* (2009), Chs. 41, 46.

[519] *U.S. Religious Landscape Survey: Religious Beliefs* (2008) pp. 33, 233. Relevant LDS teachings: *Gospel Principles* (2009), Chs. 46 and 47.

and held with greater conviction, than is the case at present. A greater proportion of the general population would become familiar with these beliefs, both in America and worldwide, and it would become more acceptable throughout society to hold these beliefs.

This does not translate into the notion that the beliefs of *evangelical* or *fundamentalist* Christians will become more common. The beliefs of any given Christian subgroup, other than the LDS faith, will not necessarily become more common in a more Mormon world; only the core Christian beliefs, particularly the ones mentioned above, will become more widely accepted, and acceptable, and perhaps some of the more distinctive LDS beliefs, as well.

The more distinctive LDS beliefs, such as those involving continuing revelation (see Chapter 1), will become more socially acceptable to the public. More to the point, the *values* that these beliefs represent will become more socially acceptable, as I described earlier in regard to the consequential dimension of religion.

Religious Practice

Various types of religious practice would be more common in a world with more Mormons in it. This is suggested by those U.S. surveys conducted by the Pew organization:

- 75% of surveyed Mormons stated that they attend religious services at least once a week, compared with 39% of the general population, 50% of Protestants (58% of Protestant evangelicals), 42% of Catholics, and 34% of Orthodox Christians.[520]

---

[520] *U.S. Religious Landscape Survey: Religious Beliefs* (2008) pp. 36, 219.

- 82% of surveyed Mormons stated that they prayed at least once daily, compared with 58% of the general population, 69% of Protestants (78% of evangelicals), 58% of Catholics, and 60% of the Orthodox.[521]

- To focus further on prayer, 66% of surveyed Mormons stated that they prayed *several times* daily, compared with 38% of the general population, 57% of evangelical Protestants, 31% of Catholics, and 33% of Orthodox Christians.[522]

- 76% of surveyed Mormons said that they studied scriptures (outside of worship services) at least once weekly, compared with 35% of the general population, 48% of Protestants (60% of evangelicals), 21% of Catholics, and 22% of Orthodox Christians.[523]

- Of those with children under the age of 18 living in the home, 91% of surveyed Mormons said that they prayed or read scripture with their children, compared with 63% of the general population, 74% of Protestants (81% of evangelical Protestants), 63% of Catholics, and 56% of Orthodox Christians.[524]

Prayer and scripture study are among those areas wherein "Mormon religious practice offers a lot of really,

---

[521] *U.S. Religious Landscape Survey: Religious Beliefs* (2008) pp. 45, 242. LDS teachings: *Gospel Principles* (2009), Chapter 8.

[522] *U.S. Religious Landscape Survey: Religious Beliefs* (2008) p. 242.

[523] *U.S. Religious Landscape Survey: Religious Beliefs* (2008) pp. 49, 244. LDS teachings: *Gospel Principles* (2009), Ch. 10.

[524] *U.S. Religious Landscape Survey: Religious Beliefs* (2008) pp. 43, 259. LDS teachings: *Gospel Principles* (2009), Chapters 36 and 37, pp. 207-217. Family prayer and scripture study have long been urged by the Church leadership; e.g., *Family Guidebook* (2006) pp. 4-7.

well, religious religion ....," as one LDS op-ed writer stated.[525] A more Mormon world would be generally more comfortable with "religious religion." This seems to be an issue especially in the West. In American popular entertainment, for example, it is the rare "normal" character who is also deeply faithful and overtly practicing his or her religion. This will change in a more Mormon world.

RELIGIOUS KNOWLEDGE

The religious studies professor Stephen Prothero has compiled much data from various sources documenting the fact that Americans are spectacularly uninformed about even their own religions. As he put it:

> Americans are both deeply religious and profoundly ignorant about religion. They are Protestants who can't name the four Gospels, Catholics who can't name the seven sacraments, and Jews who can't name the five books of Moses.... One of the most religious countries on earth is also a nation of religious illiterates.[526]

However, religious knowledge would be more widely held in a more Mormon world. This is suggested by a different survey conducted by the Pew organization:

- In a U.S. national survey of general religious knowledge using 32 questions, the overall average score was 16 correct. The highest scoring groups were atheists/agnostics, Jews, and Mormons (all av-

---

[525] Fluhman (2012) p. A25.
[526] Prothero (2007/2008) pp. 1-2.

eraging between 20 and 21 correct answers)—compared with Protestants (16 correct) and Catholics (14.7 correct).[527]

- Specifically focusing on the 12 questions addressing the Bible and Christianity, the highest scoring group was the Mormons (average 7.9 correct), compared to any other group, including the general public (6.0 correct), Protestants as a whole (6.5 correct), White evangelical Protestants specifically (7.3 correct), and Catholics (5.4 correct). (Incidentally, Jews scored an average of 6.3 correct, and atheists/agnostics an average of 6.7.)[528]

- Focusing on the 11 questions involving non-Christian religions, the Mormons scored 5.6 correct as a group, higher than the general public (5.0 correct), and higher than any other Christian group, including Protestants as a whole (4.6 correct), White evangelical Protestants specifically (4.8 correct), and Catholics (4.7 correct). (Incidentally, Jews scored an average of 7.9 correct, and atheists/agnostics an average of 7.5.)[529]

Thus, a more Mormon world would be one better informed about, not just Christianity, but world religions in general. In a world in which different religious cultures are coming into contact more frequently, greater knowledge of others' religions would be especially valuable.

---

[527] *U.S. Religious Knowledge Survey* (2010), p. 6.
[528] *U.S. Religious Knowledge Survey* (2010) p. 7.
[529] *U.S. Religious Knowledge Survey* (2010) p. 7. Many LDS missionaries serve in places with primarily non-Christian populations. E.g., this author served in the LDS Japan Okayama Mission [1978-1980].

One can only speculate about what a world with greater knowledge of the basics of the Christian religion would be like. Earlier ages are no guide in this respect; it seems that profound ignorance of even the basics of Christianity has been the norm, even in ostensibly Christian countries, for many centuries before our own era.[530] One might hope that greater understanding of Christian basics would lead to more actual living of Christian ideals.

RELIGIOUS / SPIRITUAL EXPERIENCES

In a more Mormon world, inner spiritual experiences will be somewhat more common. This is suggested by data from surveys conducted by the Pew organization:

- Of those surveyed American Mormons who pray at least several times a year, 54% stated that they received direct answers to prayers once or twice a month, or even more frequently, compared to 31% in the general population, 39% of Protestants (46% of evangelicals), 26% of Catholics, 24% of Orthodox Christians, and 12% of Jews.[531]

- Of surveyed American Mormons who believe in God, 69% said that they had witnessed or experienced divine healing, compared with 34% of the general population, 43% of Protestants (50% of evangelicals), 27% of Catholics, 34% of Orthodox Christians, and 17% of Jews.[532]

---

[530] Stark (2011).
[531] *U.S. Religious Landscape Survey: ... Beliefs and Practices* (2008) p. 53.
[532] *U.S. Religious Landscape Survey: ... Beliefs and Practices* (2008) p. 54.

Chapter 10: A 'More Mormon' World

- Among surveyed American Mormons, 71% said that they experience, weekly or more frequently, a deep sense of spiritual peace and well-being, compared with 52% of the general public, 60% of Protestants (68% of evangelicals), 47% of Catholics, 45% of Orthodox Christians, and 38% of Jews.[533]

That last item in particular does more than border on the territory of mystical experience.[534] Of course, in some quarters, personal spiritual experiences have long been considered as evidence of psychological instability.[535] However, this prejudice has little if any basis in fact, either generally,[536] or with reference to Mormons in particular.[537]

In a more Mormon world, more people would have these kinds of experiences. This would make personal spiritual experience less of an exotic thing—as it certainly seems to be, particularly in Western society at present—and more normal a part of human life. Some preliminary psychological research suggests that people who have such experiences regularly are less dogmatic, less authoritarian, and more intelligent, imaginative, relaxed, and overall have greater psychological strength than people who do not.[538] Certainly, on the face of it, a greater distribution of these characteristics would make for a better world.

---

[533] *U.S. Religious Landscape Survey: Religious Beliefs and Practices* (2008) p. 56.

[534] I have addressed mysticism from an LDS perspective in Koltko (1989).

[535] For example, Group for the Advancement of Psychiatry (1976).

[536] See references cited in Koltko (1989) notes 18 and 19.

[537] Bergin, Payne, Jenkins, Cornwall (1994); Judd (1998).

[538] E.g., Hood (1974), McClain & Andrews (1969), Sacks (1979).

Afterword:

The Meaning of Mormon Growth

There likely will be hundreds of millions—very possibly billions—of Latter-day Saints throughout the world by the early 22nd century, well within the lifespans of (very young) people now alive as I write these words.

But what does that all mean? Why does it *matter* that there will be so many Mormons? This is a question of values, and it will have different answers for different people.

For Latter-day Saints, certainly the worst possible takeaway message of what I have presented here would be the thought, "well, I guess we can all sit back and relax!" I am akin to Charles Dickens's 'Ghost of Christmas Yet to Come' character from *A Christmas Carol*: that is, my projections are only shadows of things that *may* be, **not** things that certainly *will* be.

It will require a monumental effort and immense Mormon sacrifice to make my high-growth projections a reality: a missionary effort such as the world has never seen; diligent service in the Church even beyond that hitherto observed; extending fellowship and support to new converts, and so forth.[539] If the Saints want to build a two-billion-plus member Church, they are going to have to

---

[539] It might also help if the Saints made conscious reference in their public messages, now and again, to those doctrines and practices that so positively respond to the societal preoccupations that I have described in Chapter 8.

work for it, and work hard—as hard, in many ways, as the Mormon pioneers who *walked*—often barefoot!—a third of the way across a continent and built Salt Lake City largely with their bare hands and primitive tools. Phenomenally high Mormon growth: doable, yes; easy, no.

But, assuming that the Saints exert this effort, and the Lord blesses their efforts, and this growth occurs, it will be a moment of fulfillment for the Saints. Mormons have long pondered this passage from the book of Daniel in the Jewish Bible (Old Testament), describing Daniel's interpretation of the dream of the Babylonian king Nebuchadnezzar:

> Thou, O king, sawest, and behold a great image. This great image, whose brightness was excellent, stood before thee; and the form thereof was terrible. ...
>
> Thou sawest till that a stone was cut out without hands which smote the image upon his feet that were of iron and clay, and brake them to pieces. ...
>
> ... and the stone that smote the image became a great mountain and filled the whole earth.[540]

Mormons have considered this prophecy as referring to the Church of Jesus Christ, almost from the moment that the Church was formally organized. A revelation pronounced through Joseph Smith in 1831 states:

> The keys of the kingdom of God are committed unto man on the earth, and from thence shall the gospel roll forth unto the ends of the

---

[540] LDS Standard Works: Bible, Daniel, chapter 2, verses 31, 34, 35.

Afterword: The Meaning of Mormon Growth

earth, as the stone which is cut out of the mountain without hands shall roll forth, until it has filled the whole earth.[541]

The image of the 'stone cut out of the mountain without hands' as a symbol of the restored Church[542] has been a favorite one among LDS teachers for the better part of two centuries.[543] Certainly it is an image consistent with the high-LDS-growth projections that I have described here.

If and when the Church does grow to those proportions I have predicted here, what this will mean to the Mormons is that they have fulfilled the work given to them by Christ, in the Great Commission that I described in Chapter 1. The Saints will have done their jobs, individually and collectively. And that is the dream of the faithful Saint, to be told in that Great and Final Exit Interview, as it were, "Well done, thou good and faithful servant: thou hast been faithful over a few things, I will make thee ruler over many things: enter thou into the joy of thy Lord."[544]

What about those who are not Latter-day Saints? What would massive Mormon growth mean to them?

Here again, there is a worst-possible take-away message of which one should beware. Some will think that the way to respond to the possibility that the Saints will become so extremely numerous will be to fight them at every turn, by means fair or foul.

---

[541] LDS Standard Works: Doctrine & Covenants, Section 65, verse 2.
[542] One interpretation of "without hands" is that the Church of Jesus Christ was restored by divine authority, not formed at the initiative of human beings, nor by human authority; "Lesson 46" (2001).
[543] E.g., Hinckley (2007b).
[544] Standard Works: Bible, New Test., Matthew, chapter 25, verse 21.

This would all be so much wasted and counterproductive effort. Given the rate at which various Christian churches are losing membership, their efforts are best spent in building their own faiths up, not trying to tear others down. Besides which, anti-Mormonism has sold shelf-loads of books for nearly two centuries, and in recent years anti-Mormon activity has spread to Internet videos and other visual media; nonetheless, anti-Mormonism seems to have had little effect on Mormon growth.

Far more fruitful would it be for people of other faiths to take a page or two out of the Mormon playbook. The LDS leadership makes a huge amount of very practical advice available for free on the Internet (much of which I have cited throughout this book). There is nothing to prevent any religious organization from dipping into that large electronic library and taking some ideas, for emergency preparedness, say, or for building self-reliance, or youth programs, or even for developing religious leadership. The Mormons won't mind.

From a religiously neutral position—where no positions are taken about the truth-claims of the LDS faith, where questions of what God's religion might be are suspended, or 'bracketed,' as the philosophers say—the real meaning of Mormon growth lies in what it contributes to the spiritual journey of humankind. What might that be?

As the religious studies scholar Huston Smith has put it, "the world is ambiguous.... It comes to us as a giant Rorschach inkblot."[545] A religion supplies an interpretive framework for the ambiguity presented by the world.[546]

---

[545] Huston Smith (2001) p. 205.
[546] Huston Smith (2001) Chapter 14.

Afterword: The Meaning of Mormon Growth

Such frameworks are what I have called *worldviews*.547 As I have explained elsewhere, religions influence the worldviews of individuals and entire cultures; in turn, these worldviews influence behavior, sometimes on a massive scale.548 When a religion becomes widespread, its worldview has some influence on the world at large, even among those who do not profess the religion involved.549 So, what will Mormonism contribute to the worldviews available in the world?

In the penultimate chapter of his book, *Why Religion Matters*, Huston Smith considers the notion of 'spiritual personality types,' each of which has a characteristic worldview. Smith lists these types as follows:

- The Atheist: There is no God.
- The Polytheist: There are many gods.
- The Monotheist: There is one God.
- The Mystic: There is only God.550

To these, Mormons would add another such 'type':

- The Saint: **_You are meant to become just like God._**

This is a worldview with powerful consequences. As I say in my own online "I'm a Mormon" essay:

---

547 Koltko-Rivera (2004).
548 Koltko-Rivera (2006-2007).
549 For example, I do not believe that the many people who make the writings of H.H. the Dalai Lama into best-sellers are themselves all Buddhists. In the modern world, Buddhism also has an influence on Christians, Jews, and people of no labeled faith. For example, consider the extent to which different forms of (Hindu and Buddhist) meditation have become mainstream in American society.
550 Smith (2001) Chapter 15.

> My faith affects the way that I look at other people. The LDS scriptures teach that every human being is literally a child of God, and has the potential to inherit all that our Father in Heaven has and is. That is truly awesome, in the literal sense of that word. This principle applies to every person I see all day long, including the homeless person who sleeps on a rock in Central Park, the people who strike me as rude and unmannered, the people who serve me a sandwich or who collect my trash, and the many people who live by very different principles than I do. I try to treat all people equally, with equal respect and dignity. That's living my faith.[551]

Such a vision of life has impact on one's self-image, one's image of other people, and one's sense of mission in life. Such a worldview certainly has behavioral implications, as well, in terms of interpersonal relations. If it is true that 'the personal is political'—and it certainly is—then this kind of approach to life, directed outwards to others, has political and economic implications as well. Large numbers of people living with this vision would affect the way that entire communities treated their homeless, their poor, their mentally ill, their social outcasts, the members of their minority groups.

Perhaps the most profound effect of the LDS point of view would come about when this doctrinal perspective were applied to our notions of human potential and the meaning of life. As I have mentioned earlier, anciently, the

---

[551] Koltko-Rivera (2011a).

Christian doctrine that human beings could share in the very nature of God and receive the very gift of godhood itself was called *theosis*. In our era, large numbers of people who believed that they had the seeds of godhood within them would not only treat others differently, they would treat themselves differently, too. For example, the LDS prophets have long taught their people to respect themselves, to obtain as much education as possible, to use and improve upon their talents.

Planting the 'godhood meme' in the global mindset might encourage personal development and care for others on a much larger scale, not only among Mormons, but among all people. As far as an LDS contribution to the spiritual life of humanity is concerned, I think this would all do very well.

One can also look at the LDS faith as a radical and vibrant alternative perspective on existentialism, which was arguably the dominant philosophical perspective of the twentieth century, and continues as such in the early years of the twenty-first.[552] As the psychiatrist Irvin Yalom[553] has explained it, from an existentialist perspective, there are four ultimate concerns in human life:

- *Death*. Life ultimately ends. Period.
- *Freedom*. But this is the freedom of the skydiver in free fall without a parachute, as it were: human beings are totally responsible for the design of their lives, choices, and actions, without any legitimate guidance or help available beyond themselves.

---

[552] For foundational writings of this perspective, see Kaufmann (1956).
[553] Yalom (1980) pp. 8-9.

- *Existential isolation.* Despite our desire to make contact, there is always an unbridgeable gap between each of us and all others. We are ultimately alone.
- *Meaninglessness.* The existentialist universe has no purpose, no direction, and life in it has no ultimate meaning beyond what the individual decides upon.

The existentialist perspective has become so pervasive in American and European society, particularly among our cultural elites, that its very premises are considered beyond serious discussion. This perspective underlies the wholesale hedonism that is the focus of so much of our popular culture; at the same time, it is the foundation for much contemporary literary writing and art cinema. Existentialism is certainly the major philosophical underpinning of the New Atheism. It is also arguably the basis of a pervasive, free-floating anxiety in Western civilization: God is dead, and although everything therefore may be permitted, nothing matters at all.

It is nothing unusual for a religion to distinguish itself from existentialism. What makes Mormonism unique is that *it actually agrees with some of existentialism's premises* — and yet comes to very different conclusions.[554]

The major issue to consider in this regard is the matter of human moral agency. For the Latter-day Saints, the human soul was endowed upon its creation with agency, the power of choice, as the most precious gift of God. Indeed, the War in Heaven before the Earth was created was

---

[554] There are lively discussions about the compatibility of Mormonism and existentialism on the Internet. In the printed literature, one of the earlier considerations of this theme is Stott (1989).

fought to preserve human agency.[555] Yes, the Atonement of Christ graciously opens certain possibilities for us that otherwise would be forever closed (physical resurrection and immortality for all, exaltation for the valiant). But, now that the Atonement has been accomplished, what becomes of any given human being is a matter of that person's choice, as demonstrated by her or his actions. Ultimately, even exaltation is a choice.

This placement of choice and agency at the center of the story of the universe is not a common story among the religions of the world. In a very real sense, the Mormon story is like the existentialist story, in that humankind is radically free to choose. However, instead of those choices being ultimately meaningless, as they are from the existentialist point of view, from the LDS perspective, human choice is fraught with cosmic meaning and immense consequences—indeed, eternal and infinite consequences.

This, too, would be a good meme to place into the world. It is a perspective that empowers human beings in this world, a point of view that encourages both initiative and responsibility. As guiding philosophies go, the LDS notion that choice is central to existence, and that the right choices can lead even unto godhood, is a very powerful one, with a host of positive consequences for the individual, the family, the community, and the world at large.

We have been on a long journey together. If there were three things I would have you remember from this book, these would be as follows:

---

[555] LDS Standard Works: Pearl of Great Price, Moses, Ch. 4, vv. 1-4.

1. In all likelihood, there will be more Mormons—a *lot* more Mormons—both in the United States, and in the world at large, over the next century.

2. This will be a good thing, leading to more education, less poverty, and perhaps even the spread of a more positive and productive approach to life throughout the world.

3. As far as this news is concerned:

    a. For the Mormons in the room: Be prepared to work harder than you ever have before to bring this growth about. *Or:*

    b. For those who are not Latter-day Saints: Perhaps now would be a good time to learn about these Mormons of whom we shall be seeing so many more in the future. The better we all understand each other, the better the world will be.

Good fortune to all my readers—of whatever peace-loving, positive, productive faith-tradition or philosophy you may be—as you seek to find your way in the world, and to strengthen your own communities.

— MEK-R

Appendix A

Sources of Statistical Data and Methods of Projections

Sources of Historical Statistical Data

The raw data for the statistical analyses in Chapter 1 were obtained from several sources:

- LDS figures (for membership, numbers of convert baptisms, numbers of missionaries, etc.) were largely obtained from the "Statistical Report" articles for the years 1971 through 2011. For pre-1971 data, and for some data from later years, LDS figures were obtained from the *Deseret News Church Almanac*, most especially the issue released in 2012, but supplemented by other issues as noted in the footnotes.

- Membership figures for other Christian churches in the United States were obtained from issues of the *Yearbook of American and Canadian Churches* released 1987 through 2012.

- Membership figures for religions throughout the world were obtained from the "Annual Megacensus of Religion," found in the *Encyclopedia Britannica Books of the Year*, 1991-2010.

METHODS OF STATISTICAL PROJECTION

Global Projections

- LDS: All projections begin from a base of 14,441,346 members at year-end 2011, obtained from "Statistical Report, 2011." Projections continue with one-year growth projected for 2012 of 2.10%, and one-year growth projected for 2013 of 2.00%. Thereafter:
  - In the low-growth model, the projected annual growth rate remains at 2.00%, from 2014 through the conclusion of the period covered by the projections (2120).
  - In the moderate-growth model, the projected annual growth rate from 2014 on increases by 0.05% annually, to a maximum of 4.00% (in 2053). The projected annual growth rate thereafter remains at 4.00% through 2120.
  - In the high-growth model, the projected annual growth rate from 2014 on increases by 0.10% annually, to a maximum of 5.50% (in 2048). The projected annual growth rate thereafter remains at 5.50% through 2120.
- All other religious bodies: All projections begin from a base of membership figures for year-end 2011, as given in the relevant "Annual Megacensus of Religion."
  - For each group, a nominal projected annual growth rate (NPAGR) was defined, as follows, based on the group's median growth rate for 2001-2011 (see Table 3-1), as follows:

- Roman Catholics: 0.94%
- Protestant Christians: 1.61%
- Independent Christians: 1.62%
- Orthodox Christians: 0.56%
- Anglican Christians: 1.25%
- Muslims: 2.06%
- Hindus: 1.10%
- Chinese folk religionists: 0.71%
- Buddhists: 0.90%
- New Religionists: 0.43%
- Sikhs: 1.98%
- Jews: 0.34%

> An annual fertility reduction factor (AFRF) was defined annually for 2012-2120, to account for falling fertility rates predicted for the global population at large.[556] This annual fertility reduction factor was defined at 0.75% for 2012, and increased annually thereafter by 0.75% from 2013 through 2120.

> The applied projected annual growth rate (APAGR) for each religious body was calculated as follows: APAGR = NPAGR * (1 − AFRF). The projected membership figure for any given year was thus equal to APAGR

---

[556] United Nations, Department of Economic and Social Affairs, Population Division (2004).

times the previous year's membership figure (real, in the case of 2011, or projected).[557]

United States Projections

- LDS: All projections begin from a base of 6,144,582 members at year-end 2010, obtained from adding all the U.S. state totals in the *Deseret News 2012 Church Almanac*, pp. 324-415. (The total membership figure given for the U.S.A. on p. 324 of that reference is incorrect, and reflects year-end 2009 data.)

  ➢ The low-growth model begins with an annual growth rate of 1.42%, projected for 2011. Thereafter, the projected annual growth rate increases by 0.01% annually, to a maximum of 1.67% (in 2036). The projected annual growth rate remains at 1.67% through 2120.

  ➢ The moderate-growth model begins with an annual growth rate of 1.43% in 2011. Thereafter, the projected annual growth rate increases by 0.02% annually, to a maximum of 3.43% (in 2111). The projected annual growth rate remains at 3.43% through 2120.

  ➢ The high-growth model begins with an annual growth rate of 1.45%, projected for 2011.

---

[557] The annual fertility reduction factor, or AFRF, was not applied to calculate LDS global membership because, as established in Chapter 1, LDS growth is overwhelmingly the result of convert baptisms, not so-called 'natural increase' (i.e., births of children to adherents of a given religious body). Global fertility is irrelevant to LDS growth. For most other religious bodies, at least on a global scale, natural increase seems to be the primary engine for growth.

Thereafter, the projected annual growth rate increases by 0.04% annually, to 5.17%, projected for 2104. The projected annual growth rate increases to 5.18% in 2105, and remains at that figure through 2120.

- All churches other than the Latter-day Saints: Projections begin from a base of membership figures as of year-end 2010, as given in the *Yearbook of American and Canadian Churches: 2012*. Thereafter, annual growth rates were applied that reflected median annual change, 1991-2010 (see Table 4-1), as follows:

  ➢ Roman Catholic Church: All projections begin from a base of 68,202,492 members at year-end 2010. Thereafter, the annual growth for 2011 through 2120 is projected at 0.75%.

  ➢ Southern Baptist Convention: All projections begin from a base of 16,136,044 members at year-end 2010. Thereafter, the annual growth for 2011 through 2120 is projected at 0.35%.

  ➢ United Methodist Church: All projections begin from a base of 7,679,850 members at year-end 2010. Thereafter, the annual "growth" for 2011 through 2120 is projected as a loss rate of -0.75%.

  ➢ Lutheran Churches (Combined): All projections begin from a base of 6,553,441 at year-end 2010 (combining figures for the Evangelical Lutheran Church and the Lutheran Church—Missouri Synod). Thereafter, the annual "growth" for 2011 through 2120 is projected as a loss rate of -0.60%.

- Evangelical Lutheran Church in America: All projections begin from a base of 4,274,855 members at year-end 2010. Thereafter, the annual "growth" for 2011 through 2120 is projected as a loss rate of -0.53%.

- Assemblies of God: All projections begin from a base of 3,030,944 members at year-end 2010. Thereafter, the annual growth for 2011 through 2120 is projected at 1.69%.

- Presbyterian Church USA: All projections begin from a base of 2,675,873 members at year-end 2010. Thereafter, the annual "growth" for 2011 through 2120 is projected as a loss rate of -1.50%.

- Lutheran Church—Missouri Synod: All projections begin from a base of 2,278,586 members at year-end 2010. Thereafter, the annual "growth" for 2011 through 2120 is projected as a loss rate of -0.74%.

- Episcopal Church: All projections begin from a base of 1,951,907 members at year-end 2010. Thereafter, the annual "growth" for 2011 through 2120 is projected as a loss rate of negative 0.66%.

Appendix B

The Slowing of Mormon Growth Post-1990: A Statistical Analysis

From 1991 on, the number of LDS converts has remained high. However, compared to the period 1977-1990, the *percentage* of LDS growth per year has dropped. This is apparent from Table B-1.

Year	World LDS Membership	Growth over Preceding Year	Percent Growth
1977	3,969,220	226,471	6.05%
1978	4,166,854	197,634	4.98%
1979	4,404,121	237,267	5.69%
1980	4,639,822	235,701	5.35%
1981	4,920,449	280,627	6.05%
1982	5,162,619	242,170	4.92%
1983	5,351,724	189,105	3.66%
1984	5,641,054	289,330	5.41%
1985	5,919,483	278,429	4.94%
1986	6,166,974	247,491	4.18%

Table B-1. Annual Mormon growth, 1978-2011

(continued)

Year	World LDS Membership	Growth over Preceding Year	Percent Growth
1987	6,394,314	227,340	3.69%
1988	6,721,210	326,896	5.11%
1989	7,308,444	587,234	8.74%
1990	7,761,207	452,763	6.20%
1992	8,404,087	314,239	3.88%
1993	8,689,168	285,081	3.39%
1994	9,024,368	335,200	3.86%
1995	9,338,397	314,029	3.48%
1996	9,692,441	354,044	3.79%
1997	10,071,783	379,342	3.91%
1998	10,404,448	332,665	3.30%
1999	10,724,984	320,536	3.08%
2001	11,394,518	325,657	2.94%
2002	11,721,548	327,030	2.87%
2003	11,985,254	263,706	2.25%
2004	12,275,822	290,568	2.42%
2005	12,560,869	285,047	2.32%
2006	12,868,606	307,737	2.45%
2007	13,193,999	325,393	2.53%
2008	13,508,509	314,510	2.38%
2009	13,824,854	316,345	2.34%
2010	14,131,467	306,613	2.22%
2011	14,441,346	309,879	2.19%

Table B-1 (continued). **Annual Mormon growth, 1978-2011**

Appendix B: The Slowing of Mormon Growth

The median annual growth for 1977–1990 was 5.23%; that for 1991–2011 was 2.94%, a drop in annual growth rate of 44%. Why might this have happened?

The great majority of LDS growth in a given year involves convert baptisms (see Chapter 1), so it makes sense to look at factors influencing the number of convert baptisms over this period. Consider Table B-2, for 1977–2011.

Year	Number of LDS Convert Baptisms	Number of LDS Missionaries Serving	Number of Countries in which Church is Organized
1977	167,939	25,300	54
1978	152,000	27,669	60
1979	193,000	29,454	83
1980	221,000	29,953	86
1981	224,000	29,700	105
1982	207,000	26,300	107
1983	189,419	26,565	114
1984	192,983	27,655	115
1985	197,640	29,265	122
1986	216,210	31,803	122
1987	227,284	34,750	125
1988	256,515	36,132	128
1989	318,940	39,739	130
1990	330,877	43,651	138
1991	297,770	43,395	146
1992	274,477	46,025	149

Table B-2. **LDS Convert Baptisms, 1977-2011**

(continued)

Year	Number of LDS Convert Baptisms	Number of LDS Missionaries Serving	Number of Countries in which Church is Organized
1993	304,808	48,708	156
1994	300,730	47,311	159
1995	304,330	48,631	161
1996	321,385	52,938	162
1997	317,798	56,531	164
1998	299,134	57,853	165
1999	306,171	58,593	167
2000	273,973	60,784	168
2001	292,612	60,850	170
2002	283,138	61,638	171
2003	242,923	56,237	173
2004	241,239	51,067	174
2005	243,108	52,060	176
2006	272,845	53,164	177
2007	279,218	52,686	179
2008	265,593	52,494	180
2009	280,106	51,736	182
2010	272,814	52,225	183
2011	281,312	55,410	185

Table B-2 (continued). **LDS Convert Baptisms, 1977-2011**

Notes for Tables B-1 and B-2: Sources: Figures for Church membership, numbers of convert baptisms, and number of missionaries are listed in "Statistical Report" for each year. Number of countries is listed there for some years, and in *Deseret News Church Almanac.*

I used data in Table B-2 to explore the relationship between convert baptisms, the number of missionaries serving at a given time, and the number of countries in which the Church was organized (that is, where the Church had even a single formal congregation). I considered these relationships in two different periods: (1) from 1977 to 1990, inclusive, and (2) from 1991 to 2011, inclusive.

LDS GROWTH, 1977-1990: ALL ABOUT THE MISSIONARIES

For the period from 1977 through 1990, I conducted a multiple regression with annual number of LDS converts as the dependent variable, and both annual number of missionaries serving, and the number of countries in which LDS were organized within a given year, as the two predictors. This multiple regression is reported in Tables B-3 and B-4. The two predictor variables were not too highly correlated (Pearson's $r = +0.664$, $N = 14$, $p = .005$), so the assumption of non-multicollinearity was met, using the $r < .80$ criterion.[558] However, all of the variables in the analysis are highly skewed,[559] thereby violating an important assumption of multiple regression[560]; in practical terms, this means that we should interpret the analysis cautiously.

---

[558] Licht (1995) p. 45. Given the highly skewed distribution of these variables, and the fact that they are nonlinearly related, a nonparametric measure of their association is preferable to Pearson's r; due to the small sample size, a better nonparametric measure of their association than Kendall's tau is Spearman's rho (Xu, Hou, Hung, & Zou, 2010), which here is equal to $+0.737$ ($p = .001$).

[559] For number of missionaries serving, skew = +1.185; for number of convert baptisms, skew = +1.171; for number of countries, skew = -0.980.

[560] Osborne & Waters (2002).

Variable	M	SD	1	2
Annual Convert Baptisms	221,057.6	51,052	.935**	.714*
Predictor vars.:				
1. Missionaries serving	31,281.1	5,414	—	.664*
2. Countries w/ LDS congregations	106.4	26		—

*p < .01. **p < .001.

Table B-3. **Means, standard deviations, and intercorrelations for annual LDS convert baptisms and predictor variables, 1977-1990**

Variable	B	SE B	β	t	p
Missionaries serving	7.77	1.26	.82	6.15	<.001
Countries w/ LDS congregations	357.54	261.95	.17	1.25	.237

Note. Adjusted R^2 = .87 (N = 14, p < .001).

Table B-4. **Regression analysis summary for variables predicting annual LDS convert baptisms, 1977-1990**

Appendix B: The Slowing of Mormon Growth 303

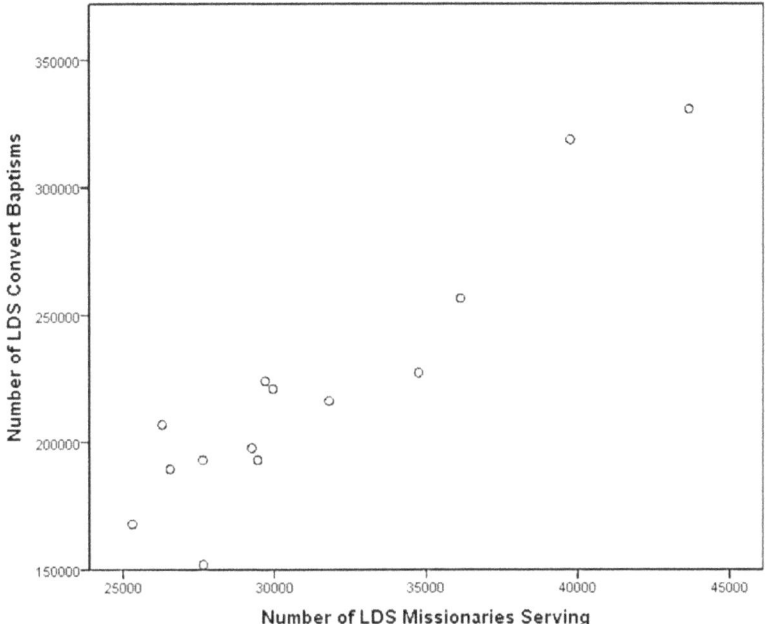

Figure B-1. **Convert baptisms and missionaries serving, 1977-1990**

For this period, the number of countries with LDS congregations simply was not a significant predictor of the number of LDS convert baptisms. The number of LDS missionaries serving, however, was a highly significant predictor, both statistically and practically. For each additional missionary in the field, between 7 and 8 additional convert baptisms occurred ($B = 7.77$). However, the actual story is a bit more complicated.

On the one hand, to judge from Figure B-1, the relationship between the number of missionaries serving and the number of convert baptisms in any given year appears to be a reasonable approximation of a linear relationship. The more missionaries there were, the more convert baptisms there were: no surprises here.

On the other hand, to judge from Figure B-2, the relationship between the number of countries with LDS congregations and the number of convert baptisms is anything *but* linear. (This is another violation of an assumption of multiple regression,[561] hence another reason that we should interpret the regression quite cautiously).

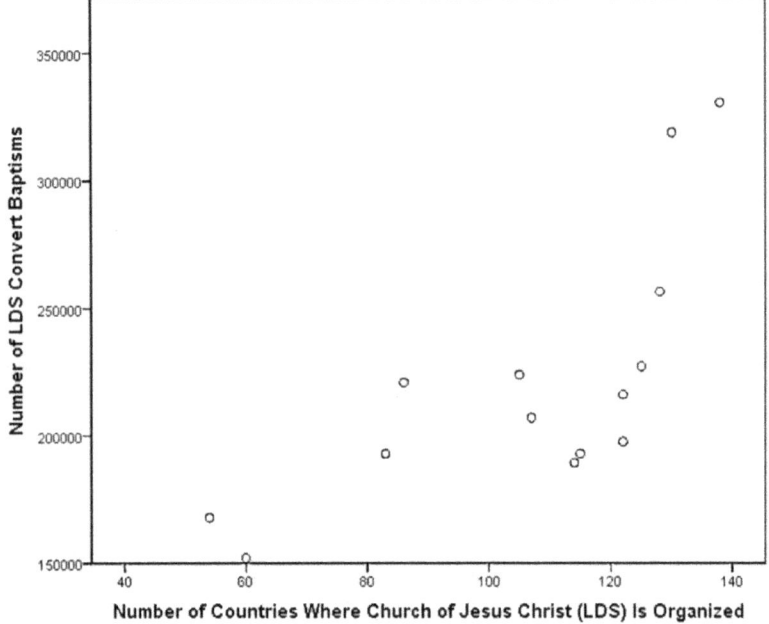

Figure B-2. **Convert baptisms and countries with LDS congregations, 1977-1990**

What we see in Figure B-2 looks like a curvilinear relationship in which the more countries there were with LDS congregations, the more convert baptisms there were—to a

---

[561] Osborne & Waters (2002).

Appendix B: The Slowing of Mormon Growth

point. Then, there was a severe dip, such that adding an LDS presence to more countries seems to result in *fewer* convert baptisms. (Here, the dip seems to occur between 100 and 120 countries.) After that point, there was a precipitous rise, such that adding an LDS presence to more countries again seemed to result in more convert baptisms (here, between 120 and 140 countries). One wonders what might happen if the LDS had a presence in even more countries, as the Saints did after 1990. That is the subject of the next multiple regression.

LDS GROWTH, 1991-2011: ALL ABOUT THE *COUNTRIES*

For the period from 1991 through 2012, I conducted a multiple regression with annual number of LDS converts as the dependent variable, and both annual number of missionaries serving, and the number of countries in which LDS were organized within a given year, as the two predictors. This multiple regression is reported in Tables B-5 and B-6. Here, the two predictor variables were not too highly correlated (Pearson's r = +0.44), so the assumption of non-multicollinearity was met here as well.[562]

For this period, all variables were approximately normally distributed; in all cases, the absolute value of skew and kurtosis were less than 0.51. However, scatterplots demonstrated that none of the variables were bivariate linearly related, violating an assumption of multiple regres-

---

[562] Licht (1995) p. 45. A scatterplot shows that these variables are non-linearly related, so a non-parametric measure of their association is preferable to Pearson's r; due to the small sample size, a better measure of their association than Kendall's tau is Spearman's rho, which here is still lower than the .80 criterion (rho = +0.306, N = 21, p = .088, setting α = .10 because we are testing assumptions).

sion[563]; in practical terms, this means we should interpret the analysis cautiously.

For this period, the number of missionaries serving simply was not a significant predictor of the number of LDS convert baptisms—a truly counterintuitive result, indeed. The number of countries where the Church had organized congregations *was* a significant predictor of convert baptisms—but in the ***negative*** direction. For each additional country added to the list where the Mormons had an organized presence, 1,300 *fewer* convert baptisms occurred ($B = -1,301.15$).

Here again, there are complications to the story.

To judge from Figure B-3, it appears that, for this period, there is nothing but a random relationship between the number of missionaries serving and the number of convert baptisms in any given year. It is not that there is a weak relationship; there is *no* relationship. The difference between this situation and that of the earlier period (compare Figure B-1) is striking.

Furthermore, to judge from Figure B-4, the relationship between the number of countries with LDS congregations and the number of convert baptisms is rather messy as well. There seems to have been a precipitous drop in convert baptisms as the number of countries with LDS congregations increased from about 162 to 176. Outside this range, the relationship between these two variables is unclear. (Here again, the lack of a clear linear relationship means that we should interpret the regression cautiously.)

---

[563] Osborne & Waters (2002).

Variable	M	SD	1	2
Annual Convert Baptisms	283,594.5	23,087	n.s.	-.499*
Predictor vars.:				
1. Missionaries serving	53,349.3	4,979	—	.443*
2. Countries w/ LDS congregations	168.9	11		—

*$p < .05$.

Table B-5. **Means, standard deviations, and intercorrelations for annual LDS convert baptisms and predictor variables, 1991-2011**

Variable	B	SE B	β	t	p
Missionaries serving	1.18	1.02	.26	1.16	.260
Countries w/ LDS congregations	-1,301.15	467.28	-.61	-2.78	.012

Note. Adjusted $R^2 = .22$ ($N = 21$, $p = .04$).

Table B-6. **Regression analysis summary for variables predicting annual LDS convert baptisms, 1991-2011**

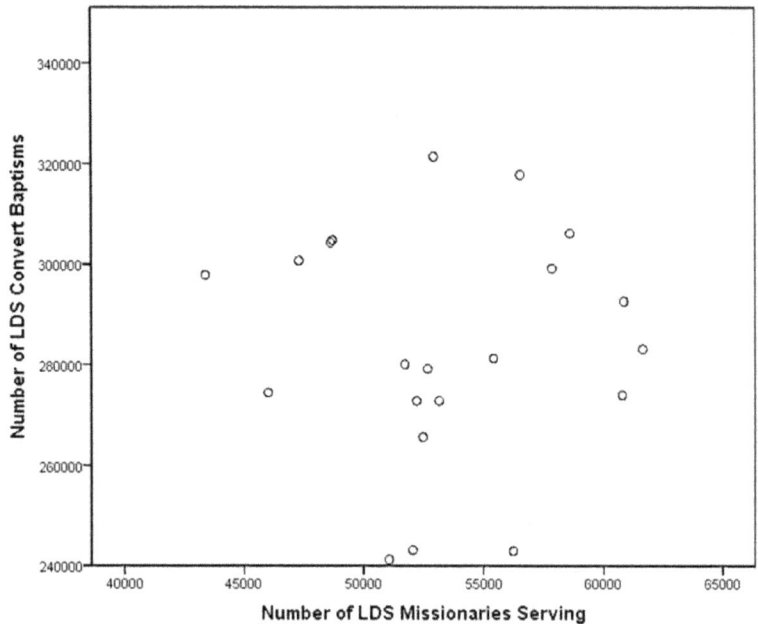

Figure B-3. Convert baptisms and missionaries serving, 1991-2012.

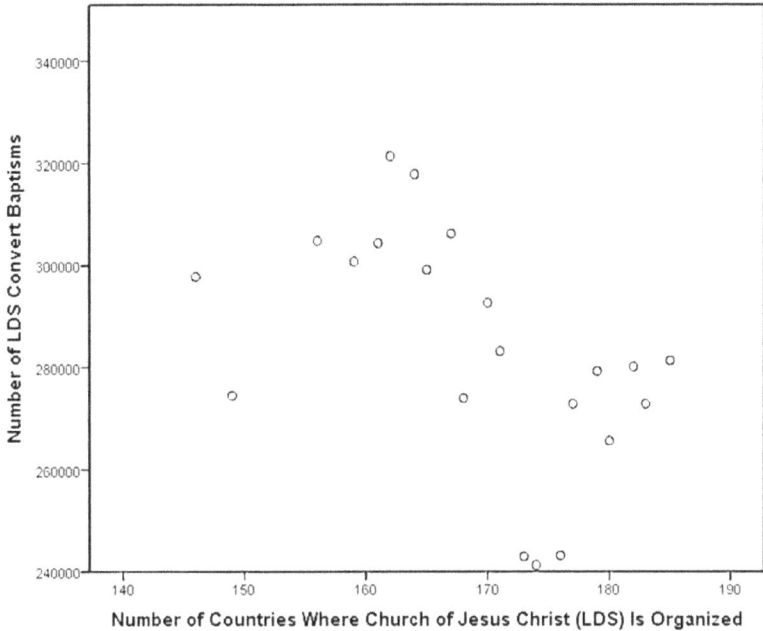

Figure B-4. Convert baptisms and countries with LDS congregations, 1991-2011.

Here is what I would tentatively conclude from this analysis:

1. The environment for LDS convert baptisms changed after 1990. I attribute this to the tremendous expansion of the Church into Eastern Europe and elsewhere, following the dissolution of the Soviet Union at the end of 1991. Thus, the evidence in this Appendix supports the contention that I made in Chapter 1, namely, that it was this expansion of the scope of LDS missionary work that slowed the rate of Mormon growth after 1990.

2. More generally, this evidence suggests that when a large number of new areas are opened for missionary work at around the same time, the overall rate of LDS growth will slow down.

3. The corollary of the preceding conclusions is that, with fewer countries seeing their *first* LDS congregations at this point [late 2012], the Saints are building up membership in countries where they have already *had* congregations. This will build the LDS "networks of faith" that Rodney Stark's model suggests are necessary for Church growth (see Chapter 1).

I would expect that, at some point post-2011, the environment for convert baptisms will be such that the more traditional relationship between the number of missionaries serving and the number of convert baptisms will reassert itself. That is, we will see a relationship between these variables that is less like Figure B-3 and more like Figure B-1. This will set the stage for major Mormon growth, as the size of the LDS missionary force grows (as I contend in Chapter 2 that it will).

Appendix C
Why Do People Convert to Mormonism?

The idea that it is the *beliefs* of a faith that result in conversion is out of favor among some researchers at present. Based on observation of the first people to join the Unification Church in San Francisco in the early 1960s, John Lofland and Rodney Stark developed a theory of conversion that emphasized the preservation of social capital:

> Eventually, Lofland and Stark realized that of all the people the Unificationists encountered in their efforts to spread their faith, the only ones who joined were those *whose interpersonal attachments to members overbalanced their attachments to nonmembers.*[564]

Stark and Finke later developed this theory to consider the preservation of both social and religious capital:

> *Definition 23.* **Social capital** consists of interpersonal attachments….
>
> PROPOSITION 29. In making religious choices [that is, choices among several alternatives among religions to join], people will attempt to conserve their **social capital**….
>
> *Definition 24.* **Religious capital** consists of the degree of mastery of and attachment to a particular religious culture….

---

[564] Stark & Finke (2000) p. 117, italics in original.

PROPOSITION 33. In making religious choices, people will attempt to conserve their religious capital.[565]

Currently, the Lofland-Stark-Finke theory is probably the most widely accepted theory of conversion in the sociology of religion. However, the available evidence shows that **this theory is a poor explanation of conversion to the LDS faith in particular.**

Contrary to what would be predicted by the Lofland-Stark-Finke theory, many LDS convert narratives involve an *increase* in tension between potential converts and their family and friends, created because of the convert's decision to become a Latter-day Saint.[566] Often, these narratives involve facing actual hostility from, and even being disowned by, the convert's non-LDS family.[567] Clearly, the preservation of social capital was *not* a primary consideration in making these converts' religious choices.

In addition, it is hard to reconcile the Lofland-Stark-Finke theory with the evidence that converts to Mormonism over the years have come from non-Christian religions, such as Buddhism,[568] Islam,[569] and Judaism.[570] Indeed,

---

[565] Stark & Finke (2000) pp. 118-121, emphases in original.

[566] E.g., Gilmour (2011); Kinnear (1973, p. 136); V.R. Ledbetter (1973, pp. 8-10); Wang (1973, Julie Wang's narrative).

[567] E.g., Borrowman (1996); I. H. Cohen (1971); Hinckley (1993); J.J. Johnson (2011); A.J.-J. Merrill (2011); "One Stalwart Pioneer" (2011).

[568] E.g., Lin (2011). Anecdotally, it appears that the vast majority of the LDS converts in Cambodia, Japan, Taiwan, and Thailand—where a total of 10 LDS missions were headquartered as of year-end 2010— were formerly Buddhist (and/or Shintō, in the case of Japan). These countries combined had an LDS population of over 205,000 at year-end 2010, an increase of 2.4% over 2009, which in turn was an increase of 33.9% over 1999. This growth occurred primarily through

many LDS converts have come from the ranks of the *clergy* of other Christian churches.[571] These are people who had quite a lot of religious capital to lose from a conversion to Mormonism: knowledge of their former church's history, religious traditions, and ceremony would be little if at all useful within their new LDS faith. Clearly, the preservation of religious capital was *not* a primary consideration when it came to making these converts' religious choices, either. Neither was the preservation of social capital; most former clergy conversion narratives mention a severing of social connections with the members of their former congregations upon the clergy's conversion to the LDS faith.

For that matter, although it is not mentioned in the Lofland-Stark-Finke theory, the preservation of *economic* capital was not the primary consideration when it came to making these converts' religious choices, either. Indeed, when the clergy of other Christian churches convert to Mormonism, the individuals involved usually lose their very livelihoods because of conversion to the LDS faith.

So why *do* LDS converts join the Church? Frequently, LDS converts cite spiritual factors, such as receiving testimony from the Holy Spirit that LDS teachings and the Church of Jesus Christ are true[572]; often, this testimony

---

convert baptisms. (Author's calculations from data in the 2001-2002, 2011, and 2012 editions of the *Deseret News Church Almanac*.)

[569] E.g., Husein (2012).

[570] E.g., I. H. Cohen (1971).

[571] E.g., Camargo (1973); Carlisle (1983); Dodds (1971); Francesca (1971, 1988); Heidenreich (1971), Herring (1983); C F. Ledbetter (1973); Novak (1976); Reiher (1983); Staley (1971); Whitlock (1973). These examples include only those who decided to convert to Mormonism *while actually serving* as clergy in other Christian churches.

[572] E.g., Baborka (1971); Brando (2010); Browning (1997) p. 174 (Reziukova narrative), pp. 205-206 (Malkova narrative), p. 221 (Kolesni-

comes in the form of a spiritual confirmation of the truth of the Book of Mormon, or of the LDS faith as approved by God.[573] Such a personal enlightenment is, in one convert's words, something "better felt than described."[574]

In other words, what leads many converts to become Mormons are *precisely* the beliefs and teachings of the Church of Jesus Christ—***but not these teachings in isolation.*** Rather, what leads to these conversions are LDS beliefs and teachings, *as these are spiritually confirmed* to the individual convert-to-be in an experience that he or she considers personal revelation, given by God to the potential convert through the Holy Spirit. This statement is consistent with the findings of a Pew Research study:

> When asked to describe in their own words their reasons for converting to Mormonism, 59% of converts cite the religion's beliefs as a reason. The most common responses within this category are general statements about the religion being true or making sense

---

kov narrative), p. 293 (Bazarskaia narr.); Cherry (1970, p. 41); Cowherd (2012); I. H. Cohen (1971) p. 62; Ford (1976) p. 171; Gibbons & Gibbons (2002) p. 8 (Snow narr.); Hamilton (2011, p. 51); Mikulina (2011); Sexton (2011); Wang (1973, p. 30, Julie Wang's narr.).

[573] E.g., Bush (1971), see also Bowen (1970); Browning (1997) p. 81 (Goncharova narrative), pp. 112-113 (Gavrilov narrative), p. 202 (Baltovskii narrative); Callister (2011); Chaffetz (2012); E. Davies (1971) p. 166; Francesca (1971, 1988); Gilardi (2012); Gillum (1973) p. 154; González (2011); Griffith (2012) esp. p. 138; "How the Book of Mormon Changed My Life" (2011); G. Jones (1976); Koltko-Rivera (2011a); Lee (2012); Lin (2011); Litster (1997, Tabango and Leaño narratives); Morris (2012), p. 31 (Leiva narrative); Romney (1971); Schulte (2010); Shipps & Welch (1994) pp. 29-30, 33-34; Whitlock (1973).

[574] Cope (2012) p. 50.

(38%), as well as statements about the Book of Mormon or other scriptures (13%). Mormonism's emphasis on the family and family values is cited as a reason for converting by 5% of converts, and 3% cite the faith's specific teaching that families can be bound together for eternity. Roughly one-quarter of converts to Mormonism (23%) cite issues of personal spirituality as reasons for their conversion, including 17% who say they felt called by God or "gained a testimony."[575]

In sum, at least for most American LDS converts, it is the religious beliefs that they cite as reasons for their conversions. About one-sixth of these converts state that they received a calling from God, or were "led by prayer" or "received a testimony" (presumably, of the truth of the Church's teachings) and that this was a factor in their conversions.

---

[575] *Mormons in America* (2012) p. 48; see also p. 118. Survey respondents were allowed to cite more than one reason for their conversion.

Appendix D

Tracking Charts: Projected Vs. Actual Mormon Growth, 2011-2040

Some readers of this book will be interested in comparing the Church's actual growth to the predictions that I have made. If nothing else, this would allow the reader to see whether the Church's real growth resembles more the beginnings of the low-growth, moderate-growth, or high-growth projections that I have put forth.

Many readers will be available to follow the performance of these projections through, say, 2040—at which point, it should be clear which of my projections most closely matches the actual growth of the Church. Below, I give the year-by-year predictions of each projection, along with a space for the reader to write the actual figure for the population of the Church in a given year.

The total worldwide membership of the Church of Jesus Christ in any given year is reported annually at the following year's Annual General Conference in April. This figure is reported in the May issue of the Church's magazine for adults, the *Ensign* (currently available online at http://www.lds.org/ensign). Thus, the year-end 2010 global membership figures were reported in the April 2011 General Conference and appeared in the May 2011 issue of the *Ensign*. The Church has published the *Ensign* since 1970, and shows every sign of intent to continue to publish it for the forseeable future.

The total membership of the Church in the United States is published in the *Deseret News Church Almanac*, typically with a lag of two years (U.S. figures being available at: http://www.ldschurchnews.com/almanac/). Thus, the year-end 2010 U.S. membership figures were published in the *Deseret News 2012 Church Almanac*. The Church-owned *Deseret News* has published the *Almanac* since 1973, and shows every sign of intent to continue to publish it for the forseeable future, as well.

The three projections for worldwide membership yield identical predictions through 2013.

MORMON GROWTH WORLDWIDE, 2012-2040

Year	Projections			Actual
	Low-Growth	Mod.-Growth	High-Growth	
2011				14,441,346
2012	14,744,614	14,744,614	14,744,614	
2013	15,039,507	15,039,507	15,039,507	
2014	15,340,297	15,347,816	15,355,336	
2015	15,647,103	15,670,121	15,693,154	
2016	15,960,045	16,007,028	16,054,096	
2017	16,279,246	16,359,183	16,439,394	
2018	16,604,830	16,727,264	16,850,379	
2019	16,936,927	17,111,991	17,288,489	
2020	17,275,666	17,514,123	17,755,278	

2021	17,621,179	17,934,462	18,252,426
2022	17,973,603	18,373,857	18,781,747
2023	18,333,075	18,833,203	19,345,199
2024	18,699,736	19,313,450	19,944,900
2025	19,073,731	19,815,599	20,583,137
2026	19,455,205	20,340,713	21,262,380
2027	19,844,310	20,889,912	21,985,301
2028	20,241,196	21,464,385	22,754,787
2029	20,646,020	22,065,387	23,573,959
2030	21,058,940	22,694,251	24,446,196
2031	21,480,119	23,352,384	25,375,151
2032	21,909,721	24,041,279	26,364,782
2033	22,347,916	24,762,518	27,419,373
2034	22,794,874	25,517,775	28,543,568
2035	23,250,771	26,308,826	29,742,397
2036	23,715,787	27,137,554	31,021,321
2037	24,190,103	28,005,955	32,386,259
2038	24,673,905	28,916,149	33,843,640
2039	25,167,383	29,870,382	35,400,448
2040	25,670,730	30,871,040	37,064,269

MORMON GROWTH IN THE UNITED STATES, 2012-2040

Year	Projections			Actual
	Low-Growth	Mod.-Growth	High-Growth	
2010				6,144,582
2011	6,231,835	6,232,450	6,233,678	
2012	6,320,950	6,322,820	6,326,560	
2013	6,411,972	6,415,765	6,423,357	
2014	6,504,946	6,511,360	6,524,203	
2015	6,599,918	6,609,682	6,629,243	
2016	6,696,937	6,710,810	6,738,626	
2017	6,796,051	6,814,828	6,852,508	
2018	6,897,312	6,921,820	6,971,057	
2019	7,000,772	7,031,877	7,094,444	
2020	7,106,484	7,145,091	7,222,854	
2021	7,214,502	7,261,556	7,356,477	
2022	7,324,884	7,381,371	7,495,514	
2023	7,437,687	7,504,640	7,640,177	
2024	7,552,972	7,631,469	7,790,689	
2025	7,670,798	7,761,967	7,947,282	
2026	7,791,229	7,896,249	8,110,201	
2027	7,914,331	8,034,433	8,279,704	

Year			
2028	8,040,169	8,176,643	8,456,062
2029	8,168,811	8,323,004	8,639,559
2030	8,300,329	8,473,651	8,830,493
2031	8,434,795	8,628,719	9,029,179
2032	8,572,282	8,788,350	9,235,947
2033	8,712,867	8,952,692	9,451,145
2034	8,856,630	9,121,898	9,675,137
2035	9,003,650	9,296,126	9,908,308
2036	9,154,011	9,475,541	10,151,061
2037	9,306,882	9,660,314	10,403,822
2038	9,462,307	9,850,623	10,667,039
2039	9,620,328	10,046,650	10,941,182
2040	9,780,987	10,248,588	11,226,747

References

Notes. The LDS scriptures ("LDS Standard Works") are available for online viewing at www.lds.org; as of late September 2012, the reader at that site need only click the "Scriptures" tab. (The LDS Standard Works include the King James Version of the Christian Bible, the Book of Mormon, the Doctrine and Covenants, and the Pearl of Great Price.)

The *Church News* is a weekly section of the *Deseret News*, a daily newspaper published in Salt Lake City, Utah, by The Church of Jesus Christ of Latter-day Saints.

The official English-language magazine for adults published by the LDS Church is *The Ensign of The Church of Jesus Christ of Latter-day Saints*, and here is indicated simply as *Ensign*.

"A Call for Missionaries." (2011, February). *Ensign*, pp. 8-9. Online at https://www.lds.org/ensign/2011/02/a-call-for-missionaries

Addiction Recovery Program: A guide to addiction recovery and healing. (2005). Salt Lake City, UT: The Church of Jesus Christ of Latter-day Saints, LDS Family Services. Available online at http://addictionrecovery.lds.org/addiction-recovery-program-guide

Agar, Nicholas. (2010). *Humanity's end: Why we should reject radical enhancement.* Cambridge, MA: The MIT Press.

Albrecht, Stan L. (1998). The consequential dimension of Mormon religiosity. In James T. Duke (Ed.), *Latter-day Saint social life: Social research on the LDS Church and its members* (pp. 253-292). Provo, UT: Brigham Young University, Religious Studies Center.

Albrecht, Stan L., and Tim B. Heaton. (1998). Secularization, higher education, and religiosity. In James T. Duke (Ed.), *Latter-day Saint social life: Social research on the LDS Church and its members* (pp. 293-314). Provo, UT: Brigham Young Univ., Religious Studies Center.

Alexander, Brian. (2003). *Rapture: How biotech became the new religion.* New York, NY: Basic Books/Perseus Books Group.

Ali, Ayaan Hirsi. (2012, February 13). The rise of Christophobia. *Newsweek*, pp. 28-35.

"Alive and well: Special report: Judaism and the Jews." (2012, July 28-August 3). *The Economist*, bound between pages 42-43.

Allen, James B., & Glen M. Leonard (1992). *The story of the Latter-day Saints* (2nd ed.). Salt Lake City, UT: Deseret Book Company.

Allison, Graham. (2004). *Nuclear terrorism: The ultimate preventable catastrophe*. New York, NY: Times Books/Henry Holt & Co.

Anti-Christian violence on the rise in India [online news release]. (1999, October 1). Retrieved March 7, 2012 from http://www.hrw.org/en/news/1999/09/29/anti-christian-violence-rise-india

"Apostle creates first stake in India." (2012, June 1, 4). Retrieved June 21, 2012 from the website of the online newsroom (headquarters edition) of The Church of Jesus Christ of Latter-day Saints, http://www.mormonnewsroom.org/article/apostle-creates-first-stake-india

Appenzeller, Tim. (2005, October). Tracking the next killer flu. *National Geographic, 208*(4), pp. 2-31.

Arrington, Leonard. (2012). *Brigham Young: American Moses*. New York, NY: Vintage/Random House. (Original work published 1985)

Arrington, Leonard J., & Davis Bitton. (1992). *The Mormon experience: A history of the Latter-day Saints* (2nd ed.). Urbana, IL: University of Illinois Press.

Arrington, Leonard J., Feramorz Y. Fox, & Dean L. May. (1976). *Building the city of God: Community and cooperation among the Mormons*. Salt Lake City, UT: Deseret Book Co.

Asimov, Isaac. (1950). *I, robot*. New York, NY: Gnome Press.

Atkin, Rebekah. (2011, December). The key to opportunity: Celebrating 10 years of the Perpetual Education Fund. *Ensign*, pp. 40-45. Online at http://www.lds.org/ensign/2011/12/the-key-to-opportunity-celebrating-10-years-of-the-perpetual-education-fund

Baborka, Clifford J., Jr. (1971). "Hired" by the Lord. In Hartman Rector & Connie Rector (Eds.), *No more strangers* ([vol. 1,] pp. 72-81). Salt Lake City, UT: Bookcraft.

Baggott, Jim. (2012). *Higgs: The invention and discovery of the 'God particle.'* Oxford, England, UK: Oxford University Press.

Bahr, Stephen J. (1994). Religion and adolescent drug use: A comparison of Mormons and other religions. In Marie Cornwall,

Tim B. Heaton, & Lawrence A. Young (Eds.), *Contemporary Mormonism: Social science perspectives* (pp. 118-137). Urbana, IL: University of Illinois Press.

Ballard, M. Russell. (2002, November). The greatest generation of missionaries. *Ensign*. Online at http://www.lds.org/ensign/2002/11/the-greatest-generation-of-missionaries

Ballard, M. Russell. (2011, November). The importance of a name. *Ensign*, pp. 79-82. Available online at http://www.lds.org/ensign/2011/11/the-importance-of-a-name

Bardi, Ugo. (2011). *The limits to growth revisited*. New York, NY: Springer Science+Business Media LLC.

Barna Group. (2011, September 28). *Six reasons young Christians leave church* [webpage]. Accessed September 8, 2012 at http://www.barna.org/teens-next-gen-articles/528-six-reasons-young-christians-leave-church

Barnett, Cynthia. (2001, December). The church's ranch. *Florida Trend*, pp. 56-61. Retrieved March 3, 2012, from http://www.cynthiabarnett.net/ clips/ChurchRanch.pdf

Barrett, David B., Todd M. Johnson, & Peter F. Crossing (2007). Worldwide adherents of all religions, mid-2006 [table]. In *Encyclopaedia Britannica 2007 book of the year*, pp. 292-293. Chicago, IL: Encyclopaedia Britannica, Inc.

Barry, John M. (2004). *The great influenza: The epic story of the deadliest plague in history*. New York, NY: Viking/Penguin.

Basic physical health with limited resources: The beginning of self-reliance. (2010). Salt Lake City, UT: The Church of Jesus Christ of Latter-day Saints.

Berger, Joseph. (2012, June 12). With Orthodox growth, city's Jewish population is climbing again. *The New York Times* [late edition], p. A18.

Berger, Peter L. (1999). The desecularization of the world: A global overview. In Peter L. Berger (Ed.), *The desecularization of the world: Resurgent religion and world politics* (pp. 1-18). Washington, DC: Ethics and Public Policy Center, and Grand Rapids, MI: Eerdmans.

Berger, Peter, Grace Davie, & Effie Fokas. (2008). *Religious America, secular Europe? A theme and variations*. Burlington, VT: Ashgate.

Bergin, Allen E., I. Reed Payne, Paul H. Jenkins, & Marie Cornwall. (1994). Religion and mental health: Mormons and other groups. In Marie Cornwall, Tim B. Heaton, & Lawrence A. Young (Eds.), *Contemporary Mormonism: Social science perspectives* (pp. 138-158). Urbana, IL: University of Illinois Press.

Bible, The: See *Notes* at the beginning of this References section.

Black, Susan Easton. (1996). *Expressions of faith: Testimonies of Latter-day Saint scholars.* Salt Lake City, UT: Deseret Book Company, and Provo, UT: Foundation for Ancient Research and Mormon Studies.

Blascovich, Jim, & Jeremy Bailenson. (2011). *Infinite reality: Avatars, eternal life, new worlds, and the dawn of the virtual revolution.* New York, NY: William Morrow/HarperCollins.

Book of Mormon, The: See *Notes* at the beginning of this References section.

Borrowman, Jerry. (1996, September). A halfpenny and a pearl. *Ensign,* pp. 23-25. Online at http://www.lds.org/ensign/1996/09/a-halfpenny-and-a-pearl

Boss, Alan. (2009). *The crowded universe: The race to find life beyond Earth.* New York, NY: Basic Books/Perseus Book Group.

Bostrom, Nick. (2005, April). A history of transhumanism. *Journal of Evolution and Technology, 14*(1). Online at http://jetpress.org/volume14/bostrom.pdf

Bowen, Donna. (1970, week ending May 16). Book of Mormon reader converted on first page. *Church News,* p. 11. Online at http://news.google.com/newspapers?nid=336&dat=19700516&id=MJBaAAAAIBAJ&sjid=WEoDAAAAIBAJ&pg=5587,3996801

Bowman, Matthew. (2012). *The Mormon people: The making of an American faith.* New York, NY: Random House.

Bowring, Finn. (2003). *Science, seeds and cyborgs: Biotechnology and the appropriation of life.* New York, NY: Verso.

Boyé, Alex. (2012). Alex Boyé. In Joseph A. Cannon (Ed.), *Why I'm a Mormon* (pp. 31-37). n.p.: Ensign Peak.

Boylan, Michael, & Kevin E. Brown. (2001). *Genetic engineering: Science and ethics on the new frontier.* Upper Saddle River, NJ: Prentice Hall.

Brand, Stewart. (2009). *Whole earth discipline: An ecopragmatist manifesto.* New York, NY: Viking/Penguin.

Brando, Maria. (2010, December). Latter-day Saint voices: I defended the Prophet Joseph. *Ensign*, p. 67. Online at http://www.lds.org/ensign/2010/12/latter-day-saint-voices

Britsch, R. Lanier. (1986). *Unto the islands of the sea: A history of the Latter-day Saints in the Pacific.* Salt Lake City, UT: Deseret Book Co.

Britsch, R. Lanier. (1998). *From the East: The history of the Latter-day Saints in Asia, 1851-1996.* Salt Lake City, UT: Deseret Book Co.

Brockman, John (Ed.). (2002). *The next fifty years: Science in the first half of the twenty-first century.* New York, NY: Vintage/Random House.

Broderick, Damien. (2001). *The spike: How our lives are being transformed by rapidly advancing technologies.* New York, NY: Forge.

Brooks, Max. (2003). *The zombie survival guide: Complete protection from the living dead.* New York, NY: Three Rivers Press/Random House.

Brooks, Max. (2006). *World War Z: An oral history of the Zombie War.* New York, NY: Crown Publishers/Random House.

Brown, Lester R. (2003). *Plan B: Rescuing a planet under stress and a civilization in trouble.* New York, NY: W. W. Norton.

Brown, Lester R. (2011). *World on the edge: How to prevent environmental and economic collapse.* New York, NY: W. W. Norton.

Brown, Matthew B., & Paul Thomas Smith. (1997). *Symbols in stone: Symbolism on the early temples of the Restoration.* American Fork, UT: Covenant Communications.

Brown, Samuel Morris. (2012). *In heaven as it is on earth: Joseph Smith and the early Mormon conquest of death.* New York, NY: Oxford University Press.

Browning, Gary. (1997). *Russia and the restored gospel.* Salt Lake City, UT: Deseret Book Co.

Browning, Gary. (2000). Russia and the Restoration. In *Out of obscurity: The LDS Church in the twentieth century: The 29th Annual Sidney B. Sperry Symposium* (pp. 63-75). Salt Lake City, UT: Deseret Book Co.

Buchanan, Allen. (2011). *Beyond humanity? The ethics of biomedical enhancement.* New York, NY: Oxford University Press.

Bueno, José M. Miguel. (2012, Week of July 8). Education moments: A better future. *Church News*, p. 16. Online at http://www.ldschurchnews.com/articles/62498/Education-moments-A-better-future.html

Burger, William C. (2003). *Perfect planet, clever species: How unique are we?* Amherst, NY: Prometheus Books.

Bush, Edna K. (1971). Blessed with the Comforter. In Hartman Rector & Connie Rector (Eds.), *No more strangers* ([vol. 1,] pp. 37-46). Salt Lake City, UT: Bookcraft.

Bushman, Claudia Lauper, & Richman Lyman Bushman. (2001). *Building the kingdom: A history of Mormons in America.* New York, NY: Oxford University Press.

Bushman, Richard Lyman. (2005). *Joseph Smith: Rough stone rolling.* New York, NY: Knopf.

Butterworth, G. W. (1919). *Clement of Alexandria: Exhortation to the Greeks, The rich man's salvation, To the newly baptized* (Loeb Classical Library vol. 92). Cambridge, MA: Harvard University Press.

"BYU Museum of Paleontology" [website]. (2006). Accessed September 11, 2012 at http://cpms.byu.edu/ESM/index.html

Callister, Tad R. (2011, November). The Book of Mormon—a book from God. *Ensign,* pp. 74-76. Online at http://www.lds.org/ensign/2011/11/the-book-of-mormon-a-book-from-god

Camargo, Helio da Rocha. (1973). I. In the fulness of light. In Hartman Rector & Connie Rector (Eds.), *No more strangers* (vol. 2, pp. 104-109). Salt Lake City, UT: Bookcraft.

Cantor, Norman F. (2001). *In the wake of the plague: The Black Death and the world it made.* New York, NY: HarperCollins.

Carlisle, Norman. (1983). I was just simply curious. In Stephen W. Gibson (Ed.), *From clergy to convert* (pp. 40-46). Salt Lake City, UT: Bookcraft.

Carlson, Rick J., & Gary Stimeling. (2002). *The terrible gift: The brave new world of genetic medicine.* New York, NY: Public Affairs/Perseus.

Casti, John. (2012). *X-events: The collapse of everything.* New York, NY: William Morrow/HarperCollins.

The Career Workshop: Participant's workbook. (2004). Salt Lake City, UT: The Church of Jesus Christ of Latter-day Saints, LDS Employment Resource Services.

Center for Applied Research in the Apostolate. (2012). *Frequently requested church statistics* [online document]. Retrieved March 3,

2012 from http://cara.georgetown.edu/CARAServices/requestedchurchstats.html

Chaffetz, Jason. (2012). Jason Chaffetz. In Joseph A. Cannon (Ed.), *Why I'm a Mormon* (pp. 47-53). n.p.: Ensign Peak.

Chapman, Audrey R., & Mark S. Frankel (Eds.). (2003). *Designing our descendants: The promises and perils of genetic modifications.* Baltimore, MD: The Johns Hopkins University Press.

Cherry, Alan Gerald. (1970). *It's you and me, Lord!* Salt Lake City, UT: Bookcraft.

Chingos, Matthew M., & Michael Henderson. (2012, May). *Does Mitt Romney have a "religion problem"?* Washington, DC: Brookings Institution. Retrieved August 8, 2012 from http://www.brookings.edu/~/media/research/files/papers/2012/5/15%20romney%20lds%20chingos/chingoshenderson%20mormon%20paper%20final.pdf

Christensen, Clayton M., James Allworth, & Karen Dillon. (2012). *How will you measure your life?* New York, NY: HarperCollins.

Christensen, Michael J., & Jeffrey A. Wittung (Eds.). (2007). *Partakers of the divine nature: The history and development of deification in the Christian traditions.* Grand Rapids, MI: Baker Academic.

"The church and its financial independence." (2012, July 12). News release from the online newsroom (headquarters edition) of The Church of Jesus Christ of Latter-day Saints. Available at http://www.mormonnewsroom.org/article/church-financial-independence

"Church in talks to 'regularize' activities in China" [online news report]. (2010, August 30). Retrieved June 22, 2012 from http://www.lds.org.hk/en/index.php/worldwide-events-2010/205-church-in-talks-with-china

"Church providing relief to Hurricane Katrina victims." (2005, September 1). News release online at http://www.mormonnewsroom.org/article/church-providing-relief-to-hurricane-katrina-victims

Clark, Andy. (2003). *Natural-born cyborgs: Minds, technologies, and the future of human intelligence.* New York, NY: Oxford University Press.

Clarke, Arthur C. (1953). *Childhood's end.* New York, NY: Ballantine.

Close, Frank. (2011). *The infinity puzzle: Quantum field theory and the hunt for an orderly universe.* New York, NY: Basic Books/Perseus.

"Closer to encounter: Extra-terrestrial life." (2012, August 4-10). *The Economist, 404*(8796), pp. 69-70, 72.

Cohen, Irving H. (1971). A Jew finds the true Messiah. In Hartman Rector & Connie Rector (Eds.), *No more strangers* ([vol. 1,] pp. 56-66). Salt Lake City, UT: Bookcraft. (Online audio versions available at http://www.ldsconverts.com/docs/cohen_short.mp3 and http://www.ldsconverts.com/docs/cohen_full.mp3)

Cohen, Jacob. (1992). A power primer. *Psychological Bulletin, 112*(1), 155-159.

Cole-Turner, Ronald (Ed.). (2011). *Transhumanism and transcendence: Christian hope in an age of technological enhancement.* Washington, DC: Georgetown University Press.

Colemere, Michael. (2012, April 2). The Church's digital communications and technology solutions. In *In the public eye: How the Church is handling increased visibility* (LDS International Society, 23rd Annual Conference; pp. 24-26). Provo, UT: Brigham Young University, David M. Kennedy Center for International Studies. Retrieved July 2012, from http://www.ldsinternationalsociety.org/

Convert from India: Letter of inquiry led to baptism. (1970, week ending May 2). *Church News*, p. 11. Online at http://news.google.com/newspapers?nid=336&dat=19700502&id=i0QKAAAAIBAJ&sjid=WEoDAAAAIBAJ&pg=3857,498126

Cope, Rachel. (2012, March). Nancy Naomi Alexander Tracy: Faithful pioneer. *Ensign*, pp. 48-51. Online at http://www.lds.org/ensign/2012/03/nancy-naomi-alexander-tracy-faithful-pioneer

Covey, Stephen R. (1989). *The 7 habits of highly effective people.* New York, NY: Simon & Schuster.

Covey, Stephen R., Merrill, A. Roger, & Merrill, Rebecca R. (1994). *First things first: To live, to love, to learn, to leave a legacy.* New York, NY: Simon & Schuster.

Cowan, Richard O. (2000). Richard Lloyd Anderson and worldwide church growth. In Stephen D. Ricks, Donald W. Parry, & Andrew H. Hedges (Eds.), *The disciple as witness: Essays on Latter-day Saint history and doctrine in honor of Richard Lloyd Anderson* (pp. 105-115). Provo, UT: The Foundation for Ancient Research and Mormon Studies at Brigham Young University.

Cowherd, Margaret (Peggy) Meade. (2012). Margaret Meade Cowherd (Peggy). In Joseph A. Cannon (Ed.), *Why I'm a Mormon* (pp. 88-93). n.p.: Ensign Peak.

Cracroft, Richard H., & Neal E. Lambert (Eds.). (1974). *A believing people: Literature of the Latter-day Saints*. Provo, UT: Brigham Young University Press.

Cranney, Charles. (2012, July/August). The church in Russia. *LDS Living, 11* (issue whole no. 60), pp. 71-77.

Cronin, Justin. (2010). *The passage: A novel*. New York NY: Ballantine.

Crosby, Alfred W. (1989). *America's forgotten pandemic: The influenza of 1918*. Cambridge, England, UK: Cambridge University Press. (Original work published 1976)

Crosby, Alfred W. (2003). *America's forgotten pandemic: The influenza of 1918* (2nd ed.). New York, NY: Cambridge University Press.

Dant, Doris R. (1999). Minerva Teichert's Manti Temple murals. *BYU Studies, 38*(3), 6-44.

Datlow, Ellen (Ed.). (2009). *Lovecraft unbound: Twenty stories*. Milwaukie, OR: Dark Horse Books.

David M. Kennedy Center for International Studies, Brigham Young University. (2012). *China Teachers Program* [online document]. Retrieved March 2012 from http://kennedy.byu.edu/chinateachers/#

Davie, Grace. (1999). Europe: The exception that proves the rule? In Peter L. Berger (Ed.), *The desecularization of the world: Resurgent religion and world politics* (pp. 65-83). Washington, DC: Ethics and Public Policy Center, and Grand Rapids, MI: Eerdmans.

Davies, Eileen. (1971). A Catholic nun discovers the Gospel. In Hartman Rector & Connie Rector (Eds.), *No more strangers* ([vol. 1,] pp. 158-168). Salt Lake City, UT: Bookcraft. Online at http://testimonies.20m.com/A%20Catholic%20Nun%20Discovers%20The%20Gospel.htm

Davies, Paul. (2003, September). E. T. and God. *The Atlantic Monthly, 292*(2), pp. 112-116, 118. Text online at http://www.theatlantic.com/past/docs/issues/2003/09/davies.htm

Davies, Pete. (2000). *The devil's flu: The world's deadliest influenza epidemic and the scientific hunt for the virus that caused it*. New York, NY: Owl/Henry Holt & Co. (Original work published 1999).

Dawkins, Richard. (2006). *The God delusion.* Boston, MA: Houghton Mifflin.

Deakyne, Kimberly Jean. (1997, January). We followed the prophets' counsel. *Ensign.* Online at http://www.lds.org/ensign/1997/01/we-followed-the-prophets-counsel

Deseret News 1974 church almanac. (1974). Salt Lake City, UT: Deseret News.

Deseret News 1976 church almanac. (1976). Salt Lake City, UT: Deseret News.

Deseret News 1982 church almanac. (1981). Salt Lake City, UT: Deseret News.

Deseret News 1989-1990 church almanac. (1988). Salt Lake City, UT: Deseret News.

Deseret News 1999-2000 church almanac. (1998). Salt Lake City, UT: Deseret News.

Deseret News 2001-2002 church almanac. (2000). Salt Lake City, UT: Deseret News.

Deseret Morning News 2004 church almanac. (2004). Salt Lake City, UT: Deseret News.

Deseret News 2011 church almanac. (2011). Salt Lake City, UT: Deseret News.

Deseret News 2012 church almanac. (2012). Salt Lake City, UT: Deseret News.

Deseret Ranches [website]. ([2012]). Site consulted March 3, 2012, at http://www.deseretranchflorida.com/index.html

Dick, Steven J. (1996). *The biological universe: The twentieth-century extraterrestrial life debate and the limits of science.* New York, NY: Cambridge University Press.

Dick, Steven J. (Ed.). (2000). *Many worlds: The new universe, extraterrestrial life, and the theological implications.* Philadelphia, PA: Templeton Foundation Press.

Doctrine and Covenants, The: See *Notes* at the beginning of this References section.

Dodds, Erika. (1971). Conversion in Kashmir [Mangal Dan Dipty]. In Hartman Rector & Connie Rector (Eds.), *No more strangers* ([vol. 1,] pp. 139-144). Salt Lake City, UT: Bookcraft.

Doring, Adolfo (Director). (2008). *Blind spot* [documentary motion picture]. n.p.: Dislexic Films.

Dubuffet, Jean. (1996). Anticultural positions (1951). In Kristine Stiles & Peter Selz (Eds.) *Theories and documents of contemporary art: A sourcebook of artists' writings* (pp. 192-197). Berkeley, CA: University of California Press. (Original work published 1960)

Duffy, John-Charles. (2005, September). The new missionary discussions and the future of correlation. *Sunstone*, pp. 28-39. 42-46. Online at https://www.sunstonemagazine.com/pdf/138-28-46.pdf

Duncan, Kirsty. (2003). *Hunting the 1918 flu: One scientist's search for a killer virus*. Toronto, Ontario, Canada: University of Toronto Press.

Durham, W. Cole, Jr. (2008). The impact of secularization on proselytism in Europe: A minority religion perspective. In Reid L. Neilson (Ed.), *Global Mormonism in the 21st century* (pp. 114-133). Provo, UT: Brigham Young University, Religious Studies Center. (Original paper delivered 1999)

Eagleman, David. (2011). *Incognito: The secret lives of the brain*. New York, NY: Pantheon/Random House.

"Ebola outbreak in DRC risks spreading to towns: WHO" [online news story] (2012, September 13). Reuters website [U.S. edition]. Accessed September 15, 2012 at http://www.reuters.com/article/2012/09/13/us-congo-democratic-ebola-idUSBRE88C0LS20120913

Ehrlich, Paul R., Carl Sagan, & Donald Kennedy. (1984). *The cold and the dark: The world after nuclear war*. New York, NY: W. W. Norton.

"Elder Oaks establishes first stake in India." (2012, July/August). *LDS Living, 11*, whole no. 60, p. 20.

Eldredge, Niles. (1997). *Dominion*. Berkeley, CA: University of California Press. (Original work published 1995)

Eldredge, Niles. (1998). *Life in the balance: Humanity and the biodiversity crisis*. Princeton, NJ: Princeton University Press.

Elliott, Carl. (2003, Autumn). Humanity 2.0. *The Wilson Quarterly, 27*(4), 13-20.

Ellis, Stanley G. (2012, August). Natural disasters: We don't have to be afraid. *Ensign*, pp. 22-25. Online at http://www.lds.org/ensign/2012/08/natural-disasters-we-dont-have-to-be-afraid

England, Eugene (Ed.). (1992). *Bright angels and familiars: Contemporary Mormon stories.* Salt Lake City, UT: Signature Books.

Enstrom, James E. (1998a). Health practices and cancer mortality among active California Mormons. In James T. Duke (Ed.), *Latter-day Saint social life: Social research on the LDS Church and its members* (pp. 441-460). Provo, UT: Brigham Young University, Religious Studies Center.

Enstrom, James E. (1998b). Health practices and mortality among active California Mormons, 1980-93. In James T. Duke (Ed.), *Latter-day Saint social life: Social research on the LDS Church and its members* (pp. 461-471). Provo, UT: Brigham Young University, Religious Studies Center.

Evans, Gary LeRoy. (2012, January). My journey from alcoholism to sobriety. *Ensign,* pp. 61-65. Online at http://www.lds.org/ensign/2012/01/my-journey-from-alcoholism-to-sobriety

Evenson, William E. (Ed.). (1992a). [BYU evolution packet]. Accessed September 10, 2012 at http://www.sciencebysteve.net/wp-content/papers/EvolutionPacket.pdf

Evenson, William E. (1992b). Evolution. In Daniel H. Ludlow (Ed.), *Encyclopedia of Mormonism* (Vol. 1, p. 478). New York, NY: Macmillan. Accessed September 10, 2012 at http://eom.byu.edu/index.php/Evolution

Evenson, William E., & Duane E. Jeffery (Eds.). (2005) *Mormonism and evolution: The authoritative LDS statements.* Salt Lake City, UT: Greg Kofford Books.

"Extremely Low Attention Demand Information Systems (ELADIS)" [webpage]. (2006). *SITIS Archives—Topic Details* [website]. Accessed September 8, 2012 at http://www.dodsbir.net/sitis/archives_display_topic.asp?Bookmark=29100

Eyring, Henry. (1967). *The faith of a scientist.* Salt Lake City, UT: Bookcraft.

Eyring, Henry B. (1999). *Learning in the light of faith: The compatibility of scholarship and discipleship.* West Valley City, UT: Bookcraft.

Faivre, Antoine. (1994). *Access to Western esotericism.* Albany, NY: State University of New York Press.

Faivre, Antoine. (1998). Renaissance Hermeticism and the concept of Western esotericism. In Roelf van den Broek & Wouter J.

Hanegraaff (Eds.), *Gnosis and Hermeticism: From antiquity to modern times* (pp. 109-123). Albany, NY: State University of NY Press.

The family finance workshop: Facilitator's guide. (2010). Salt Lake City, UT: The Church of Jesus Christ of Latter-day Saints, LDS Employment Resource Services.

The family finance workshop: Participant's guide. (2010). Salt Lake City, UT: The Church of Jesus Christ of Latter-day Saints, LDS Employment Resource Services.

Family first [booklet]. (1992). Salt Lake City, UT: The Church of Jesus Christ of Latter-day Saints.

Family guidebook. (2006). Salt Lake City, UT: The Church of Jesus Christ of Latter-day Saints. Online at http://www.lds.org/bc/content/shared/content/english/pdf/31180_FamilyGuidebook/fg-2010-00-complete-eng.pdf

Family Home [website]. (2010). Online at http://www.lds.org/ldsorg/v/index.jsp?locale=0&vgnextoid=2164d7f57d716010VgnVCM1000004e94610aRCRD

Family Home Evening [website]. (2012). Online at http://www.lds.org/topics/family-home-evening

Family Home Evening resource book. (1997). Salt Lake City, UT: The Church of Jesus Christ of Latter-day Saints. Online at http://www.lds.org/ ldsorg/v/index.jsp?locale=0&sourceId=ba20a41f6cc20110VgnVCM100000176f620a____&vgnextoid=7b2a5f74db46c010VgnVCM1000004d82620aRCRD

Fassihi, Farnaz. (2012, September 15-16). Amid chaos, extremists spur violence. *The Wall Street Journal*, p. A6.

Finke, Roger, & Rodney Stark. (2005). *The churching of America, 1776-2005: Winners and losers in our religious economy* (2nd ed.). New Brunswick, NJ: Rutgers University Press.

Finlan, Stephen, & Vladimir Kharlamov (Eds.). (2006). *Theōsis: Deification in Christian theology.* Eugene, OR: Pickwick Publications/Wipf & Stock.

Fischer, Bryan. (2011). *First Amendments according to the founding fathers* (online video). Retrieved February 24, 2012 from http://www.youtube.com/watch?v=LPz8kmPpRsM

Fluhman, J. Spencer. (2012, June 4). Why we fear Mormons. *The New York Times*, p. A25. Available online at http://www.nytimes.com/2012/06/04/opinion/anti-mormonism-past-and-present.html

Ford, Vivian. (1976). Ask and ye shall receive. In Hartman Rector & Connie Rector (Eds.), *No more strangers* (vol. 3, pp. 160-178). Salt Lake City, UT: Bookcraft.

Forstchen, William R. (2009). *One second after*. New York, NY: Forge.

Francesca, Vincenzo Di. (1971). Forty-year wait for baptism. In Hartman Rector & Connie Rector (Eds.), *No more strangers* ([vol. 1,] pp. 82-89). Salt Lake City, UT: Bookcraft.

Francesca, Vincenzo Di. (1988, January). "I will not burn the book!" *Ensign*. Online at http://www.lds.org/ensign/1988/01/i-will-not-burn-the-book

Frank, Pat [pseud. for Harry Hart Frank]. (1959). *Alas, Babylon*. Philadelphia, PA: J. B. Lippincott.

French, David. (2012, July 10). Six reasons why Mormons are beating Baptists (in church growth) [blog post]. *The French Revolution: The French guide to American faith, politics, and culture* [blog]. Accessed September 8, 2012 at http://www.patheos.com/blogs/frenchrevolution/2012/07/10/six-reasons-why-mormons-are-beating-baptists-in-church-growth/

Friedman, George. (2010). *The next 100 years: A forecast for the 21st century*. New York, NY: Anchor/Random House. (Original work published 2009)

Fukuyama, Francis. (2002). *Our posthuman future: Consequences of the biotechnology revolution*. New York, NY: Farrar, Straus, & Giroux.

Garreau, Joel. (2005). *Radical evolution: The promise and peril of enhancing our minds, our bodies—and what it means to be human*. New York, NY: Doubleday/Random House.

Garrett, Laurie. (1994). *The coming plague: Newly emerging diseases in a world out of balance*. New York, NY: Farrar, Straus & Giroux.

Garrett, Laurie. (2005, July/August). The next pandemic? *Foreign Affairs*, 84(4), pp. 3-23.

Garrett, Natasia. (2011, May). Perpetual Education Fund fulfills prophetic promises. *Ensign*, pp. 141-143. Online at https://

www.lds.org/ensign/2011/05/perpetual-education-fund-fulfills-prophetic-promises

Gibbons, Francis M., & Daniel Bay Gibbons. (2002). *A gathering of eagles: Conversions from the four quarters of the earth*. Lincoln, NB: Writers Club Press /iUniverse.

Gibson, William. (1984). *Neuromancer*. New York, NY: Ace.

Gilardi, Umberto. (2012, August). I thought it was all nonsense. *Ensign*, pp. 42-43. Online at http://www.lds.org/ensign/2012/08/i-thought-it-was-all-nonsense

Gillum, Gary. (1973). Guidance along the way. In Hartman Rector & Connie Rector (Eds.), *No more strangers* (vol. 2, pp. 145-158). Salt Lake City, UT: Bookcraft.

Gilmour, Lorraine. (2011, July). Latter-day Saint voices: My pioneer days in Calgary. *Ensign*, p. 70. Online at http://www.lds.org/ensign/print/2011/07/latter-day-saint-voices

Gladstone, Rick. (2012,, September 15). Anti-American protests flare beyond the Mideast. *The New York Times* [late edition], pp. A1, A10.

Glock, Charles Y. (1962). On the study of religious commitment. *Religious Education, 57* [Supplement], S98-S109.

Glynn, Alan. (2001). *The dark fields*. New York, NY: Bloomsbury, USA.

Godwin, Joscelyn. (2007). *The golden thread: The ageless wisdom of the Western mystery traditions*. Wheaton, IL: Quest.

Goldsmith, Donald (1997). *The hunt for life on Mars*. New York, NY: Dutton/Penguin.

González, Walter F. (2011, October). If you really want to know, you will know. *Ensign*, pp. 60-64. Online at http://www.lds.org/ensign/2011/10/if-you-really-want-to-know-you-will-know

Goodrick-Clarke, Nicholas. (2008). *The Western esoteric traditions: A historical introduction*. New York, NY: Oxford University Press.

Goodstein, David. (2004). *Out of gas: The end of the age of oil*. New York, NY: W. W. Norton.

Gorman, Michael J. (2009). *Inhabiting the cruciform God: Kenosis, justification, and theosis in Paul's narrative soteriology*. Grand Rapids, MI: Eerdman's.

Gospel principles. (2009). Salt Lake City, UT: The Church of Jesus Christ of Latter-day Saints. Available online at http://www.lds.org/manual/gospel-principles

The gospel and the productive life: Student Manual, Religion 150. (2004). Salt Lake City, UT: The Church of Jesus Christ of Latter-day Saints.

Gray, Chris Hables, with Heidi J. Figueroa-Sarriera & Steven Mentor (Eds.). (1995). *The cyborg handbook.* New York, NY: Routledge.

Gray, Chris Hables. (2001). *Cyborg citizen.* New York, NY: Routledge.

Greer, John Michael. (2008). *The long descent: A user's guide to the end of the Industrial Age.* Gabriola Island, British Columbia, Canada: New Society Publishers.

Greer, John Michael. (2009). *The ecotechnic future: Envisioning a post-peak world.* Gabriola Island, British Columbia, Canada: New Society Publishers.

Griffith, Thomas B. (2012). Thomas B. Griffith. In Joseph A. Cannon (Ed.), *Why I'm a Mormon* (pp. 137-145). n.p.: Ensign Peak.

Grossman, Lev (2009). *The magicians: A novel.* New York, NY: Viking.

Grossman, Lev. (2011, February 21). 2045: The year man becomes immortal. *Time,* pp. 42-49. Online at http://www.time.com/time/magazine/article/0,9171,2048299,00.html

Group for the Advancement of Psychiatry. (1976). *Mysticism: Spiritual quest or psychic disorder?* [GAP Publication No. 97]. New York, NY: Author.

Grover, Mark L. (2000). The miracle of the rose and the oak in Latin America. In *Out of obscurity: The LDS Church in the twentieth century: The 29th Annual Sidney B. Sperry Symposium* (pp. 138-150). Salt Lake City, UT: Deseret Book Co.

Guarente, Lenny. (2003). *Ageless quest: One scientist's search for genes that prolong youth.* Cold Spring Harbor, NY: Cold Spring Harbor Laboratory Press.

Hall, Stephen S. (2003). *Merchants of immortality: Chasing the dream of human life extension.* Boston, MA: Houghton Mifflin.

Hallstrom, Angela (Ed.). (2010). *Dispensation: Latter-day fiction.* Provo, UT: Zarahemla Books.

Hallwas, John E., & Roger D. Launius. (1995). *Cultures in conflict: A documentary history of the Mormon War in Illinois*. Logan, UT: Utah State University Press.

Hamilton, Keith N. (2011). *Last laborer: Thoughts and reflections of a Black Mormon*. Salt Lake City, UT: Ammon Works LLC.

Handbook 2: Administering the Church. (2010). Salt Lake City, UT: The Church of Jesus Christ of Latter-day Saints. Online at http://www.lds.org/manual/handbook

Hansell, Gregory R., & William Grassie (Eds.). (2011). *H±: Transhumanism and its critics*. Philadelphia, PA: Metanexus Institute.

Harper, Steven C. (2000, Winter). Infallible proofs, both human and divine: The persuasiveness of Mormonism for early converts. *Religion and American Culture, 10*, 99-118.

Harris, John. (2010). *Enhancing evolution: The ethical case for making better people*. Princeton, NJ: Princeton University Press. (Original work published 2007)

Harrison, Albert A. (1997). *After contact: The human response to extraterrestrial life*. New York, NY: Plenum.

Harrop, Froma. (2008, August 26). Parties dither as Intermountain West bears brunt of population bomb. *The Seattle Times* [electronic edition]. Accessed September 7, 2012 at http://seattletimes.com/html/opinion/ 2008137644_froma26.html

Hart, John L. (2005, September 17). After Katrina's fury, relief on a grand scale. *Church News*. Online at http://www.ldschurchnews.com/articles/47826/After-Katrinas-fury-relief-on-a-grand-scale.html

Hartley, William G. (1975, July). Coming to Zion: Saga of the gathering. *Ensign*. Online at http://www.lds.org/ensign/1975/07/coming-to-zion-saga-of-the-gathering

Heaton, Tim B., Kristen L. Goodman, & Thomas B. Holman. (1994). In search of a peculiar people: Are Mormon families really different? In Marie Cornwall, Tim B. Heaton, & Lawrence A. Young (Eds.), *Contemporary Mormonism: Social science perspectives* (p. 87-117). Urbana, IL: University of Illinois Press.

Heidenreich, John F. (1971). The Gospel transforms a minister's life. In Hartman Rector & Connie Rector (Eds.), *No more strangers* ([vol. 1,] pp. 104-120). Salt Lake City, UT: Bookcraft.

Heidenreich, John F. (1976, September). Mormon journal: It taught me the Bible. *Ensign*, pp. 22-23. Online at http://www.lds.org/ensign/1976/09/mormon-journal

Heim, Michael. (1993). *The metaphysics of virtual reality*. New York, NY: Oxford University Press.

Heinberg, Richard. (2011). *The end of growth: Adapting to our new economic reality*. Gabriola Island, British Columbia, Canada: New Society Publishers.

Heinerman, John, & Anson Shupe. (1985). *The Mormon corporate empire*. Boston, MA: Beacon Press.

Henderson, Peter, & Kristina Cooke. (2012, January 30). Special report –Mormonism besieged by the modern age (online news story). Retrieved July 15, 2012, from the Reuters website, http://uk.reuters.com/assets/print?aid=UKTRE80T1CP20120130

Herbert, Frank. (1965). *Dune*. Philadelphia, PA: Chilton.

Herring, John. (1983). What will become of me? In Stephen W. Gibson (Ed.), *From clergy to convert* (pp. 1-8). Salt Lake City, UT: Bookcraft.

Hilbig, Keith K. (2008). The Prophet's impact on Europe, then and now. In Reid L. Neilson (Ed.), *Global Mormonism in the 21st century* (pp. 47-64). Provo, UT: Brigham Young University, Religious Studies Center. (Original paper delivered 2005)

Hinckley, Gordon B. (1993, July). "It's true, isn't it?" *Ensign*. Online at http://www.lds.org/ensign/1993/07/its-true-isnt-it

Hinckley, Gordon B. (2001, May). The Perpetual Education Fund. *Ensign*. Online at http://www.lds.org/ensign/2001/05/the-perpetual-education-fund

Hinckley, Gordon B. (2007a, September). Words of the Prophet: Seek learning. *New Era*. Online at http://www.lds.org/new-era/2007/09/words-of-the-prophet-seek-learning

Hinckley, Gordon B. (2007b, November). The stone cut out of the mountain. *Ensign*. Online at http://www.lds.org/ensign/2007/11/the-stone-cut-out-of-the-mountain

Hitchens, Christopher. (2007a). *god is not great: How religion poisons everything*. New York, NY: Twelve/Warner Books/Hachette Group.

Hitchens, Christopher (Ed.). (2007b). *The portable atheist: Essential readings for the nonbeliever*. Da Capo Press/Perseus.

Hood, Ralph W., Jr. (1974). Psychological strength and the report of intense religious experience. *Journal for the Scientific Study of Religion, 13,* 65-71.

Horn, Thomas, Nita Horn, Gary Stearman, Noah Hutchings, Chuck Missler, et al. (2011). *Pandemonium's engine: How the end of the Church Age, the rise of transhumanism, and the coming of the Übermensch (Overman) herald Satan's imminent and final assault on the creation of God.* Crane, MO: Defender.

"How the Book of Mormon changed my life." (2011, October). *Ensign,* pp. 68-71. Online at http://www.lds.org/ensign/2011/10/how-the-book-of-mormon-changed-my-life

"How the Lord provides for His own." (2004). In *Deseret Morning News 2004 Church almanac* (pp. 124-144). Salt Lake City, UT: Deseret News.

Hudson, Michael. (2012, April 22). Productivity, the miracle of compound interest, and poverty (webpage). From the *Naked Capitalism* blog, available at http://www.nakedcapitalism.com/2012/04/michael-hudson-productivity-the-miracle-of-compound-interest-and-poverty.html

Hudson, Nancy J. (2007). *Becoming God: The doctrine of theosis in Nicholas of Cusa.* Washington, DC: The Catholic University of America Press.

Hudson, Valerie M., & Andrea M. den Boer (2004). *Bare branches: The security implications of Asia's surplus male population.* Cambridge, MA: MIT Press.

Hughes, James. (2004). *Citizen cyborg: Why democratic societies must respond to the redesigned human of the future.* Cambridge, MA: Westview/Perseus.

"Humanitarian aid" [web page]. (2011). Retrieved July 19, 2012 from http://mormon.org/humanitarian-aid/

"Humanitarian services." (2012). Topic sheet at the online newsroom (headquarters edition) of The Church of Jesus Christ of Latter-day Saints, retrieved July 19, 2012 at http://www.mormonnewsroom.org/topic/humanitarian-services

Husein, Firoz King. (2012). Firoz King Husein. In Joseph A. Cannon (Ed.), *Why I'm a Mormon* (pp. 185-191). N.p.: Ensign Peak.

"I have a question." (1988, January). *Ensign*. Accessed September 11, 2012 at http://www.lds.org/ensign/1988/01/i-have-a-question

Internet world stats: Usage and population statistics [website]. Retrieved June 10, 2012 from http://www.internetworldstats.com/stats.htm

Introvigne, Massimo. (2001). *The future of religion and the future of new religions* [online document]. Retrieved February 29, 2012 from http://www.cesnur.org/2001/mi_june03.htm

"Is God disappearing?" [online, newspaper article]. *The Guardian* [online edition]. Available at http://www.guardian.co.uk/commentisfree/belief/2010/oct/11/god-disappearing-christianity

Jackson, Tim. (2011). *Prosperity without growth: Economics for a finite planet*. London, UK and Washington, DC: Earthscan. (Original work published 2009)

Jaroff, Leon. (1992, October 15). Seeking a godlike power. *Time*. Accessed September 14, 2012 at http://www.time.com/time/magazine/article/0,9171,976747,00.html

Jensen, Derrick. (2006a). *Endgame, Vol. I: The problem of civilization*. New York, NY: Seven Stories Press.

Jensen, Derrick. (2006b). *Endgame, Vol. II: Resistance*. New York, NY: Seven Stories Press.

Jensen, Richard L., and William G. Hartley. (n.d.). *Immigration and emigration* [webpage]. Retrieved June 8, 2012 from http://ldsfaq.byu.edu/viewEM.aspx?number=103

Jesus Christ is the way [website]. (2012). Online at http://www.lds.org/plan/jesus-christ-is-the-way

Johnson, Janiece Lyn. (2011, April). Rebecca Swain Williams: Steadfast & immovable. *Ensign*, pp. 38-41. Online at http://www.lds.org/ensign/2011/04/rebecca-swain-williams-steadfast-and-immovable

Johnson, Jill. (1994, January). Mormon Journal: I couldn't ignore the voice. *Ensign*, pp. 62-53. Online at http://www.lds.org/ensign/1994/01/mormon-journal

Jonas, Hans. (2001). *The gnostic religion: The message of the alien god and the beginnings of Christianity* (3rd ed.). Boston, MA: Beacon.

Jones, Christopher C. (2012). Mormonism in the Methodist marketplace: James Covel and the historical background of

Doctrine and Covenants 39-40. *BYU Studies Quarterly, 51*(1), 67-98. Online at https://byustudies.byu.edu/showTitle.aspx?title=8964

Jones, Gerald E. (1976, September). Mormon journal: A South Dakota Swede and the Book of Mormon. *Ensign*, pp. 19-20. Online at http://www.lds.org/ensign/1976/09/mormon-journal

Joshi, S. T. (Ed.). (1997). *The annotated H.P. Lovecraft*. New York, NY: Dell.

Joshi, S. T. (Ed.). (2000). *Atheism: A reader*. Amherst, NY: Prometheus.

Joshi, S. T. (Ed.). (2011). *The call of Cthulhu and other weird stories*. New York, NY: Penguin. (Original work published 1999)

Joshi, S. T., & Peter Cannon (Eds.). (1999). *More annotated Lovecraft*. New York, NY: Dell.

Judd, Daniel K. (1998). Religiosity, mental health, and the Latter-day Saints: A preliminary review of literature (1923-95). In James T. Duke (Ed.), *Latter-day Saint social life: Social research on the LDS Church and its members* (pp. 473-497). Provo, UT: Brigham Young University, Religious Studies Center.

Jung, C. G. (1953). *Psychology and alchemy* [vol. 12, *Collected Works*]. New York, NY: Bollingen Foundation & Pantheon Books.

Kahn, Herman. (1960). *On thermonuclear war*. Princeton, NJ: Princeton University Press.

Kahneman, Daniel. (2011). *Thinking, fast and slow*. New York, NY: Farrar, Straus & Giroux.

Kaku, Michio. (2012). *Physics of the future: How science will shape human destiny and our daily lives by the year 2100*. New York, NY: Anchor/Random House. (Original work published 2011)

"Kansas City Missouri Temple dedicated." (2012, July). *Ensign*, p. 78. Online at http://www.lds.org/ensign/2012/07/temple-news

Kärkkäinen, Veli-Matti. (2004). *One with God: Salvation as deification and justification*. Collegeville, MN: Liturgical Press.

Kaufman, Marc. (2009, November 8). When E.T. phones the pope. *The Washington Post*. Electronic version accessed September 8, 2012 at http://www.washingtonpost.com/wp-dyn/content/article/2009/11/06/AR2009110601899_pf.html

Kaufmann, Walter (Ed.). (1956). *Existentialism from Dostoevsky to Sartre*. Cleveland, OH: Meridian/World Publishing Co.

Keating, Daniel A. (2007). *Deification and grace*. Ave Maria, FL: Sapientia Press of Ave Maria University.

Keyes, Daniel. (1966). *Flowers for Algernon*. New York, NY: Harcourt, Brace & World.

Khan, Ali A. (2009). Social media: Preparedness 101: Zombie apocalypse [online document]. Retrieved August 30, 2011 from the website of the Centers for Disease Control and Prevention, http://www.bt.cdc.gov/ socialmedia/zombies_blog.asp

Kharlamov, Vladimir (Ed.). (2011). *Theosis: Deification in Christian theology: Vol. 2*. Eugene, OR: Pickwick Publications/Wipf & Stock.

Kim, Sebastian C. H. (2003). *In search of identity: Debates on religious conversion in India*. New Delhi, India: Oxford University Press.

Kimball, Edward L. (2005). *Lengthen your stride: The presidency of Spencer W. Kimball*. Salt Lake City, UT: Deseret Book Co.

Kimball, Edward L. (2008). Spencer W. Kimball and the Revelation on Priesthood. *BYU Studies, 47*(2), 4-78.

Kimball, Edward L., & Andrew E. Kimball, Jr. (1977). *Spencer W. Kimball: Twelfth president of The Church of Jesus Christ of Latter-day Saints*. Salt Lake City, UT: Bookcraft.

Kimball, Spencer W. (1974, October). "When the world will be converted": From an address delivered at a Regional Representatives Seminar, Thursday, April 4, 1974. *Ensign*. Online at http://lds.org/ensign/print/1974/10/when-the-world-will-be-converted

King, Stephen. (1990). *The stand: The complete and uncut version*. New York, NY: Doubleday.

King, Stephen. (2006). *Cell: A novel*. New York, NY: Scribner.

Kinnaman, David, with Aly Hawkins. (2011). *You lost me: Why young Christians are leaving church ... and rethinking faith*. Grand Rapids, MI: Baker Books/Baker Publishing Group.

Kinnear, John G. (1973). Conquered by love. In Hartman Rector & Connie Rector (Eds.), *No more strangers* (vol. 2, pp. 130-140). Salt Lake City, UT: Bookcraft.

Kinney, Brandon G. (2011). *The Mormon War: Zion and the Missouri extermination order of 1838*. Yardley, PA: Westholme.

Kirsch, Jonathan. (2006). *A history of the end of the world: How the most controversial book in the Bible changed the course of Western civilization.* New York, NY: HarperCollins.

Knobler, Stacey L., Alison Mack, Adel Mahmoud, & Stanley M. Lemon (Eds.). (2005). *The threat of pandemic influenza: Are we ready? Workshop summary.* Washington, DC: National Academies Press.

Knowles, Christopher. (2007). *Our gods wear spandex: The secret history of comic book heroes.* San Francisco, CA: Red Wheel/Weiser.

Koerner, David, & Simon LeVay. (2000). *Here be dragons: The scientific quest for extraterrestrial life.* New York, NY: Oxford University Press.

Kolata, Gina. (1999). *Flu: The story of the great influenza pandemic of 1918 and the search for the virus that caused it.* New York, NY: Farrar, Straus & Giroux.

Koltko, Mark Edward. (1989, April). Mysticism and Mormonism: An LDS perspective on transcendence and higher consciousness. *Sunstone,* pp. 13-19. Online at https://www.sunstonemagazine.com/pdf/070-13-19.pdf

Koltko-Rivera, Mark E. (2004). The psychology of worldviews. *Review of General Psychology, 8,* 3-58. (On-line at http://www.filedby.com/author/mark_e_koltko_rivera/572961/documents/)

Koltko-Rivera, Mark E. (2005). The potential societal impact of virtual reality. In K. M. Stanney & M. Zyda (Eds.), *Advances in virtual environments technology: Musings on design, evaluation, and applications. Volume 9 in G. Salvendy (Series Ed.), HCI International 2005: 11th International Conference on Human-Computer Interaction* [CD-ROM, unpaginated]. Mahwah, NJ: Erlbaum. Accessed September 5, 2012 at http://www.haverford.edu/psych/ddavis/psych214/koltko-rivera_2005_VR-rev.pdf

Koltko-Rivera, Mark E. (2006). Rediscovering the later version of Maslow's hierarchy of needs: Self-transcendence and opportunities for theory, research, and unification. *Review of General Psychology, 10,* 302-317. Online at http://docbk.com/a/download/rediscovering-the-later-version-of-maslow-shierarchyof-needs-self.pdf

Koltko-Rivera, Mark E. (2006-2007, Winter). Religions influence worldviews; worldviews influence behavior: A model with research agenda. *Psychology of Religion Newsletter, 32*(1), 1-10. (On-line at http://www.division36.org/Newsletters/v32n1.pdf)

[Koltko-Rivera, Mark E.] (2011a). *Hi, I'm Mark* [web page]. http://mormon.org/me/1777/

Koltko-Rivera, Mark. (2011b, February 13). The Singularity—and why it must be stopped [blog post]. *On the Mark*™ [blog]. http://markkrblog.blogspot.com/2011/02/ singularity-and-why-it-must-be-stopped.html

Kotlikoff, Laurence J., & Scott Burns. (2004). *The coming generational storm: What you need to know about America's economic future.* Cambridge, MA: MIT Press.

Krausz, Michael (Ed.). (2010). *Relativism: A contemporary anthology.* New York, NY: Columbia University Press.

Kress, Nancy. (1993). *Beggars in Spain.* New York, NY: Wm. Morrow.

Kueshana, Eklal [pseud., Richard Kieninger]. (1963). *The ultimate frontier.* Stelle, IL: The Stelle Group.

Kunstler, James Howard. (2005). *The long emergency: Surviving the converging catastrophes of the twenty-first century.* New York, NY: Atlantic Monthly Press.

Kunstler, James Howard. (2008). *World made by hand.* New York, NY: Atlantic Monthly Press.

Kunstler, James Howard. (2010). *The witch of Hebron: A World Made by Hand novel.* New York, NY: Atlantic Monthly Press.

Kurzweil, Ray. (2005). *The singularity is near: When humans transcend biology.* New York, NY: Viking/Penguin.

Kuspit, Donald. (2000). *Redeeming art: Critical reveries.* New York, NY: Allworth Press and the School of Visual Arts.

Kuspit, Donald. (2004). *The end of art.* New York, NY: Cambridge University Press.

LaHaye, Tim. (1999). *Revelation unveiled: A revised and updated edition of Revelation illustrated and made plain.* Grand Rapids, MI: Zondervan.

Langewiesche, William. (2007). *The atomic bazaar: The rise of the nuclear poor.* New York, NY: Farrar, Straus, & Giroux.

LDS Standard Works: See *Note* at the beginning of this References section.

Leadership training library [website]. Online at http://www.lds.org/service/leadership

LeBaron, E. Dale. (2000). The church in Africa. In *Out of obscurity: The LDS Church in the twentieth century: The 29th Annual Sidney B. Sperry Symposium* (pp. 177-189). Salt Lake City, UT: Deseret Book Co.

Ledbetter, Curtis E. (1973). III. The chaplain. In Hartman Rector & Connie Rector (Eds.), *No more strangers* (vol. 2, pp. 12-20). Salt Lake City, UT: Bookcraft.

Ledbetter, Virginia R. (1973). II. The chaplain's wife. In Hartman Rector & Connie Rector (Eds.), *No more strangers* (vol. 2, pp. 4-12). Salt Lake City, UT: Bookcraft.

Lee, Cynthia Ann. (2012, February). Latter-day Saint voices: Is this book from You? *Ensign*, pp. 66-67. Online at http://www.lds.org/ensign/2012/02/latter-day-saint-voices

Lemonick, Michael D. (2012). E.T., are you calling us? In Jeffrey Kluger, Michael D. Lemonick, et alia, *New space discoveries* (pp. 50-57). New York, NY: TIME Books.

"Lesson 46: 'A kingdom, which shall never be destroyed.'" (2001). In *Old Testament: Gospel Doctrine teacher's manual* (pp. 216-219). Salt Lake City, UT: The Church of Jesus Christ of Latter-day Saints. Online at https://www.lds.org/manual/old-testament-gospel-doctrine-teachers-manual/lesson-46-a-kingdom-which-shall-never-be-destroyed

Levy, Elinor, & Mark Fischetti. (2003). *The new killer diseases: How the alarming evolution of mutant germs threatens us all.* New York, NY: Crown/Random House.

Lewis, M. Paul. (Ed.). (2009). *Ethnologue: Languages of the world* (16th ed.). Dallas, TX: SIL International Publications. Online edition consulted June 10, 2012 at http://www.ethnologue.org/ethno_docs/distribution.asp?by=size

Licht, Mark H. (1995). Multiple regression and correlation. In Laurence G. Grimm & Paul R Yarnold (Eds.), *Reading and understanding multivariate statistics* (pp. 19-64). Washington, DC: American Psychological Association.

Lin, Chiao-yi. (2011, January). Gospel in my life: From believing to knowing. *Ensign*, p. 41. Online at http://www.lds.org/ensign/2011/01/from-believing-to-knowing

Lindner, Eileen W. (2012). Can the church log in with the "connected generation"? The church and young adults. In *Yearbook of American & Canadian churches* (pp. 16-20). Nashville, TN: Abingdon.

Lindsey, Hal, with C.C. Carlson. (1970). *The late great planet Earth*. Grand Rapids, MI: Zondervan.

Lindsey, Hal. (1984). *There's a new world coming: An in-depth analysis of the Book of Revelation* (updated ed.). Eugene, OR: Harvest House.

Linker, Damon. (2006). *The theocons: Secular America under siege*. New York, NY: Doubleday.

Litster, Allen. (1997, January). Pioneering in the Andes. *Ensign*, pp. 16-22. Online at http://www.lds.org/ensign/1997/01/pioneering-in-the-andes

Lomborg, Bjørn (Ed.). (2010). *Smart solutions to climate change: Comparing costs and benefits*. New York, NY: Cambridge Univ. Press.

Longman, Phillip. (2004). *The empty cradle: How falling birthrates threaten world prosperity and what to do about it*. New York, NY: Basic Books.

Lopez, Franklin (Director). (2011). *END:CIV: Resist or die* [documentary motion picture]. Oakland, CA: PM Press.

"Lorenzo Snow, served 1898-1901" [webpage]. (2004). Accessed June 4, 2012, at http://www.lds.org/churchhistory/presidents/controllers/potcController.jsp?leader=5&topic=quotes

Lovecraft, H. P. (1982). *The best of H. P. Lovecraft: Bloodcurdling tales of horror and the macabre*. New York, NY: Ballantine Books.

Lucas, James W., & Warner P. Woodworth. (1999). *Working toward Zion: Principles of the United Order for the modern world*. Salt Lake City, UT: Aspen Books.

Mansfield, Stephen. (2012). *The Mormonizing of America: How the Mormon religion became a dominant force in politics, entertainment, and pop culture*. Nashville, TN: Worthy Publishing.

Marriott, Edward. (2002). *Plague: A story of science, rivalry, and the scourge that won't go away*. New York, NY: Metropolitan Books.

Maruyama, Magoroh, & Arthur Harkins (Eds.). (1975). *Cultures beyond the Earth: The role of anthropology in outer space*. New York, NY: Vintage/Random House.

Martel, F[rances]. (2011, August 10). Rachel Maddow: Rick Perry's 2012 run is power grab for Christian conspiracy group. *Mediaite* [online site]. Accessed February 5, 2012 at http://www.mediaite.com/tv/rachel-maddow-rick-perrys-2012-run-is-power-grab-for-christian-conspiracy-group/

Martenson, Chris. (2011). *The crash course: The unsustainable future of our economy, energy, and environment.* Hoboken, NJ: Wiley.

Martin, David. (1999). The evangelical upsurge and its political implications. In Peter L. Berger (Ed.), *The desecularization of the world: Resurgent religion and world politics* (pp. 37-49). Washington, DC: Ethics and Public Policy Center & Eerdmans.

Martin, James. (2006). *The meaning of the 21st century: A vital blueprint for ensuring our future.* New York, NY: Riverhead/Penguin.

Martin, Roger. (2011, November 10). The limits of the scientific method in economics and the world. *The Great Debate* [online opinion column]. Accessed February 29, 2012 at http://blogs.reuters.com/great-debate/2011/11/10/a-better-blueprint-for-economics/

Mason, Patrick Q. (2011). *The Mormon menace: Violence and anti-Mormonism in the postbellum South.* New York, NY: Oxford University Press.

Matheson, Richard. (1954). *I am legend.* New York, NY: Gold Medal.

Maxwell, Neal A. (2001). A wonderful flood of light. In *The Collected Works of Neal A Maxwell* (vol. 4). Salt Lake City, UT: Eagle Gate/Deseret Book. (Original work published 1990)

Mazlish, Bruce. (1993). *The fourth discontinuity: The co-evolution of humans and machines.* New Haven, CT: Yale University Press.

McBay, Aric, Lierre Keith, & Derrick Jensen. (2011). *Deep green resistance: Strategy to save the planet.* New York, NY: Seven Stories Press.

McClain, E.W., & Henry B. Andrews. (1969). Some personality correlates of peak experiences—a study in self-actualization. *Journal of Clinical Psychology, 25,* 36-38.

McGuire, Bill. (2002). *A guide to the end of the world: Everything you never wanted to know.* New York, NY: Oxford University Press.

McMurtrie, Beth. (2011, November 14). International enrollments at U.S. colleges grow but still rely on China. *The Chronicle of Higher Education.* Online version retrieved March 6, 2011 from http://chronicle.com/ article/International-Enrollments-at/129747/

Meadows, Donella, Jorgen Randers, & Dennis Meadows. (2004). *Limits to growth: The 30-year update.* White River Junction, VT: Chelsea Green.

Mehlman, Maxwell J. (2003). *Wondergenes: Genetic enhancement and the future of society.* Bloomington, IN: Indiana University Press.

Merrill, Allison Ji-Jen. (2011, August). Two pioneers across two centuries. *Ensign*, pp. 22-23. Online at http://www.lds.org/ensign/2011/08/two-pioneers-across-two-centuries

Meyer, Stephenie. (2005). *Twilight.* New York, NY: Little, Brown & Co.

Michaud, Michael A. G. (2007). *Contact with alien civilizations: Our hopes and fears about encountering extraterrestrials.* New York, NY: Copernicus Books/Springer Science + Business Media.

Micklethwait, John, and Adrian Wooldridge. (2010). *God is back: How the global revival of faith is changing the world.* New York: Penguin Books. (Original work published 2009)

Mikulina, Victoria. (2011, August). Latter-day Saint voices: I missed feeling the Spirit. *Ensign*, p. 67. Online at http://www.lds.org/ensign/2011/08/ latter-day-saint-voices

Miller, Walter M., Jr. (1960). *A canticle for Leibowitz.* Philadelphia, PA: J.B. Lippincott & Co.

Millet, Robert L. (2004). *Getting at the truth: Responding to difficult questions about LDS beliefs.* Salt Lake City, UT: Deseret Book.

Millet, Robert L. (2005). *A different Jesus? The Christ of the Latter-day Saints.* Grand Rapids, MI: Eerdmans.

Millet, Robert L. (2010). *Modern Mormonism: Myths and realities.* Salt Lake City, UT: Greg Kofford Books.

Millet, Robert L. (Ed.). (2011). *No weapon shall prosper: New light on sensitive issues.* Salt Lake City, UT: Deseret Book, and Provo, UT: Brigham Young University, Religious Studies Center.

Millet, Robert L., Camille Fronk Olson, Andrew C. Skinner, & Brent L. Top. (2011). *LDS beliefs: A doctrinal reference.* Salt Lake City, UT: Deseret Book.

Missionary Preparation Student Manual: Religion 130. (2005). Salt Lake City, UT: The Church of Jesus Christ of Latter-day Saints. Online at http://www.lds.org/manual/institute/

Monson, Thomas S. (2010, November). As we meet together again. *Ensign*, pp. 4-6. Online at https://www.lds.org/ensign/2010/11/as-we-meet-together-again

Monson, Thomas S. (2011a, May). The holy temple—a beacon to the world. *Ensign*, pp. 90-94. Online at https://www.lds.org/ensign/2011/05/the-holy-temple-a-beacon-to-the-world

Monson, Thomas S. (2011b, January.). The Lord needs missionaries. *Ensign*, pp. 4-5. Online at https://www.lds.org/ensign/2011/01/the-lord-needs-missionaries

"Mormon and modern" [online commentary]. (2012, July 6). Retrieved July 19, 2012 from the online newsroom (headquarters edition) of The Church of Jesus Christ of Latter-day Saints, at http://www.mormonnewsroom.org/article/mormon-and-modern

"The Mormon way of doing business" [Schumpeter column]. (2012, May 5). *The Economist*. Accessed September 17, 2012 at http://www.economist.com/node/21554173

Mormons in America: Certain in their beliefs, uncertain of their place in society. (2012). Washington, DC: Pew Research Center, Pew Forum on Religion & Public Life. Available online at http://www.pewforum.org/mormons-in-america/

Morris, Michael R. (2012, August). Finding faith at the ends of the earth. *Ensign*, pp. 30-33. Online at http://www.lds.org/ensign/2012/08/finding-faith-at-the-ends-of-the-earth

Morrison, Grant. (2012). *Supergods: What masked vigilantes, mutants, and a sun god from Smallville can teach us about being human.* New York, NY: Spiegel & Grau. (Original work published 2011)

Mosser, Carl. (2002). And the Saints go marching on: The new Mormon challenge for world missions, apologetics, and theology. In Francis J. Beckwith, Carl Mosser, & Paul Owen (Eds.), *The new Mormon challenge: Responding to the latest defenses of a fast-growing movement* (pp. 59-93). Grand Rapids, MI: Zondervan

Mosteller, Timothy. (2008). *Relativism: A guide for the perplexed*. New York, NY: Continuum.

Munkittrick, Kyle. (2010, March 29). Transhumanism and superheroes. *h+ Magazine* [online publication]. Online at http://hplusmagazine.com/2010/03/29/transhumanism-and-superheroes/

Munz, Philip, Ioan Hudea, Joe Imad, & Robert J. Smith. (2009). When zombies attack! Mathematical modelling of an outbreak of zombie infection. In J. M Tchuenche & C. Chiyaka (Eds.), *Infectious disease modelling research progress* (pp. 133-150). n.p.: Nova Science Publishers, Inc. Retrieved August 30, 2011 from http://mysite.science.uottawa.ca/ rsmith43/Zombies.pdf

Myers, B. R. (2002). *A reader's manifesto: An attack on the growing pretentiousness in American literary prose*. Hoboken, NJ: Melville House.

Naam, Ramez. (2005). *More than human: Embracing the promise of biological enhancement*. New York, NY: Broadway Books.

A national survey of families and households [website]. (2008). Accessed September 8, 2012 at http://www.ssc.wisc.edu/nsfh/

Neilson, Reid L. (Ed.). (2008). *Global Mormonism in the 21st century*. Provo, UT: Brigham Young University, Religious Studies Center.

Nelson, Victoria. (2012). *Gothicka: Vampire heroes, human gods, and the new supernatural*. Cambridge, MA: Harvard University Press.

"News of the Church: The Church in Northern Europe." (1994, January). *Ensign*, pp. 79-80. Online at http://www.lds.org/ensign/1994/01/news-of-the-church

Nibley, Hugh. (1987). The passing of the primitive church: Forty variations on an unpopular theme. In Hugh Nibley, *Mormonism and early Christianity* [The Collected Works of Hugh Nibley: Volume 4] (pp. 168-208). Salt Lake City, UT: Deseret Book Co. (Reprinted from *Church History*, June 1961, 20, 131-154)

Nibley, Hugh. (1989). *Approaching Zion* [The Collected Works of Hugh Nibley: Vol. 9]. Salt Lake City, UT: Deseret Book Co.

Nield, Reeve A. (2012). Reeve A. Nield. In Joseph A. Cannon (Ed.), *Why I'm a Mormon* (pp. 250-256). n.p.: Ensign Peak.

Noone, Richard W. (n.d. [ca. 1982]). *Ice: The ultimate disaster*. Dunwoody, GA: Genesis Publishers, Inc.

Nossiter, Adam. (2011, December 26). Bomb attacks on churches across Nigeria. *The New York Times* [late edition], pp. A1, A10.

Novak, Louis. (1976). What's in a decision? In Hartman Rector & Connie Rector, *No More Strangers* (vol. 3, pp. 40-53). Salt Lake City, UT: Bookcraft.

Nussbaum, Martha C. (2007). *The clash within: Democracy, religious violence, and India's future.* Cambridge, MA: Belknap/Harvard University Press.

Oaks, Dallin H. (1991, March 12). *Getting to know China.* Devotional address presented at Brigham Young University. Available online at http://speeches.byu.edu/reader/reader.php?id=7070

Oaks, Dallin H. (2011, January). Fundamental to our faith. *Ensign*, pp. 22-29. Online at https://www.lds.org/ensign/2011/01/fundamental-to-our-faith

Oaks, Dallin H. (2012, May). Sacrifice. *Ensign*, pp. 19-22. Online at https://www.lds.org/ensign/2012/05/sacrifice

Oliver, Paul. (2012, September). UK members celebrate Queen's diamond jubilee with day of service. *Ensign*, pp. 74-75. Online at http://www.lds.org/ensign/2012/09/uk-members-celebrate-queens-diamond-jubilee-with-day-of-service

Olson, Kathryn H. (2012, August). Celebrating a day of service. *Ensign*, pp. 66-69. Online at http://www.lds.org/ensign/2012/08/celebrating-a-day-of-service

"One stalwart pioneer, many generations blessed." (2011, August). *Ensign*, pp. 12-13. Online at http://www.lds.org/ensign/2011/08/one-stalwart-pioneer-many-generations-blessed

O'Neil, Dennis. (2012). *Archaic human culture* [webpage]. Accessed September 18, 2012 at http://anthro.palomar.edu/homo2/mod_homo_3.htm

OpenDoors 2011 "Fast Facts." (2011, November). Obtained June 10, 2012, from the website of the Institute of International Education, at http://www.iie.org/en/Research-and-Publications/Open-Doors

Orent, Wendy. (2004). *Plague: The mysterious past and terrifying future of the world's most dangerous disease.* New York, NY: Free Press.

"The origin of man: By the First Presidency of the Church." (2002, February). *Ensign.* (Original work published 1909). Online at http://www.lds.org/ensign/2002/02/the-origin-of-man

Osborne, Jason, & Elaine Waters. (2002). Four assumptions of multiple regression that researchers should always test. *Practical Assessment, Research & Evaluation, 8*(2). Accessed September 15, 2012 from http://pareonline.net/getvn.asp?v=8&n=2

Osterholm, Michael T. (2005, July/August). Preparing for the next pandemic. *Foreign Affairs, 84*(4), pp. 24-37.

Ostling, Richard N., & Joan K. Ostling. (2007). *Mormon America: The power and the promise* (rev. ed.). New York, NY: HarperCollins.

Otterson, Michael. (2012, April 2). In the public eye: How the Church is handling increased global visibility. In *In the public eye: How the Church is handling increased visibility* (LDS International Society, 23rd Annual Conference; pp. 16-23). Provo, UT: Brigham Young University, David M. Kennedy Center for International Studies. Online at http://www.ldsinternationalsociety.org/

Our heritage: A brief history of The Church of Jesus Christ of Latter-day Saints. (1996). Salt Lake City, UT: The Church of Jesus Christ of Latter-day Saints. Online at http://www.lds.org/Static%20Files/PDF/Manuals/OurHeritage_35448_eng.pdf

Pearl of Great Price, The: See *Notes* at the beginning of this References section.

Penrose, Roger. (2011). *Cycles of time: An extraordinary new view of the universe.* New York, NY: Knopf/Random House.

Perkins, Anthony D. (2012, April 2). Out of obscurity: Perspectives from Asia. In *In the public eye: How the Church is handling increased visibility* (LDS International Society, 23rd Annual Conference; pp. 3-15). Provo, UT: Brigham Young University, David M. Kennedy Center for International Studies. Retrieved July 21, 2012, from http://www.ldsinternationalsociety.org/

Peterson, Daniel C., & Stephen D. Ricks. (1992). *Offenders for a word: How anti-Mormons play word games to attack the Latter-day Saints.* Salt Lake City, UT: Aspen Books.

Pew Forum on Religion & Public Life. (2008, May). *Religion in China on the Eve of the 2008 Beijing Olympics* [online document]. Online at http://www.pewforum.org/Importance-of-Religion/Religion-in-China-on-the-Eve-of-the-2008-Beijing-Olympics.aspx

Pew Forum on Religion & Public Life. (2010, April). *Tolerance and tension: Islam and Christianity in sub-Saharan Africa.* Washington, DC: Pew Research Center. Retrieved June 15, 2012 from http://www.pewforum.org/uploadedFiles/Topics/Belief_and_Practices/sub-saharan-africa-full-report.pdf

Pew Research Center. (2010, February). *Millennials: A portrait of Generation Next: Confident. Connected. Open to change*. Washington, DC: Author. Retrieved June 10, 2012 from http://pewresearch.org/millennials/ ; http://pewsocialtrends.org/files/2010/10/millennials-confident-connected-open-to-change.pdf

Phillips, Kevin. (2006). *American theocracy: The peril and politics of radical religion, oil, and borrowed money in the 21st century*. New York, NY: Viking/Penguin.

Pope, Margaret McConkie. (1992). Exaltation. In Daniel H. Ludlow (Ed.), *Encyclopedia of Mormonism* (vol. 1, p. 479). New York, NY: Macmillan. Accessed September 10, 2012 at http://eom.byu.edu/index.php/Exaltation

Population Division of the Department of Economic and Social Affairs of the United Nations Secretariat. (2010). *World population prospects: The 2010 revision*. Retrieved February 16, 2012 from http://esa.un.org/unpd/wpp/index.htm

Prensky, Marc. (2012). *Brain gain: Technology and the quest for digital wisdom*. New York, NY: Palgrave Macmillan/St. Martin's Press.

Prince, Gregory A., & Wm. Robert Wright. (2005). *David O. McKay and the rise of modern Mormonism*. Salt Lake City, UT: University of Utah Press.

President's Council on Bioethics, The. (2003). *Beyond therapy: Biotechnology and the pursuit of happiness*. New York, NY: HarperCollins.

Prothero, Stephen. (2008). *Religious literacy: What every American needs to know—and doesn't*. New York, NY: HarperOne. (Original work published 2007)

Quammen, David. (2012). *Spillover: Animal infections and the next human pandemic*. New York, NY: W.W. Norton.

Reed, Jessica. (2010, October 14). Christianity in France is fading. *The Guardian* [online edition]. Online at http://www.guardian.co.uk/commentisfree/belief/2010/oct/14/christianity-france-fading

Regardie, Israel. (1989). *The Golden Dawn* (6th ed.). St. Paul, MN: Llewellyn.

Regis, Edward, Jr. (Ed.). (1985). *Extraterrestrials: Science and alien intelligence*. New York, NY: Cambridge University Press.

Reich, Robert B. (2011). *Aftershock: The next economy and America's future* (updated ed.). New York, NY: Vintage/Random House.

Reiher, John. (1983). I didn't want to change. In Stephen W. Gibson (Ed.), *From clergy to convert* (pp. 31-39). Salt Lake City, UT: Bookcraft.

Reynolds, Noel B. (Ed.). (2005). *Early Christians in disarray: Contemporary LDS perspectives on the Christian apostasy.* Provo, UT: Brigham Young University, Foundation for Ancient Research and Mormon Studies.

Rheingold, Howard. (1991). *Virtual reality.* New York: Simon & Schuster.

Rich, Frank. (2012, July 30). Mayberry R.I.P. *New York Magazine, 45*(24), pp. 18-24.

Roberts, B[righam]. H. (2001). *The Missouri persecutions.* Heber City, UT: Archive Publishers. (Original work published 1900 in Salt Lake City, UT, by George Q. Cannon & Son Co., Publishers)

Roberts, B[righam]. H. (1996). *The truth, the way, the life: An elementary treatise on theology* (2nd ed., John W. Welch, Ed.). Provo, UT: BYU Studies. (Original work completed 1928)

Roberts, Paul. (2004). *The end of oil: On the edge of a perilous new world.* Boston, MA: Houghton Mifflin Co.

Robertson, Pat. (1994). *The collected works of Pat Robertson: The new millennium, The New World Order, The secret kingdom.* New York, NY: Inspiration Press/Budget Book Service.

Robinson, Rowena, & Sathianathan Clarke (Eds.). (2003). *Religious conversion in India: Modes, motivations, and meanings.* New Delhi, India: Oxford University Press.

Romney, Beth. (1971). Juan Soriano: The shining words. In Hartman Rector & Connie Rector (Eds.), *No more strangers* ([vol. 1,] pp. 154-157). Salt Lake City, UT: Bookcraft.

Rothman, Sheila M., & David J. Rothman. (2003). *The pursuit of perfection: The promise and perils of medical enhancement.* New York: Pantheon/Random House.

Rowling, J. K. (1997). *Harry Potter and the philosopher's stone.* London, England, UK: Bloomsbury.

Rudd, Glen L. (1995). *Pure religion: The story of Church Welfare since 1930*. Salt Lake City, UT: The Church of Jesus Christ of Latter-day Saints.

Rudd, Glen L. (2011). *Pure religion epilogue: The story of Church Welfare from 1995 to 2010*. Salt Lake City, UT: The Church of Jesus Christ of Latter-day Saints.

Rudolph, Kurt. (1987). *Gnosis: The nature and history of gnosticism*. San Francisco, CA: HarperSanFrancisco/HarperCollins.

Ruppert, Michael C. (2009). *Confronting collapse: The crisis of energy and money in a post peak oil world: A 25-point program for action*. White River Junction, VT: Chelsea Green Publishing.

Russell, Norman. (2005). *The doctrine of deification in the Greek patristic tradition*. New York, NY: Oxford University Press.

Russell, Norman. (2009). *Fellow workers with God: Orthodox thinking on theosis*. Crestwood, NY: St. Vladimir's Seminary Press.

Sacks, Howard L. (1979). The effect of spiritual exercises on the integration of self-system. *Journal for the Scientific Study of Religion, 18*, 46-50.

Sagan, Carl, John E. Mack, J. Bryan Hehir, & Stephen Jay Gould. (1986). *The long darkness: Psychological and moral perspectives on nuclear winter*. New Haven, CT: Yale University Press.

Schell, Jonathan. (1982). *The fate of the Earth*. New York, NY: Knopf.

Schell, Jonathan. (1986). *The abolition*. New York, NY: Avon Books.

Schell, Jonathan. (2007). *The seventh decade: The new shape of nuclear danger*. New York, NY: Metropolitan Books/Henry Holt & Co.

Schmorrow, Dylan, Kay M. Stanney, Kelly S. Hale, Sven Fuchs, Glen Wilson, & Peter Young. (2012). Neuroergonomics in human-system interaction. In Gavriel Salvendy (Ed.), *Handbook of human factors & ergonomics* (4th ed., pp. 1057-1082). Hoboken, NJ: Wiley.

Schulte, Allie. (2010, December). Free to smile. *Ensign*, pp. 63-65. Online at http://www.lds.org/ensign/2010/12/free-to-smile

Scott, Susan, & Christopher Duncan. (2004). *Return of the Black Death: The world's greatest serial killer*. Chichester, England, UK: John Wiley.

Searle, Don L. (1996, March). Ghana—A household of faith. *Ensign*. Online at http://www.lds.org/ensign/1996/03/ghana-a-household-of-faith

Sexton, Tanintoa. (2011, April). Latter-day Saint voices: I'm not interested in the Church. *Ensign*, p. 66. Online at http://www.lds.org/ensign/2011/04/latter-day-saint-voices

Sherlock, Richard. (1980, Fall). "We can see no advantage to a continuation of the discussion:" The Roberts/Smith/Talmage affair. *Dialogue: A Journal of Mormon Thought, 13*(3), 63-78. Accessed September 10, 2012 at http://www.dialoguejournal.com/wp-content/uploads/sbi/articles/Dialogue_V13N03_65.pdf

Sherman, William R., & Alan B. Craig. (2003). *Understanding virtual reality: Interface, application, and design.* San Francisco, CA: Morgan Kaufmann/ Elsevier.

Shipps, Jan. (1985). *Mormonism: The story of a new religious tradition.* Urbana, IL: University of Illinois Press.

Shipps, Jan, & John W. Welch (Eds.). (1994). *The journals of William E. McLellin, 1831-1836.* Provo, UT: Brigham Young University, BYU Studies, and Urbana, IL: University of Illinois Press.

Shuster, Eric, & Charles Sale. (2010). *The biblical roots of Mormonism.* Springville, UT: CFI/Cedar Fort, Inc.

Shute, Neville. (1957). *On the beach.* London, England, UK: Heinemann.

Smita, Narula. (1999, September). Politics by other means: Attacks against Christians in India. *Human Rights Watch, 11*(6)(C).

Smith, Christian, with Melinda Lundquist Denton. (2005). *Soul searching: The religious and spiritual lives of American teenagers.* New York, NY: Oxford University Press.

Smith, Huston. (2001). *Why religion matters: The fate of the human spirit in an age of disbelief.* San Francisco, CA: HarperCollins.

Smith, Hyrum W. (1994). *The 10 natural laws of successful time and life management: Proven strategies for increased productivity and inner peace.* New York, NY: Warner Books.

Smith, Joseph Fielding. (1954). *Man: His origin and destiny.* Salt Lake City, UT: Deseret Book Company.

Smith? [sic], Robert. (2009, December 8) A report on the zombie outbreak of 2009: How mathematics can save us (no, really). *Canadian Medical Association Journal, 181*(12), E297-E300. Online at http://mysite.science.uottawa.ca/rsmith43/CMAJZombies.pdf

Smithsonian Institution. (n.d.). The mystery of the Pit of Bones, Atapuerca, Spain [webpage]. *Smithsonian: National Museum of Natural History* [website]. Accessed September 18, 2012 at http://humanorigins.si.edu/resources/whats-hot/mystery-pit-bones-atapuerca-spain

Solomon, Jay, & Carol E. Lee. (2012, September 15-16). Anti-U.S. mobs on rampage. *The Wall Street Journal*, pp. A1, A6.

Sorell, Tom. (1994). *Scientism: Philosophy and the infatuation with science*. New York, NY: Routledge. (Original work published 1991)

Stack, Peggy Fletcher. (2012, February 3). Mormons tackling tough questions in their history. *The Salt Lake Tribune* (electronic edition). Accessed July 15, 2012 at http://www.sltrib.com/sltrib/news/53408134-78/church-lds-mormon-faith.html.csp

Staley, John S. (1971). A Catholic monk finds Gospel brotherhood. In Hartman Rector & Connie Rector (Eds.), *No more strangers* ([vol. 1,] pp. 19-36). Salt Lake City, UT: Bookcraft.

Standard Works, LDS: See *Notes* at the beginning of this References section.

Stanney, Kay M. (Ed.). (2002). *Handbook of virtual environments: Design, implementation, and applications*. Mahwah, NJ: Erlbaum.

Stanney, Kay M., & Joseph V. Cohn. (2012). Virtual environments. In Gavriel Salvendy (Ed.), *Handbook of human factors and ergonomics* (4th ed., pp. 1031-1056). Hoboken, NJ: Wiley.

Stark, Rodney. (1984). The rise of a new world faith. *Review of Religious Research, 26*, 18-27.

Stark, Rodney. (1994). Modernization and Mormon growth: The secularization thesis revisited. In Marie Cornwall, Tim B. Heaton, & Lawrence A. Young (Eds.), *Contemporary Mormonism: Social science perspectives* (pp. 13-23). Urbana, IL: University of Illinois Press.

Stark, Rodney. (1996). So far, so good: A brief assessment of Mormon membership projections. *Review of Religious Research, 38*, 175-178.

Stark, Rodney. (1996). *The rise of Christianity: How the obscure, marginal Jesus movement became the dominant religious force in the Western world in a few centuries*. Princeton, NJ: Princeton University Press.

Stark, Rodney. (2005). *The rise of Mormonism* (Reid L. Neilson, Ed.). New York, NY: Columbia University Press.

Stark, Rodney. (2008). *What Americans really believe*. Waco, TX: Baylor University Press.

Stark, Rodney. (2011). *The triumph of Christianity: How the Jesus movement became the world's largest religion*. New York, NY: HarperCollins.

Stark, Rodney, & Roger Finke. (2000). *Acts of faith: Explaining the human side of religion*. Berkeley, CA: University of California Press.

[Statistical report 1971]. "The annual report of the church." (1972, July). *Ensign*. Online at http://www.lds.org/ensign/print/1972/07/the-annual-report-of-the-church

"Statistical report 1973." (1974, May). *Ensign*. Online at http://www.lds.org/ensign/1974/05/statistical-report-1973

"Statistical report 1974." (1975, May). *Ensign*. Online at http://www.lds.org/ensign/1975/05/statistical-report-1974

"Statistical report 1975." (1976, May). *Ensign*. Online at http://www.lds.org/ensign/1976/05/statistical-report-1975

"Statistical report 1976." (1977, May). *Ensign*. Online at http://www.lds.org/ensign/1977/05/statistical-report-1976

"Statistical report 1977." (1978, May). *Ensign*. Online at http://www.lds.org/ensign/1978/05/statistical-report-1977

"Statistical report 1978." (1979, May). *Ensign*. Online at http://www.lds.org/ensign/1979/05/statistical-report-1978

"Statistical report 1979." (1980, May). *Ensign*. Online at http://www.lds.org/ensign/1980/05/statistical-report-1979

"Statistical report 1980." (1981, May). *Ensign*. Online at http://www.lds.org/ensign/1981/05/statistical-report-1980

"Statistical report 1981." (1982, May). *Ensign*. Online at http://www.lds.org/ensign/1982/05/statistical-report-1981

"Statistical report 1982." (1983, May). *Ensign*. Online at http://www.lds.org/ensign/1983/05/statistical-report-1982

"Statistical report 1983." (1984, May). *Ensign*. Online at http://www.lds.org/ensign/1984/05/statistical-report-1983

"Statistical report 1984." (1985, May). *Ensign*. Online at http://www.lds.org/ensign/1985/05/statistical-report-1984

"Statistical report 1985." (1986, May). *Ensign*. Online at http://www.lds.org/ensign/1986/05/statistical-report-1985

"Statistical report 1986." (1987, May). *Ensign*. Online at http://www.lds.org/ensign/1987/05/statistical-report-1986

"Statistical report 1987." (1988, May). *Ensign*. Online at http://www.lds.org/ensign/1988/05/statistical-report-1987

"Statistical report 1988." (1989, May). *Ensign*. Online at http://www.lds.org/ensign/1989/05/statistical-report-1988

"Statistical report 1989." (1990, May). *Ensign*. Online at http://www.lds.org/ensign/1990/05/statistical-report-1989

"Statistical report 1990." (1991, May). *Ensign*. Online at http://www.lds.org/ensign/1991/05/statistical-report-1990

"Statistical report 1991." (1992, May). *Ensign*. Online at http://www.lds.org/ensign/1992/05/statistical-report-1991

"Statistical report 1992." (1993, May). *Ensign*. Online at http://www.lds.org/ensign/1993/05/statistical-report-1992

"Statistical report 1993." (1994, May). *Ensign*. Online at http://www.lds.org/ensign/1994/05/statistical-report-1993

"Statistical report 1994." (1995, May). *Ensign*. Online at http://www.lds.org/ensign/1995/05/statistical-report-1994

"Statistical report 1995." (1996, May). *Ensign*. Online at http://www.lds.org/ensign/1996/05/statistical-report-1995

"Statistical report 1996." (1997, May). *Ensign*. Online at http://www.lds.org/ensign/1997/05/statistical-report-1996

"Statistical report, 1997." (1998, May). *Ensign*. Online at http://www.lds.org/ensign/1998/05/statistical-report-1997

"Statistical report, 1998." (1999, May). *Ensign*. Online at http://www.lds.org/ensign/1999/05/statistical-report-1998

"Statistical report, 1999." (2000, May). *Ensign*. Online at http://www.lds.org/ensign/2000/05/statistical-report-1999

"Statistical report, 2000." (2001, May). *Ensign*. Online at http://www.lds.org/ensign/2001/05/statistical-report-2000

"Statistical report, 2001." (2002, May). *Ensign*. Online at http://www.lds.org/ensign/2002/05/statistical-report-2001

"Statistical report, 2002." (2003, May). *Ensign*. Online at http://www.lds.org/ensign/2003/05/statistical-report-2002

"Statistical report, 2003." (2004, May). *Ensign*. Online at http://www.lds.org/ensign/2004/05/statistical-report-2003

"Statistical report, 2004." (2005, May). *Ensign*. Online at http://www.lds.org/ensign/2005/05/statistical-report-2004

"Statistical report, 2005." (2006, May). *Ensign*. Online at http://www.lds.org/ensign/2006/05/statistical-report-2005

"Statistical report, 2006." (2007, May). *Ensign*. Online at http://www.lds.org/ensign/2007/05/statistical-report-2006

"Statistical report, 2007." (2008, May). *Ensign*. Online at http://www.lds.org/ensign/2008/05/statistical-report-2007

"Statistical report, 2008." (2009, May). *Ensign*. Online at http://www.lds.org/ensign/2009/05/statistical-report-2008

"Statistical report, 2009." (2010, May). *Ensign*. Online at http://www.lds.org/ensign/2010/05/statistical-report-2009

"Statistical report, 2010." (2011, May). *Ensign*. Online at http://www.lds.org/ensign/2011/05/statistical-report-2010

"Statistical report, 2011." (2012, May). *Ensign*, p. 30. Online at http://www.lds.org/ensign/2012/05/statistical-report-2011

Stegeby, E. Kenneth. (1999). An analysis of the impending disestablishment of the Church of Sweden. *Brigham Young University Law Review*, issue 2. Online at http://lawreview.byu.edu/archives/1999/2/ste-fin.pdf

Stenger, Victor J. (2009). *The new atheism: Taking a stand for science and reason*. Amherst, NY: Prometheus Books.

Stewart, George R. (1949). *Earth abides*. New York, NY: Random House.

Stock, Gregory. (2002). *Redesigning humans: Choosing our genes, changing our future*. Boston, MA: Houghton Mifflin.

Stott, Michelle. (1989, Winter). Of truth and passion: Mormonism and existential thought. *Dialogue: A Journal of Mormon Thought*, 22(4), 76-88. Accessed September 18, 2012 at https://www.dialoguejournal.com/wp-content/uploads/sbi/articles/Dialogue_V22N04_78.pdf

"Strengthening the family: Multiply and replenish the Earth." (2005, April). *Ensign*. Online at https://www.lds.org/ensign/2005/04/strengthening-the-family-multiply-and-replenish-the-earth

Strieber, Whitley, & James Kunetka. (1984). *Warday*. New York, NY: Holt, Rinehart, & Winston.

"The sustaining of church officers." (2012, May). *Ensign*, pp. 27-28. Available online at http://www.lds.org/ensign/2012/05

Talmage, James E. (1994). *The great apostasy; Considered in the light of scriptural and secular history*. Salt Lake City, UT: Deseret Book. (Original work published 1909)

Teachings of presidents of the church: Brigham Young. (1997). Salt Lake City, UT: The Church of Jesus Christ of Latter-day Saints. Online at https://www.lds.org/manual/teachings-brigham-young

Teachings of presidents of the church: Joseph F. Smith. (1998). Salt Lake City, UT: The Church of Jesus Christ of Latter-day Saints. Online at http://www.lds.org/manual/teachings-joseph-f-smith

Teachings of presidents of the church: Spencer W. Kimball. (2006). Salt Lake City, UT: The Church of Jesus Christ of Latter-day Saints. Online at https://www.lds.org/manual/teachings-spencer-w-kimball

Teitelbaum, Michael S., & Jay Winter. (1998). *A question of numbers: High migration, low fertility, and the politics of national identity*. New York, NY: Hill & Wang/Farrar, Straus & Giroux.

"Testifying of Christ." (2012, September). *Ensign*, pp. 40-43. Online at http://www.lds.org/ensign/2012/09/testifying-of-christ

Thoma, Mark. (2011, November 14). Should economists be "imagineers" of our future? *The Great Debate* [online opinion column]. Retrieved February 29, 2012 from http://blogs.reuters.com/great-debate/2011/11/14/should-economists-be-%E2%80%9Cimagineers-of-our-future/

Tillich, Paul. (1996). Each period has its peculiar image of man (1996). In Kristine Stiles & Peter Selz (Eds.) *Theories and documents of contemporary art: A sourcebook of artists' writings* (pp. 183-185). Berkeley, CA: University of California Press. (Original work published 1959)

Toronto, James A. (2008). Challenges to establishing the Church in the Middle East. In Reid L. Neilson (Ed.), *Global Mormonism in the 21st century* (pp. 134-145). Provo, UT: Brigham Young University, Religious Studies Center. (Original work published 1999)

Trumbower, Jeffrey A. (2001). *Rescue for the dead: The posthumous salvation of non-Christians in early Christianity*. New York, NY: Oxford University Press.

Tullis, F. LaMond (Ed.). (1978). *Mormonism: A faith for all cultures.* Provo, UT: Brigham Young University Press.

Tumulty, Karen. (2012, June 20). Mormonism good for the body as well as the soul? *The Washington Post* [online edition]. Retrieved June 22, 2012, http://www.washingtonpost.com/blogs/she-the-people/post/ mormonism-good-for-the-body-as-well-as-the-soul/2012/06/20/gJQARk3IqV_blog.html

Turley, Richard E., Jr., & Ronald W. Walker (Eds.). (2009). *Mountain Meadows Massacre: The Andrew Jenson and David H. Morris Collections.* Provo, UT: Brigham Young University Press, and Salt Lake City, UT: University of Utah Press.

United Nations, Department of Economic and Social Affairs, Population Division. (2004). *World population to 2300.* New York, NY: Author. Accessed July 20, 2012 at http://www.un.org/esa/population/publications/longrange2/WorldPop2300final.pdf

United States Census Bureau. (2000). *(NP-T1) Annual projections of the total resident population as of July 1: Middle, lowest, highest, and zero international migration series 1999 to 2100.* Retrieved February 28, 2012 from http://www.census.gov/population/www/projections/natsum-T1.html

United States Census Bureau. (2012a). Table 1336: Marriage and divorce rates by country: 1980 to 2008. In *Statistical abstract of the United States: 2012* (p. 840). Online at http://www.census.gov/compendia/statab/2012/tables/12s1336.pdf

United States Census Bureau. (2012b, July 20). *U.S. and world population clocks* [web page]. Retrieved 10:05 p.m., July 20, 2012, from http://www.census.gov/main/www/popclock.html

United States Department of Commerce, Economics and Statistics Administration, United States Census Bureau. (n.d.). *Census regions and divisions of the United States* [online document]. Accessed September 7, 2012 at http://www.census.gov/geo/www/us_regdiv.pdf

U.S. religious knowledge survey. (2010, September). Washington, DC: Pew Research Center, Pew Forum on Religion & Public Life. Available online at http://www.pewforum.org/uploadedFiles/Topics/ Belief_and_Practices/religious-knowledge-full-report.pdf

U.S. religious landscape survey: Religious affiliation: Diverse and dynamic. (2008, February). Washington, DC: Pew Research Center, Pew Forum on Religion & Public Life. Online at http://religions.pewforum.org/pdf/report-religious-landscape-study-full.pdf

U.S. religious landscape survey: Religious beliefs and practices: Diverse and politically relevant. (2008, June). Washington, DC: Pew Research Center, Pew Forum on Religion & Public Life. Online at http://religions.pewforum.org/pdf/report2-religious-landscape-study-full.pdf

Vajda, Jordan. (2002). *"Partakers of the divine nature": A comparative analysis of patristic and Mormon doctrines of divinization* [FARMS Occasional Paper No. 2]. Provo, UT: Brigham Young University, Foundation for Ancient Research and Mormon Studies.

van den Broek, Roelof. (1998). Gnosticism and Hermeticism in antiquity: Two roads to salvation. In Roelf van den Broek & Wouter J. Hanegraaff (Eds.), *Gnosis and Hermeticism: From antiquity to modern times* (pp. 1-20). Albany, NY: State University of NY Press.

Vogel, Dan. (1988). *Religious seekers and the advent of Mormonism*. Salt Lake City, UT: Signature Books.

Wade, Nicholas. (2001). *Life script: How the human genome discoveries will transform medicine and enhance your health*. New York, NY: Simon & Schuster.

Wagner, C. Peter. (2008). *Dominion! How Kingdom action can change the world*. Grand Rapids, MI: Chosen Books/Baker Publishing Group.

Walker, Joseph. (2012, June 1). LDS Church organizes first stake in India. *Deseret News* [online edition]. Online at http://www.deseretnews.com/article/865556827/LDS-Church-organizes-first-stake-in-India.html

Walker, Ronald W., Richard E. Turley Jr., & Glen M. Leonard. (2008). *Massacre at Mountain Meadows*. New York, NY: Oxford Univ. Press.

Wallerstein, Judith S., Julia M. Lewis, & Sandra Blakeslee. (2000). *The unexpected legacy of divorce: A 25 year landmark study*. New York, NY: Hyperion.

Wallis Budge, E. A. (1979). *Egyptian religion: Egyptian ideas of the future life*. London, England, UK: Routledge & Kegan Paul. (Original work published 1899)

Wang Tien Te. (1973). Taiwan congregation follows teen-ager. In Hartman Rector & Connie Rector (Eds.), *No more strangers* (vol. 2, pp. 26-32). Salt Lake City, UT: Bookcraft.

Warwick, Kevin. (2002). *I, cyborg*. London, England, UK: Century.

Watson, Ian. (2012). *The universal machine: From the dawn of computing to digital consciousness*. New York, NY: Copernicus Books/Springer Science + Business Media.

Weaver, Sarah Jane. (2012, Week of July 22). Educating the future of Manaus. *Church News*, pp. 8-10. Online at http://www.ldschurch news.com/articles/62561/Educating-the-future-of-Manaus.html

Webb, Stephen. (2002). *If the universe is teeming with aliens... where is everybody? Fifty solutions to the Fermi paradox and the problem of extraterrestrial life*. New York, NY: Copernicus Books.

Welch, John W., & Doris R. Dant. (1997). *The Book of Mormon paintings of Minerva Teichert*. Provo, UT: BYU Studies & Bookcraft.

West, Michael D. (2003). *The immortal cell: One scientist's quest to solve the mystery of human aging*. New York, NY: Doubleday.

White, Michael. (1997). *Isaac Newton: The last sorcerer*. New York, NY: Basic Books.

Whitlock, F. Woodworth, Jr. (1973). Paying the price. In Hartman Rector & Connie Rector (Eds.), *No more strangers* (vol. 2, pp. 33-58). Salt Lake City, UT: Bookcraft.

Whitney, Orson F. (1974). Home literature. In Richard H. Cracroft & Neal E. Lambert (Eds.), *A believing people: Literature of the Latter-day Saints* (pp. 203-207). Provo, UT: Brigham Young University Press. (Original work published 1888)

Widtsoe, John A. (Ed.). (1954). *Discourses of Brigham Young*. Salt Lake City, UT: Deseret Book Company.

Wilson, Daniel H. (2011). *Robopocalypse*. New York, NY: Doubleday.

Wilson, Edward O. (2002). *The future of life*. New York, NY: Knopf.

Wilson, Keith J. (2000). A nation in a day: The Church in Guatemala. In *Out of obscurity: The LDS Church in the twentieth century* (pp. 363-378). Salt Lake City, UT: Deseret Book Co.

Winchel, Beki. (2012, June 9). Missionary work goes viral thanks to 'I'm a Mormon' campaign. *Deseret News*. Retrieved June 10, 2012 from http://www.deseretnews.com/article/865557169/Missionary-work-goes-viral-thanks-to-Im-a-Mormon-campaign.html

Winter, Caroline. (2012, July 16-22). Latter-day lucre: How the Mormon Church makes its billions. *Bloomberg Businessweek*, pp. 40-47.

Wrigley, Heather. (2012, May). Celebrating 75 years of welfare. *Ensign*, pp. 139-140. Online at https://www.lds.org/ensign/2011/05/celebrating-75-years-of-welfare

Xu, Weichao, Yunhe Hou, Y.S. Hung, & Yuexian Zou. (2010, November). Comparison of Spearman's rho and Kendall's tau in normal and contaminated normal models. Paper submitted to *IEEE Transactions on Information Theory*. Available at eprint arXiv:1011.2009. Accessed September 15, 2012 at http://arxiv.org/abs/1011.2009d

Yalom, Irvin D. (1980). *Existential psychotherapy*. New York, NY: Basic Books/Perseus Books Group.

Yearbook of American & Canadian churches: 2002 (Eileen W. Lindner, Ed.). (2002). Nashville, TN: Abingdon Press.

Yearbook of American & Canadian churches: 2012 (Eileen W. Lindner, Ed.). (2012). Nashville, TN: Abingdon Press.

Young, Simon. (2006). *Designer evolution: A transhumanist manifesto*. Amherst, NY: Prometheus Books.

Zakaria, Fareed. (2012). *The post-American world: Release 2.0*. New York, NY: Norton. (Original work published 2011)

Zimmerman, Barry E., & David J. Zimmerman. (2003). *Killer germs: Microbes and diseases that threaten humanity* (rev. ed.). Chicago, IL: Contemporary Books/McGraw-Hill.

Index

19th century, 6, 7, 15, 18, 19, 106, 108, 109, 119, 127, 162, 177, 199, 250, 271

21st century, xix, 15, 39, 109, 114, 126, 167, 177, 178, 185, 261

666 (number of the Beast), 185

Africa, 43, 46, 47, 61, 62, 65, 72, 116, 139, 140, 141, 142, 263

agency, moral, 288, 289

agnostics, agnosticism, 20, 149, 276, 277

Albania, 41, 43

alchemy, 199, 200

alcohol, 4, 49, 50, 242, 253, 266, 267

American culture, 5, 178, 185, 203, 204, 233

American Family Association, 109

Amharic (language), 225

Anglicans, 64, 65, 74, 77, 293

anthropology, 184

Antichrist, 131

anti-Mormonism, xxii, 10, 107, 108, 109, 110, 284

Apocalypse. *See* Revelation, Book of

apocalypticism, 186

apostasy, 9, 177

apostles, 8, 9, 10, 11, 15, 16, 30, 31, 42, 48, 107, 224

apotheosis. *See* theosis

Arabic (language), 225

archaeological discoveries, 103

archaeology, 184

Argentina, 140, 227

Aristotle, 179

Arizona, 20, 30, 239

artificial intelligence, 191, 209, 210

Asia, 33, 42, 43, 46, 47, 61, 62, 65, 72, 116, 171, 172, 223, 224, 231

Aslan, Reza, xxii

Assemblies of God, 86, 88, 93, 121, 122, 123, 296

Atapuerca (Spain), 98

atheists, atheism, 2, 125, 148, 159, 181, 276, 277, 285, 288

Atonement of Jesus Christ, 20, 214, 289

attrition, 1, 128, 129, 130, 131

augmented cognition, 206

Australia, 33

Austria, 156
Baby Boomers, 232, 234
Ballard, M. Russell, 48, 49, 50, 51, 54, 55, 58, 101
Bangalore (India), 168, 169
Bangladesh, 33, 169
baptism, 8, 10, 17, 19, 21, 27, 57, 59
Barna Group, 129, 180, 181
Beast, number of the, 185
Belarus, 41, 43
Belgium, 155, 156
Bengali (language), 225
Berger, Peter L., 113
Bhutan, 169
Bible, 7, 13, 16, 19, 31, 47, 172, 182, 185, 273, 277, 282, 283, 323
bioenhancement, 206
biology, 184
bishop (LDS Church officer), xxi, 11, 194, 263, 385
Bishop's Storehouse, 260
Bloggernacle, LDS, 230
blogosphere, LDS, 230
Boggs, Lilburn W., 106
Book of Mormon, 7, 9, 13, 17, 18, 20, 34, 49, 117, 131, 132, 177, 223, 224, 228, 255, 258, 314, 315, 323
Book of the Dead (Egyptian), 198
Boyé, Alex, 20

branch (LDS congregation), 11, 106, 167, 263
Brazil, 119, 140, 141, 142
Brigham Young University, 59, 118, 163, 174, 184, 257
   Middle Eastern Texts Initiative, 174
   Museum of Paleontology, 184
Brookings Institution, 3
Browning, Gary, 43
Buddha, 103
Buddhism, 25, 47, 147, 285, 312
Buddhists, 64, 68, 78, 80, 124, 132, 146, 285, 293
Bulgaria, 41, 43
Burma, 33
California, 20, 44, 167
calling (LDS church job), 4
Cambodia, 33, 34, 42, 44, 312
Cambodian (language), 224
Cana, miracle at, 182
Canada, 11, 164
Carpenter, John, 191
Catholicism, xxii, 46, 64, 68, 74, 96, 127, 132
Catholics, 97, 126, 127, 128, 145, 147, 151, 152, 165, 185, 245, 259, 273, 274, 275, 276, 277, 278, 279, 293
Central America, 44, 62, 72, 139, 140, 142, 262
Chabon, Michael, 191
Chaffetz, Jason, 20

children of record, 27, 57, 58
children of record, number of and missionaries, correlation, 57
Chile, 140, 164
China, 33, 34, 139, 162, 163, 164, 165, 166, 167, 170, 175, 247, 248
China, People's Republic of, 34, 162, 163, 165, 166, 167
Chinatown (New York City neighborhood), 44, 45
Chinese (language), 224, 225, 227
Chinese folk religionists, 68, 80, 124, 132, 293
Chinese Red Army, 10
Christian Science, 65
Christianity, 13, 17, 25, 65, 73, 76, 111, 121, 122, 158, 159, 162, 177, 180, 213, 268, 273, 277, 278, *See* evangelical Christianity, *See* Orthodox Christianity, *See* Roman Catholicism and specific churches
   ancient, 7, 8, 9, 13, 15, 16, 17, 19, 31, 164, 177, 179, 183, 198, 213, 214, 217, 253, 254
   fundamentalist, 274
   Latter-day Saint faith, 6, 7
Christians, 13, 18, 64, 65, 68, 109, 124, 146, 158, 165, 169, 171, 172, 174, 180, 245, 274, 285, 293
   Latter-day Saints, 6, 7

Christians, independent, 76, 132
Church Internet Committee (LDS), 224
Church of Jesus Christ, 12, 38, 41
Church of Jesus Christ of Latter-day Saints, The, xix, 86
   terms used to designate, 12
Church of Sweden, 161
Church Office Building (LDS), 31, 48
Civil War, American, 10
Civilization, end of, 185, 221
   through asteroid strikes, 190
   through energy crisis, 187
   through environmental catastrophe, 187, 192, 261
   through global pandemic, 188, 189
   through natural catastrophes, 186
   through nuclear war, 189
Clement of Alexandria, 214
Club of Rome report, 187
coffee, 4, 242, 259
Colorado, 20, 239
comic book superheroes, 200, 201, 202, 209
computing, quantum, 98
Confucianism, 65
Confucius, 103, 249
Congregationalists, 89

Constantine (Roman emperor), 112
conversion
    LDS, 313, 314
    Lofland-Stark-Finke theory of, 312, 313
    religious capital and, 311, 313
    social capital and, 311, 313
converts (LDS), number of
    and missionaries, correlation, 51
    and missionaries, number of, 299
Côte d'Ivoire, 61
Cowherd, Peggy, 20
cyborgs, 208, 215
Czech Republic, 43, 155, 156
Czechoslovakia, 41
Da Vinci, 268
Daedalus, 179
Dalai Lama, 285
damnation, 19, 261, 267
Daniel (ancient prophet), 282
Dante, 268
Davie, Grace, 160
death
    in existentialism, 287
Declaration of Independence, 127
declinist panic, 114
del Toro, Guillermo, 191
Democratic Republic of the Congo, 43, 62, 140, 189
Depression, Great, 89, 101

Deseret News Church Almanac, 318
Deseret Ranches, 120
deseret, Deseret, 10, 117, 118, 120, 194, 239
Dialogue, A Journal of Mormon Thought (independent LDS periodical), xxi, 271
disaster relief, 174
disestablishmentarianism, 160
divorce, 246
Doctrine and Covenants, 7, 243, 323
Dominican Republic, 119
drugs, 4, 50, 242, 266, 267
Dubuffet, Jean, 268
Dürer, 268
E! (television program), 5
Eastern Bloc, 41
economic inequality, 254, 258
Economist, The (magazine), 165, 252
economists, 105
Ecuador, 140
education
    LDS emphasis on, 2, 243
egotism, 5
Egypt, 198
El Salvador, 140
Employment Resource Services, LDS, 257
England, 152, 154, 155, 156, 157, 159, 167, 199
English (language), 225, 227

enhancement of human capacities, artificial, 206
Enlightenment, European, 112, 180, 269
Enoch (ancient prophet), 254
Ensign (official LDS magazine), 115, 317
Episcopal Church, xxi, 86, 88, 89, 93, 296
Episcopalians, 89
Estonia, 41, 42, 43
eternal life, 6, 7
Ethiopia, 263
Europe, 11, 34, 42, 43, 44, 46, 47, 61, 62, 72, 108, 113, 116, 117, 139, 152, 153, 154, 155, 156, 157, 158, 159, 160, 161, 173, 175, 188, 271, 309
evangelical Christianity, 22, 109, 110, 121, 151, 169, 180, 185, 186, 213, 274
  authors, xxii
evangelical Christians, 274, 275, 277, 278, 279
evolution, 180, 182, 183, 184
exaltation, 6, 7, 8, 10, 211, 212, 213, 214, 215, 289
Exhortation to the Greeks (Clement of Alexandria), 214
existential uncertainty, 104
existentialism, 287, 288
experiences, spiritual, 20, 21, 278, 279

extermination order, Missouri, 106
extraterrestrial life, 103, 179, 191, 201, 212, 215, 216, 217, 219, 220, 221
  discovery of, 103, 221
families are forever, 19, 212
Family Home Evening, 246, 257
family stability, 246
Fanti (language), 225
Finke, Roger, 311
Finland, 42
First Amendment rights, 109
First Presidency, LDS, 11, 39, 183, 184, 214, 227, 249
Fischer, Bryan, 109
Florida, 49, 120, 195
forces on religious choice
  external or pulling, 136, 137, 139
  internal or pushing, 136, 137, 178, 221
  knowledge, 136, 137, 223
Fordham University, 385
forever families, 19, 212
France, 154, 156
freedom
  in existentialism, 287
French (language), 225
genealogical research, LDS, 212
General Authorities (LDS Church officers), 11, 223
General Conference, LDS, 48, 58, 193, 317

Generation Y, 159
geology, 184
German (language), 225
Germany, 41, 127, 155, 156, 157, 246
Ghana, 43, 62, 107, 140, 263
global financial crisis (2007+), 258
Glock, Charles, 241
Gnosticism, 198, 199
God, 2, 6, 7, 9, 16, 17, 20, 22, 31, 32, 49, 118, 148, 149, 181, 183, 193, 194, 212, 213, 214, 217, 218, 219, 220, 232, 243, 249, 250, 251, 253, 258, 269, 271, 272, 273, 278, 282, 284, 285, 286, 287, 288, 296, 314, 315
God, glory of, is intelligence, 118
Godhead, 6
godhood meme, 287
Golden Dawn (magical order), 199, 200
Google Apostasy, 130
Gospel and the Productive Life, The (academic class), 257
gospel of Jesus Christ (LDS), 8, 19, 32, 39, 50, 178, 270, 282
restored, 166, 184, 249
Great Britain, 34
Great Commission, 31, 48, 283
Greeley, Andrew, 158
growth, Mormon, projections
  United States of America, 90
  worldwide, 69
Guatemala, 140
handcarts, 117
Hansen's disease (leprosy), 259
Harlem (New York City neighborhood), 45
Harry Potter (book and movie series), 203
Haverford College, 385
hedonism, 5, 221
hell, 19
Hephaestos, 179
Hermeticism, 198
Hindi (language), 225, 227
Hinduism, 25, 147, 169, 242
Hindus, 64, 68, 78, 124, 132, 146, 168, 169, 171, 172, 293
Holy Spirit, 6, 15, 17, 31, 49, 59, 313, 314
home teachers (LDS lay pastoral visitors), 4, 194, 263, 385
Honduras, 140, 141
Hong Kong, 33, 43, 163, 167, 227
human life, ultimate concerns of, 287
Human Rights Watch, 169
humanism, 268
humanitarian aid, 129, 263
humanity, offspring of God, 214

Hungary, 41, 42, 43
Hyderabad (India), 168, 169, 170
Idaho, 239
Igbo (language), 225
Illinois, 10, 19, 117, 153, 192
immortality, 289
Independent Christianity, 74
Independent Christians, 64
India, 33, 34, 44, 62, 139, 167, 168, 169, 170, 171, 172, 175, 227, 248
Indonesia, 44, 61, 174
Indonesian (language), 224, 225
Industrial Revolution, 180
Institute program (LDS), 119
intelligence, the glory of God is, 2
Intermountain West, 117, 193, 238, 239, 240
Internet, 130, 288
Inwood (New York City neighborhood), 45
Iraq, 262
Ireland, 127
Irreantum (independent LDS periodical), 271
Isaiah, 34
Islam, xxii, 25, 139, 147, 172, 173, 174, 175, 312
isolation
 in existentialism, 288
Italian (language), 225
Italy, 36, 154, 156

Itri, John Kyle "Jack", 35
Itri, Nicholas "Nick", 36
Ivory Coast, 43, 62
Japan, xxi, 33, 36, 43, 61, 247, 312
Japanese (language), 225
Jehovah's Witnesses, 65, 146
Jerusalem, 9, 31
Jesus Christ, 6, 7, 8, 13, 17, 31, 49, 50, 103, 112, 131, 158, 182, 214, 219, 220, 224, 228, 255, 273, 283
 Atonement of, 7, 20, 214, 289
 life of, on LDS video series, 225
 Savior, 182
 taught theosis, 214
Jews, 64, 77, 146, 147, 241, 245, 276, 277, 278, 279, 285, 293
Jonas, Hans, 199
Judaism, xxii, 312
Jung, Carl Gustav, 199
Kansas City (Missouri), 106
Kazakh (language), 225
Kenya, 43, 60
Kimball, Spencer W., 30, 31, 32, 33, 34, 35, 36, 38, 40, 48, 58, 72, 101, 252
Kirtland (Ohio), 9
Knowles, Christopher, 202
Koltko, Emil, 99, 100, 102
Koltko, Viktor, 36
Koltko, Zygmunt, 99
Koltko-Rivera models of LDS growth

United States, 91, 92
worldwide, 70, 71
Koltko-Rivera, Mark E., xxi, 385
Koran, 158
Korea, 33, 43, 61
Korean (language), 225
Korean War, 38, 101
Kripal, Jeffrey J., 203
Kufuor, John Ageykum, 107
Kuspit, Donald, 267
Lamb of God, 131, 132
language expertise, LDS, 248
Late Great Planet Earth, The (H. Lindsey), 186
Latter-day Saint. *See* LDS
helping the poor essential to being a good, 259
Latvia, 41, 42, 43, 45, 60, 155, 156, 227
Latvian (language), 225
LDS. *See* missions, stakes, temples, wards and branches, websites
Addiction Recovery Program, 266
beliefs, 6
Church Educational System, 257
Church Welfare Program, 194, 256, 258
disaster relief, 5, 262
education emphasis, 5
Employment Resource Services, 257
ethic of initiative, 261

ethic of preparation, 262
ethic of provident living, 263
ethic of self-reliance, 264, 284
ethic of work, 250, 252, 253
history, 8
humanitarian aid, 5, 262
Institute program, 119
International Art Competition, 271
International Youth Art Competition, 271
leadership training programs, 257
lifestyle, 3
meaning of abbreviation, 13
organization, 11
practices, religious, 3
Renaissance, potential for new, 267, 272
Seminary program, 5, 259
service to the poor and needy, 258
work ethic, 250, 252, 253
LDS 101™ (blog), xxi, 230, 231
Lee, Harold B., 30
Left Behind (book series), 186
leprosy. *See* Hansen's disease
Liberia, 43
Limits to Growth, The (book), 187
Lincoln Center (New York City neighborhood), 44, 45
Lindsey, Hal, 186
Lithuania, 41, 42, 43
Lofland, John, 311

Lord's Supper, 8, 17
Louisiana, 127, 195
Louisiana Purchase, 127
Lovecraft, Howard Philips, 191
Lower East Side (New York City neighborhood), 385
Lucas, Robert, 105
Lutheran Church, 86, 88, 89, 93, 95, 213, 295, 296
Lutherans, 89
Macau, 163, 167
Madagascar, 43, 47, 61
Maddow, Rachel, 109
Malay (language), 225
Malaysia, 174
Manaus (Brazil), 119
Manhattan (New York City, USA), xxi, 4, 44, 241, 260, 385
Manhattan Mormon™, The (blog), xxi, 230
Manila (Philippines), 4
Mansfield, Stephen, 237
Martin, Roger, 105
materialism, 5
Mauss, Armand, 25
Maxwell, Neal A., 220
McKay, David O., 182
meaninglessness
  in existentialism, 288
Mecham, Steven Ray, 42
Melbourne (Australia), 167
memes, 221, 287, 289

mental health, 242
Merton, Thomas, xxii
metathemes, 179
Methodist Church, 47, 86, 88, 93, 95, 295
Mexican-American War, 127
Mexico, 10, 140, 141, 142, 227, 262
Meyer, Stephenie, 204
Michelangelo, 268
Middle Ages, 213, 268
Middle Paleolithic era, 98
Millennial generation, 129, 231, 232, 233, 235
Miltons and Shakespeares of our own, we will yet have, 271
miracles, 181
missionaries (LDS), number of
  and children of record, correlation, 57
  and converts, correlation, 51
  and converts, number of, 299
missionary preparation, 29, 40, 51, 58, 59, 60
Missionary Preparation Student Manual, 60
missionary service, 4, 27, 29, 35, 36, 48, 50, 51, 54, 58
Missionary Training Center, 59
missionary work, 10, 29, 31, 34, 35, 37, 41, 42, 46, 47, 52, 58, 72, 107, 108, 109, 114, 152,

159, 168, 234, 250, 253, 309, 310

missions, LDS, specific
   Baltic States Mission, v
   India New Delhi Mission, 169
   Japan Okayama Mission, 58, 277, 385
   Mongolia Ulaanbaatar Mission, 44

Missouri, 9, 106, 117

modernization, 97, 112, 113

Mohammed, 25, 103, 249

Mongolia, 33, 34, 42, 44, 60, 116

Mongolian (language), 224, 225

Monson, Thomas S., 55, 58, 194

Montana, 239

more Mormon world, a, 2, 238, 241, 242, 243, 246, 247, 248, 249, 250, 254, 257, 258, 261, 262, 265, 266, 267, 269, 272, 273, 274, 276, 277, 278, 279

Mormon go-go years (1960s), 72

Mormon Helping Hands, 195

Mormonizing of America, The (S. Mansfield), 130, 237

Morningside Heights (New York City neighborhood), 45

Moroni, 9, 17

Morrison, Grant, 202

Moscow (Idaho, USA), 46

Moscow (Russia), 46, 107

Moses, 103, 217, 218, 219, 276

Mother, Heavenly, 7

Mountain Meadows Massacre, 130

Mozambique, 43, 45

MTV News (television program), 5

multicultural expertise, LDS, 248, 249

multiculturalism, 161

Muslims, 64, 68, 78, 80, 124, 132, 146, 147, 158, 168, 171, 172, 173, 174, 241, 262, 293

mysticism, 279, 285

nanotechnology, 98, 209

Nauvoo (Illinois), 10, 19, 118, 192, 193

Nebuchadnezzar, 282

Nelson, Russell M., 42

Nelson, Victoria, 204, 205, 213

Nepal, 169

networks of faith, 45, 54, 60, 72, 142, 154, 171, 310

Neuenschwander, Dennis B., 174

Nevada, 239

New Delhi (India), 168

New Hampshire, 127

New Mexico, 239

New Mormon Challenge, The (book), xxiii

New Religionists, 78, 80, 124, 293

new religious movements, 25, 26

New York City, xxiii, 77, 167, 265, 385
New York New York Stake (LDS), 260
New York State, xix, 9, 44
New York University, xxi, 385
New Zealand, 33
Newton, Isaac, 269
Nield, Reeve, 21
Nigeria, 21, 43, 62, 140, 141
Nixon, Jay, 106
No god but God (Aslan), xxii
North America, 44, 62
Oaks, Dallin H., 162, 164, 166
Oates, Joyce Carol, 191
obsessions, societal, 136, 137, 178, 221
Ohio, 9, 117, 152, 153
Oregon, 37
Orthodox Christianity, 46, 65, 68, 74, 77, 146, 213, 245, 259, 273, 274, 275, 278, 279, 293
Otterson, Michael, 164
Pakistan, 169, 174
Paraguay, 227
Pearl of Great Price, 7, 9, 177, 219, 255, 289, 323
Pennsylvania, xxi, 9
Pentecostal Church, 97, 121, 122
Pentecostalism, 121
Perkins, Anthony D., 167, 223
Perpetual Education Fund (PEF), 118, 119, 245, 256, 258

Peru, 140, 141
Pew organization, 148, 278, 314
Philippines, 33, 61
Plato, 179, 249
plural marriage, 10
Poland, 41, 43, 45, 99, 127, 155, 156, 157
Polish (language), 225
popular entertainment, 1, 2, 5, 179, 186, 187, 188, 189, 191, 204, 215, 216, 276
population shrinkage, 247
pornography, 50, 266, 267
Portugal, 154, 156
Portuguese (language), 225
post-American world, 97
posthumans, 209
Preach My Gospel, 40
Presbyterian Church, 86, 88, 89, 93, 296
Presbyterians, 89, 110
Presiding Bishopric (LDS Church officers), 11
priesthood, 7, 8, 9, 11, 12, 19, 35, 48, 194, 263, 385
productivity, 250
projections, straight-line, 97, 102, 105
prophets, 7, 9, 11, 16, 17, 183, 287
Protestants, 65, 74, 77, 88, 97, 108, 110, 125, 126, 128, 129, 132, 145, 147, 151, 165, 185,

245, 259, 273, 274, 275, 276, 277, 278, 279, 293
Prothero, Stephen, 276
Provo (Utah), 45
Psychological Blog™, The (blog), xxii
questions
    addressed by this book, xix
Raimi, Sam, 191
Red Scare, xxiii
Reformers, Protestant, 249
Regis High School (NYC), 385
relativism, 159, 161
Relief Society, 11, 12, 194, 259, 263
religion
    Belief dimension, 272
    Consequential dimension, 241
    Experiential dimension, 278
    Glock's five dimensional model of, 241
    ignorance about, 276
    Knowledge dimension, 276
    older than human technology, 98
    Practice dimension, 274
religious capital, 45, 46, 47, 136, 137, 147, 148, 150, 172, 311, 312
Religious Science, 65
Renaissance, European, 199, 268
Renaissance, new LDS-related, 267
resurrection, 7, 20, 31, 255, 289

revelation, 7, 17, 19, 183, 193, 211, 217, 260, 274, 282, 314
Revelation, Book of (Bible), 185
Revolutions of 1989, 41, 42, 43
Rhodesia, 21
Rice, Anne, 204
Rise of a New World Faith, The (article, R. Stark), 25, 26
risk management, 104
Roberts, Brigham H., 182
Roman Catholic Church, 76, 86, 110, 152, 295
Roman Catholicism, 76, 86, 93, 110, 152, 213, 295
Roman Empire, 111, 112
Romania, 41, 43
Rowling, J. K., 203
Russia, 33, 34, 41, 42, 43, 60, 61, 107, 155, 156, 157
Russian (language), 225
Sabbath, 4
Sacrament Meeting, 12
Saint, meaning of term, 13
Salt Lake City (Utah), 10, 48, 117, 195, 282
salvation, 184
Sargent, Thomas, 105
Schumpeter (columnist, pseud.), 252
science, xxi, 2, 160, 179, 180, 181, 184, 185, 210, 221, 269, 272
scientism, 160, 161, 180
secularization, 97, 112, 113, 233

seekers, 1
self-reliance, LDS value, 195, 253
self-transcendence, 197, 205, 211
Seminary program, LDS, 5, 259
service, LDS day of, 129, 254
Seven Storey Mountain, The (Merton), xxii
Seventy, the (LDS Church officers), 11
sexual relationships, 3
Sierra Leone, 43
Sikhs, 64, 77, 168, 172, 293
Singularity, 103, 209, 210, 211, 215
Smith, Huston, 284
Smith, Joseph Fielding, 182
Smith, Joseph, Jr., 9, 16, 17, 18, 19, 99, 177, 192, 193, 211, 217, 219, 253, 255, 260, 282
assassinated, 10
So what?, 96, 103, 237, 281
social capital, 136, 137
Socrates, 249
South Africa, 43, 62, 140
South America, 44, 62, 72, 140, 142
Southern Baptist Convention, 86, 88, 93, 95, 110, 295
Soviet Union, 34, 41, 42, 43, 112, 154, 155, 190, 309
Spain, 98, 154, 155, 156, 157
Spanish (language), 225, 227

Staines, Graham, 169
stake (LDS), xxi, 11, 12, 35, 61, 62, 107, 170, 171, 385
stakes (LDS), specific
Hyderabad India Stake, 168, 169
New York New York Stake, 45, 254
Stark, Rodney, 21, 24, 25, 26, 45, 46, 54, 60, 72, 81, 89, 102, 104, 111, 112, 113, 137, 147, 148, 153, 155, 158, 171, 172, 310, 311
Stark, Tony (character), 208
Statement of the First Presidency Regarding God's Love for All Mankind (official statement, LDS First Presidency), 249
stone cut out of the mountain without hands, 282
Sunday School, 12, 47, 130, 385
Sunstone (independent LDS periodical), 271
Sunstone (LDS periodical), xxi
Swan, Bella (character), 205
Sydney (Australia), 167
Systematic Program for Teaching the Gospel, A, 37
Taiwan, 33, 43, 62, 312
Tamil (language), 225, 227
Taoism, 65
tea, 4, 242, 259
technology, 179, 205
Telugu (language), 227
temple ceremonies, LDS, 10

baptism for the dead, proxy, 8, 10, 19
endowment, 211
sealings (weddings), 19, 211
temples, LDS, 2, 5, 8, 22, 118, 154, 211, 212, 225, 250, 270
temples, LDS, specific
　Accra Ghana Temple, 107
　Buenos Aires Argentina Temple, 227
　Hong Kong China Temple, 163
　Kansas City Missouri temple, 106
　Kirtland Temple, 9
　London England temple, 154
　Manhattan New York Temple, xxi
　Nauvoo Temple (original), 10, 19
　Salt Lake Temple, 118
　St. Louis Missouri Temple, 106
testimony (LDS), 20, 49, 50, 219, 313, 315
Thai (language), 225
Thailand, 33, 43, 312
theosis, 213, 287
This Is My God (Wouk), xxii
Tillich, Paul, 269
tithe, tithing, 4, 22, 119
TMZ (television program), 5
tobacco, 4, 50, 242, 266, 267
Toronto (Canada), 167
tracting, 37

transcend human limits, ambition to, 197, 221
transhumanism, 201, 202, 208, 209, 211, 215
True Blood (television series), 204
Turkish (language), 225
Twi (language), 225
Twilight (book and movie series), 204, 205
Uganda, 43, 61
Ukraine, 43, 155, 156, 157
Ukrainian (language), 225
Ulaanbaatar (Mongolia), 44, 47, 116
Unaffiliateds, 145, 147, 148, 149, 150, 151, 159, 165, 167
Uniform System for Teaching Families, The, 37
Uniform System for Teaching Investigators, A, 37
Union Square (New York City neighborhood), 45
Unitarians, 65
United Order, LDS, 192, 193
United States, xix, 1, 10, 11, 15, 29, 33, 35, 62, 68, 72, 85, 86, 88, 89, 93, 96, 97, 99, 108, 109, 114, 115, 116, 117, 118, 122, 125, 126, 127, 139, 142, 147, 153, 154, 157, 165, 170, 173, 175, 177, 178, 186, 188, 201, 226, 231, 233, 235, 237, 238, 239, 240, 241, 245, 246, 265, 274, 290, 291, 294

University of Central Florida, 385

University of Utah, 118

Upanishads, 103

Upper East Side (New York City neighborhood), 45

Urdu (language), 225

Uruguay, 227

Utah, 10, 20, 45, 115, 117, 118, 119, 153, 192, 193, 238, 239, 240

Vajda, Jordan, 213

Vampire Chronicles, The (book and movie series), 204

vampire plague, 191

Vancouver (Canada), 167

Vatican, 220

Vietnam, 29, 33, 34

Vietnam War, 29

Vietnamese (language), 225

virtual reality, 207, 208

visiting teachers (LDS lay pastoral visitors), 4, 194, 263

War in Heaven, 288

War of Independence, 126

ward (LDS congregation), xxi, 11, 12, 194, 263

wards/branches (LDS), specific
  Canal Street Branch, 44
  Goldenrod Ward, 195
  Manhattan First Ward, 44
  Winter Park Ward, 195

Warsaw (Indiana, USA), 46

Warsaw (Poland), 46

Wayland the Smith, 179

We will yet have Miltons and Shakespeares of our own, 271

wealth, societal obsession with, 221

Weber, Max, 252

websites, LDS
  country websites, 227
  FamilySearch.org, 225
  language pages, 225
  lds.org, 224
  mormon.org, 225, 228
  MormonChannel.org, 225
  MormonNewsroom.org, 225
  youth-oriented, 225

Western civilization, 103, 111, 185, 188, 200, 288

Whitney, Orson F., 271

Why Religion Matters (Huston Smith), 285

Word of Wisdom, 266

World Made by Hand (novel series), 188

World War I, 101

World War II, 32, 101, 114, 154, 189

worldviews, 285

Wouk, Herman, xxii

Wyoming, 239

Xhosa (language), 225

Yalom, Irvin, 287

Yellow Peril, xxiii

yoga, 242

Yoruba (language), 225

Young, Brigham, 10, 141, 153, 181, 182, 193, 251
youth, 5, 12, 59, 119, 128, 129, 161, 162, 185, 225, 243, 245, 246, 254, 256, 284
YouTube, xxi, 234
Yugoslavia, 42

Zakaria, Fareed, 114
Zimbabwe, 21, 43, 140
Zion (LDS), 254, 255, 256
zombie apocalypse, 191
Zulu (language), 225

About the Author

Mark Koltko-Rivera holds a doctoral degree from the Department of Applied Psychology at New York University (NYU). He is an elected Fellow of the American Psychological Association. For his scholarship, he has received several awards: the Margaret Gorman Early Career Award in the psychology of religion (from the Society for the Psychology of Religion and Spirituality), the Carmi Harari Early Career Award for Inquiry (Society for Humanistic Psychology), and, on two occasions, the George A. Miller Award for an outstanding recent article on general psychology (Society for General Psychology). He has taught at NYU, the University of Central Florida, and elsewhere.

He was born and raised on the Lower East Side of Manhattan in New York City, where he long lived in the East Village. He graduated from Regis High School (NYC), and holds an undergraduate degree from Haverford College and a masters degree from Fordham University.

Mark Koltko-Rivera converted to The Church of Jesus Christ of Latter-day Saints while attending college. He served for two years as an LDS missionary in the Japan Okayama Mission. He has served in the Church as a home teacher (i.e., priesthood visitor), a Sunday School teacher, a member of a stake high council, and a bishop's counselor (the rough equivalent of an associate pastor).

Dr. Koltko-Rivera is married with four grown children and two grandchildren (and counting). He and his wife live in New York City, where they are active in the Church.

His websites and e-mail address are listed at the conclusion of the Preface of this book.

www.ingramcontent.com/pod-product-compliance
Lightning Source LLC
Chambersburg PA
CBHW071645090426
42738CB00009B/1430